Life Under the Microscope as an African-American

Life Under the Microscope as an African-American

James M. Mosley

Copyright © 2011 by James M. Mosley.

Library of Congress Control Number: 2011914476
ISBN: Hardcover   978-1-4653-5108-1
              Softcover   978-1-4653-5107-4
              Ebook   978-1-4653-5109-8

All rights reserved. No part of this book may be reproduced or transmitted in any form or by any means, electronic or mechanical, including photocopying, recording, or by any information storage and retrieval system, without permission in writing from the copyright owner.

This book was printed in the United States of America.

To order additional copies of this book, contact:
Xlibris Corporation
1-888-795-4274
www.Xlibris.com
Orders@Xlibris.com

CONTENTS

Introduction 9

Preface 11

Chapter 1: Early years and Elementary School 13

Chapter 2: Junior High School 18

Chapter 3: High School years and desire to be a Physician 21

Chapter 4: Enlistment in the US Navy and Recruit Training 24

Chapter 5: Service Schools, career path and first duty station 26

Chapter 6: First Shipboard Duty (Surface Ship)
    and focus on education 40

Chapter 7: Second Shipboard Duty) (Submarine) 56

Chapter 8: Nuclear Power School, (First and Second
    Nuclear Submarines) 69

Chapter 9: Shore Duty 81

Chapter 10: Last Duty Station in the US Navy (Surface Ship) 86

Chapter 11: Transition from Military to Civilian life and working
    for General Dynamics/ Electric Boat Division 98

Chapter 12: Responding to the results of my complaint 207

Chapter 13: Life in Retirement 213

Chapter 14: Breaking Barriers: African-American
    Firsts Reflections and Summary 240

This book is dedicated to my parents: Mervin McKinley Mosley Sr. and Queen Vashti Taylor Mosley.

INTRODUCTION

My parents had a difficult time bringing up their children particularly during the decades of the 1920s and the 1930s. If you recall, the Great Depression was ushered in on October 29th 1929. This period of our history was particularly turbulent due to the racial unrest in the country. Lack of opportunities in employment, education and various socio-economic areas such as housing exacerbated the period of major economic struggles.

My parents had faith in God and stressed the value of education on all their children. My father and mother were sad when their eldest son, Mervin Jr. graduated from college with degrees in Physics and Electrical Engineering, magna cum laude, and was informed during his job interviews at three major corporations that they could not hire "colored" engineers. Mervin Jr. was the first member of the Mosley or Taylor families to graduate from college. This event occurred in the early 1950s. Mervin Jr. was left with one option, to work for the federal government. He was interviewed and accepted a position with the National Bureau of Standards. I am proud to dedicate this book to my parents. My father was a very positive person. I never heard anyone make a negative comment about him, only praise. Additionally, I never heard him make a negative comment about anyone. My father always presented himself as a role model to me. There is no one in the world I respected more than my father.

PREFACE

When I look back on my life, I feel blessed. I had no intention of writing an autobiography. Friends and members of my family convinced me to share my story with others and educate my children and grand-children about the life and journey of various relatives.

I hope this book will prove useful to all who read it. When you examine a life closely, the positive events clearly outweigh the negative ones. I want to share my story primarily with my children, grand-children and great-grand-children. My journey is a part of their history. This is a story of a "negro" as we were called at the time, brought up in poverty and motivated by the desire to make my parents proud of me and to attempt to reach my full potential in life as a citizen of the United States. My life will be divided into three major eras. The period from my birth in 1929 until 1948 when I went into the military, the twenty years I served on active duty in the United States Navy until 1968 and remained in the reserves until 1978, and the period of my civilian employment with a major defense contractor until I retired in 1991 and life in my retirement years.

A Chronology of my life and how certain events shaped the individual that I am today.

My father lived to see some of his thirteen children graduate from college and two of his daughters awarded doctoral degrees. My mother died at a very young age—eleven days after her fortieth birthday. My father was forty one at the time and vowed to keep his family together. At the time of my mother's death I had been in the military about five months. My older brother was also in the military and my older sister Alma Mosley Kitchings was married. My father was left with ten children, at home three boys, William 17, Harold 15, Donald 14, seven girls, Norma 12, Franciene, 10, Yvonne 8, Phyllis 7, Madge 5, Lorraine 22 months and Marvina a new born. My mother died in childbirth. The baby lived three years after the death of my mother. I have always been very proud of my father's perseverance and his love of family. He epitomized the role of a husband and father in the home during difficult periods in our history.

All five of his sons served at various times in the United States military, during World War II, Korean and Vietnam Wars. The branches of the Armed Forces were represented well by his sons. There were two in the Navy, two in the Air Force and one in the Army. The tradition continued as I had three sons and two were in the military, one in the Air Force and one in the Marine Corp.

When my father's sons graduated from high school, there were limited opportunities in the area. I recall the school advisor or guidance counselor directed me to apply to the steel mill for a job as a laborer. The steel mill was not hiring at the time. The only jobs available were as a dishwasher or a janitor. I was able to obtain a job as an Orderly at the Homestead Hospital. I knew at the time, one day I wanted to obtain a college education and pursue the field of medicine. I always loved the fields of chemistry and biology. My male siblings and I ended up in the military because it was the only jobs program available at the time.

My journey in life has been rewarding because I have always placed my faith in God despite circumstances along the way. I can truly say I have been blessed. I will now start my journey in life and travel a path that leads to my peaks and valleys as I matured as an individual.

CHAPTER 1

I was born on August 12th 1929 in Homestead, Pennsylvania, a small suburb of Pittsburgh. We lived in a small house, 111 Oak Way situated behind the Second Baptist Church which was located on 12th Avenue. Oak Way was a very narrow thoroughfare between 12th and 13th Avenues. I was the third of three children at the time. I had a sister (Alma) who was three years older and a brother (Mervin Jr.) who was twenty three months old.

Two months after my birth the stock market tumbled and the Great Depression was ushered in and devastated our society. During this period practically everyone was unemployed. There were bread lines to help the unemployed feed their families. My parents explained at a later date how they stood in line to receive flour, molasses and salted herring fish. This was a difficult time for everyone. This negative event in our history was triggered after the collapse of stock prices on the New York Stock Exchange.

I have no recollection of the period from my birth until 1932 when I was three years old. I recall visiting a friend of my parents who lived on 12th Avenue. Mr. Campbell was a very large dark skinned man who was bald, wore wire rimmed glasses and smoked cigars. I enjoyed our visits to his house because he always gave me and my brother candy. I don't remember anyone else living with Mr. Campbell. He appeared to be living a comfortable life at the time when most people were struggling to make a living.

During the first few years of the depression, my parents sent Mervin Jr. and me to Virginia to stay with my uncle and maternal grandparents. The reason for this was our relatives living in the South were farmers and grew their food. This allowed me and my brother to have nourishing food which was unavailable to us in Pittsburgh. I recall my father and his friend Mr. Tyler would drive us from Pittsburgh to Valentines, Virginia, leave us and drive back. We would stay most of the summer and my father and Mr.

Tyler would return to Virginia and drive us back home. My father had a 1929 Model A Ford.

This scenario happened practically every summer prior to our enrollment in school. Most people living in our area of the North during the depression years were on public assistance.

This was a difficult period for my parents trying to support a family. I was fortunate for the opportunity to have a relationship with my grandparents. I was exposed to church services and Sunday school at a very early age by my parents and grandparents. My grandfather was a deacon in his church.

My aunt Endiana James, an older sister of my mother was a member of the Second Baptist Church. My aunt and her husband Henry informed my parents of a vacant house on their street. They were living at 545 East Third Avenue and the vacant house was at 532 East Third Avenue. East Third Avenue ended with the United States Steel Mill (Homestead Works) wall on City Farm Lane.

In the summer of 1932, our family of six moved from Oak Way to Third Avenue. The baby at this time was William Roger who was born on July 4th 1931. Uncle Henry carried William Roger down the hill to our new residence. He also carried my mother's mantle clock. This trip covered a distance of approximately nine city blocks primarily down hill. I was told later that my mother informed Uncle Henry "don't drop my baby or my clock". We settled into our new residence. We were on public assistance for a considerable period of time. My aunt and uncle provided some assistance to our family. They had one child, Willa Mae who was approximately ten years old.

In January of 1933 my mother was scheduled to deliver her fifth child. It appeared to be a complicated pregnancy therefore she was admitted to the Homestead Hospital and delivered a son whom she named Harold Lloyd. If you recall, a famous movie actor at the time was Harold Lloyd. When my mother was discharged from the hospital there was a bill for the medical services. My father was unemployed during this period however the hospital and my father reached an agreement on how to resolve the issue of payment for the medical services rendered. My father and Uncle Maguire Taylor agreed to work for two weeks as janitors to pay off the hospital bill. This apparently worked out fine. It is ironic that I would work in this hospital as an Orderly fifteen years later prior to my military service.

Later that year my father was re-hired at United States Steel Corporation in the Open Hearth furnace area. This corporation was non-union at this time and resisted collective bargaining. My father told us at a later date about open wars between labor and management occurring in the streets outside the plant gates. In 1936 there was a major riot which occurred on 8th Avenue in Homestead. I started school in September of 1935. I remember our new neighbors were immigrants to the United States from England. My mother became friendly with the Walker family. Everyone was poor at this time and sharing was a common practice. Margaret Walker, whom my mother called Peg had three children, Ralph and two girls, Anna Mae and Violet. We all went to school together. The girls were in my class and Ralph was in my sister's class. My brother Mervin was in the third grade and my sister Alma was in the fourth grade.

During this school year my brother suffered a severe injury of his left thigh when he was attacked by a stray dog. It was a tragic event for an eight year old. The following year we moved to the town of Braddock. I had to make friends all over again. Our new home was a small apartment at 1017 ½ Willow Way. My school was on Talbot Avenue. During most of the school year our classes were conducted in temporary classrooms while the building was being renovated. I will always remember when I was in third grade my teacher Mrs. Morgan, required each student to recite a verse of scripture on a rotating basis. We are aware of the fact this classroom activity is no longer allowed.

I enjoyed my time in elementary school. The winters were harsh and we had to walk to the school despite the weather. I recall my feet being so cold they were numb. When our shoes had holes in the bottom, we put pieces of cardboard inside the shoe to protect our feet against the snow and ice. We accepted this as a fact of life. My parents did everything in their power to make life a little easier for the family. Our parents insisted, do your best in school and obey the teachers. If any of the children disobeyed a teacher, my mother would discipline the guilty party. A familiar phrase from my mother was "the teachers have their education and you have yours to get". My parents were very serious about education because they knew the value of getting a high school education. They never had the opportunity to finish school.

We moved to 1116 River Street when I was in the fourth grade. This new residence was two blocks away from our previous house therefore, we attended the same school. This house was very near the Monongahela River. The railroad tracks were located between our house and the river. There were many major events in my life that occurred during this time period. I wanted to learn to swim but my mother warned me and my older brother to stay away from the river. I occasionally slipped away and went to the river and my mother never caught me disobeying her orders. A few of my friends along with myself were involved in a lot of dangerous behavior when we went to the river to learn how to swim. Before we were able to swim we crossed the river on inner tubes and logs. This was very dangerous, but at the age of eight and nine years old my friends and I never thought of the danger we were putting ourselves in by engaging in this type of activity.

A sobering event occurred which gave me a serious reality check. It happened during this time period. Two of my friends Ralph and Robert, twin boys who lived in the neighborhood drowned. It appeared that one got into trouble and his brother tried to save him and both drowned. My mother took me to the wake in order to see the twins in identical caskets. Despite the fact that I was eight years old, I learned a hard lesson which changed my life.

In order to get spending money, my brothers and I sold scrap iron, paper, cardboard and glass for one cent per pound. The buyers of these items were very strict during the inspection of the material. The glass had to be transparent or translucent, no colored glass. The iron could not contain railroad track spikes and the paper and cardboard had to be bundled. After a day's work we probably earned less than twenty cents.

Across the street from our house was a vacant lot we used to play baseball. There was a wall on one end which was the only remaining part of an old building structure. We used broom handles and mop handles for bats. We made the balls out of rags and placed a small rock inside for the core. The cover was made from part of a woman's nylon stocking. We eventually received a couple of used baseball bats.

Later we found a better area to play ball at the end of River Street. A vacant field had been cleared by the town for some future project. Very close to the lot was a house occupied by a Mr. Coleman who appeared to have mental problems. One day while playing ball, one of the players hit the ball into Mr. Coleman's yard. He told us not to enter his yard again. Later that day, the ball was again hit into his yard. My younger brother Harold Lloyd climbed over the fence to retrieve the ball. Mr. Coleman was the owner of a large German shepherd dog. He released the dog to attack my brother. The dog severed part of his right ear and made a severe laceration on his chest and right arm.

We were able to fight off the dog with our bats and had a neighbor call the police. My brother was taken to the hospital and my parents were notified. The police removed the dog and he was tested for rabies. I found out later the dog was euthanized because he had attacked a person before. After this incident, a court case was initiated relative to the medical treatment and the ultimate hospital bill.

I have a vivid memory of my life while our family was living in this small borough of Braddock, Pennsylvania. This was a difficult time in our history. I remember many of my friends and neighbors. The Blands, Siebles, Carringtons, Hendersons, Rileys, Bryants, Kisaks and Havrillas were a few of my friends.

While reflecting on my life in Braddock in the year 2001, I went to a book signing at the Garde Arts Theater in New London, Connecticut. My friend Linwood Bland Jr. wrote a book, "The Black Experience in Southeastern Connecticut". Despite knowing Mr. Bland since 1958, I never knew his personal history.

The day of the book signing on February 25th 2001 during Black History Month, I started a dialogue with Mr. Bland. We found out we had a lot in common. He informed me his family left Weldon, North Carolina, to obtain a better life in the North. My parents and grandparents came from this area of North Carolina. Many African-Americans left the South during the periods of the 1920s and 1930s to attain employment in the industrialized North, primarily the steel mills. Some members of Mr. Bland's family moved to Pittsburgh, Pa. to get jobs in the steel industry instead of settling in the New England area. Upon further discussion, I found out one of his relatives was a neighbor of my family in Braddock, Pa. in the 1930s. Mr. William Bland and his family lived at 1110 River Street. My family lived at 1116 River Street.

I was fortunate to obtain this information prior to the death of my friend, Linwood W. Bland Jr. on March 15th of 2005.

In the spring of 1937 the river overflowed its banks and our family had to temporarily leave our home. We stayed with relatives and friends until the water subsided. I recall staying with our Aunt Julia and Uncle Sam Hayes. We spent time at their house on a regular basis previously because Uncle Sam would always cut the boys' hair.

I remember stories about his military service during World War I. He spoke of being exposed to chemical weapons that were being used on the battlefield in Europe. The military was segregated at this time and his unit was responsible for bringing supplies and equipment to the front line troops. Uncle Sam eventually died in a Veterans Administration Hospital in July of 1965, but not from any service connected disability.

CHAPTER 2

When I was in the seventh grade, my English teacher was Miss Kelley, the sister of the actor / dancer Gene Kelly. Miss Kelly was a major influence on my handwriting as it appears today.

Another important event in my life was when I advanced to the eighth grade. We moved to 32-H Midway Drive in Whitaker, Pa. on April 8th 1943. This was a new housing project that was segregated by race. One side of this housing complex was for African-Americans. This was the first time we lived in segregated housing. When I started school in September, some of the white students gave the African-American students a difficult adjustment period. The teachers made a good effort to smooth the transition period for the new students.

My parents had eleven children at this time. The baby, Madge Marie was two months old. The apartment we lived in was the largest unit in each sectional complex. There were two bedroom units, three bedroom units and four bedroom units. I recall that the rent was $37.00 per month for the four bedroom units, $32.00 per month for the three bedroom units and $25.00 per month for the two bedroom units. This new housing was a major improvement over any housing we previously occupied. These units were heated by coal furnaces. We had a coal box in front of the house to store the coal. When my father purchased the coal, generally a ton at a time, it was dumped on the street and we carried it down the hill to the storage box, baskets at a time. With the size of our family it is easy to see my parents had a difficult time taking care of their family during this difficult era. In order to refrigerate food we had ice boxes and purchased blocks of ice. We purchased ice in blocks of twenty-five, fifty or one hundred pounds. One of our neighbors, Mr. Crump delivered our ice on a regular basis.

My older brother Mervin Jr. and I would go to North Braddock to find old apple trees and elderberry bushes in order to gather the apples and berries to bring back home. The apples we found were small and very hard. My mother used them to make apple pies. Occasionally we found raspberry bushes and pies were made of the berries. This was a difficult economic period and any food found was a positive event.

We walked to school which was about one mile away. In the winter it was very uncomfortable commuting this distance when the weather was inclement. In the spring when the weather was nice, we enjoyed walking down to an amusement park which was close to our school. Kennywood Park is one of the top amusement parks in the country. When the school term ended in May, there was always a school picnic at Kennywood. I remember there was always a truant officer located at the amusement park. I think we understood why a truant officer would have duty at this location.

The African-American students at this junior high school were discouraged from participating in the competition to be members of the athletic teams. I recall some of my classmates would say, "there are no colored baseball players". I felt insulted because my white classmates were unaware of the fact that an adjacent town had one of the top baseball teams in the country and was a member of the Negro Baseball League. The team was the Homestead Grays which happened to be the town where I was born. We decided to form athletic teams to represent our housing project. I felt that once I advanced to high school the circumstances would change. It was very interesting at one point while in high school our project baseball team had four Mosley family members playing at the same time. Mervin Sr. was in right field, Mervin Jr. was at second base, I was at first base and William Roger was at shortstop. My father was not a regular team member but our coach decided to put him in the lineup with three of his sons. My father played for two innings.

I decided if I was not going to be involved in athletics at the high school, I would try to get a job. When I was in junior high school at the age of thirteen, I obtained my first job delivering papers for the Pittsburgh Post Gazette. I enjoyed my independence as a carrier. I earned one dollar per week. I made my monetary collections from my customers on a weekly basis. There was an incident I will never forget. One week while collecting from my customers, I approached a house and knocked on the door. In a short period of time a small boy opened the door. Shortly thereafter, his mother appeared at the door. The small boy said "mother is that a nigger". The mother slapped the young boy and apologized to me for the incident. It was easy to see the undercurrent of racism that was prevalent in this housing project. My paper route included customers on the white as well as the African-American side of the housing project.

CHAPTER 3

I graduated from junior high school in 1944 and advanced to Homestead High School. My desire upon entering high school was to become a medical doctor some day.

When the school term started in September, I decided to try out for the football team. I was told I was too small because I weighed only 120 lbs. There was one African-American on the football team. When the basketball season began, one African-American was a member of the team. I wanted to try out for the baseball team but I was discouraged by the coach and by some of the players. I was advised to try out for the track team. I joined the team as a sophomore and had good seasons through my senior year. I participated in the long jump, hurdles, sprints and sprint relay teams. I ended my high school career undefeated in the high hurdles and one loss in my senior year in the low hurdles. I received a lot of experience playing football, basketball and baseball as a member of the teams we formed in the housing project. Our baseball team was one of the best in the area. We challenged the high school team to an exhibition game but the athletic director declined the offer. I was a member of the football team in my junior and senior years of high school however I did not get to play much.

Despite my love of athletics, I loved the academic areas also. My favorite subjects were biology and chemistry. I had a strong desire to have a future career in medicine. This motivated me to excel in the sciences. My mother always told me to follow a medical career because I loved the medical profession.

I had a job after school working at a drug store as a dishwasher and janitor. The drug stores at the time had dinettes that served food including an ice cream bar. I worked four hours per day during the week and eight hours on Saturday. I made approximately $30.00 per week which was pretty good money at the time. During my time in high school I also worked at a hardware store and as a pin setter in a bowling alley.

Mr. Gibson who lived next door offered me a job working in his automobile repair shop on weekends. I accepted and enjoyed the work. I received experience working on engines and installing manual transmissions. This experience has served me well.

The nation was still at war during my sophomore and junior years. War bonds were being bought as a patriotic gesture. I purchased saving bond stamps with money I earned from my employment. The stamps were purchased with a value of twenty five cents, fifty cents or one dollar. These stamps were placed in a book and redeemed as a bond when the book was filled. Patriotism was a common virtue among the citizens during the period of the war. School students were made aware of the sacrifice being made by military personnel. The segregation of the armed forces was rarely discussed despite the fact we lived in a segregated housing project and many African-American servicemen were losing their lives in the defense of this country. Ironically, some of the casualties from the war lived in this project prior to enlisting or being drafted into the military.

During my last two years of high school I started to seriously think about my future relative to career aspirations. I knew money would not be available to start a college education. My plan was to gain employment probably in the steel mill and save for my future college education. When I was in my junior year, I asked my mother if I could quit school and get a "real job". She said absolutely not because you will have all of your life to work after you get an education.

On May 22nd 1947 I graduated from high school and immediately started to search for employment. The steel mill was not hiring at this time so I looked for prospects elsewhere. The next few months I had failed to find a job other than a dishwasher or a janitor. I continued to search until I was offered a job at the Homestead Hospital as an Orderly. I felt optimistic because I would be working in an area where I could learn more about medicine. My shift was from 11 PM until 7 AM six days per week. I enjoyed my work because the medical profession was the goal I had planned to follow as a medical doctor. The doctors and nurses for whom I worked were extremely helpful in exposing me to knowledge which is necessary in gaining an understanding in the field of medicine. During some post-mortem examinations, the pathologist would explain how some of the organs functioned in the human body. I accompanied the night nurse around the ward and in the rooms while she took the patients' vital signs and dispensed the medications.

After working in the hospital for approximately eight months, I felt it was necessary to follow another path if I ever wanted to fulfill my dream of going to medical school. The pay was very low and I felt I was just spinning my wheels. When I decided to give my notice to the hospital administration that I was terminating my employment, I was offered a meager raise in pay but I informed the administrator I was contemplating joining the military. A significant problem I experienced during my period of employment at the hospital was my insomnia. It was very difficult for me to get the proper amount of sleep and appropriate rest due to my working hours of 11:00 PM to 7:00 AM. I arrived home after work at approximately 8:00 AM. I was never able to get more than four or five hours of sleep. It is easy to understand that eventually the lack of proper sleep and rest would ultimately affect my health. The day I left the hospital, the pathologist gave me a book on Bacteriology as a present and wished me well on my future aspirations. I still have this book today.

CHAPTER 4

Two of my high school classmates had been to the Navy Recruiting Office and informed me the recruiter was looking to recruit for the Naval Aviation Cadet Program. The Blue Angel Exhibition flight team was formed in 1946 after the war. We enlisted and were to complete basic training prior to examinations which included a battery of tests in addition to medical and dental. Upon completion we would be transferred to the Naval Air Station at Pensacola, Florida for flight training.

Upon graduation from flight school and commissioning we would be obligated to serve for a specific period of time.

I felt this would fit into my plans. After my obligated service, I would be eligible for the GI bill and this would give me the opportunity to obtain a four year degree prior to medical school. I was very optimistic about the road I was ready to travel. The recruiters informed the enlistees our compensation would be $78.00 per month.

I entered the United States Navy on May 2nd 1948 and departed for the United States Naval Training Center, Great Lakes in the state of Illinois. This was my first trip traveling on a passenger railroad train. When we arrived at the facility, there were seven African-Americans in our group. Our unit was to be Company 162. We were informed by our Company Commander that we were the first integrated unit to train at Camp John Paul Jones. In the past African-Americans were trained at Camp Robert Small or Camp Moffett. I realized at this time the military was still segregated. There were seven African-Americans in Company 162 out of 104 recruits. We were treated fairly and had a cohesive unit. I realized this was a groundbreaking time to enter the military. When our basic training ended on July 21st 1948, I was selected as the top recruit (Honor Man) for Company 162. Prior to our company graduation, my father received a letter dated July 15th, 1948 from F.J. Grandfield, Captain, U.S. Navy, the Commanding Officer of the Recruit Training Command, informing him, his son has been chosen as the "Honor Man" of Company 162. "James will complete training with his company on July 21st, 1948. He is to be commended upon his conscientious attention to duty which has led to this high honor". I felt this was a great honor at this particular time. The month I graduated, the Truman Administration issued executive order 9981, dated July 26th, 1948 de-segregating the military. I felt only good things were going to happen. After basic training I was to be examined for my next duty which was to attend the Naval Aviation Cadet School. I was informed after my dental examination I was disqualified because my teeth did not "occlude properly". I was extremely disappointed with my failure to qualify for flight school. I felt I was qualified. I found out later there was one African-American pilot in the US Navy. He lost his life during an air support operation in support of United Nation troops around the Chosin Reservoir in North Korea when his plane, a Corsair F4U-4 was shot down on December 4th, 1950. He was attached to the 32nd fighter squadron aboard the aircraft carrier USS Leyte (CV-32). This pilot was Ensign Jesse L. Brown of Hattiesburg, Mississippi. When I was not chosen for flight school maybe it was a blessing in disguise. I can never affirm my case was racially motivated, but all evidence points in that direction.

The services interpreted racial policies to impose segregation on the great majority of African-American personnel after World War II. Generally the Navy channeled its African-American enlistees into the steward's branch. The services justified segregation, inherently unequal and unjust in terms of treatment and opportunity, in the name of military efficiency.

These policies were based on the myth of racial inferiority. During this period of time some military leaders argued that the fewer the number of African-American servicemen, the less the armed forces would be burdened by the inept and un-teachable. I had noticed during this period many of the recruits and senior petty officers were from the South.

CHAPTER 5

I was given an option to choose a service school. I chose the Hospital Corps School which was located here at Great Lakes. I chose this school because my ultimate plan was to attend medical school sometime in the future.

The Hospital Corps School (Class A) convened in August 1948. The curriculum consisted of Anatomy and Physiology, Nursing Procedures, Sanitation, Immunizations, Basic Laboratory Procedures, Preventative Medicine, Pharmacology, Toxicology, Pharmacy, Chemistry, Field service with the US Marine Corp, Embalming, Atomic, Biological and Chemical Warfare and additionally, the preparation of the Operating Room for Surgery. This school prepared graduates to work in military hospitals treating patients directly and indirectly such as duty in the Operating Room, Sanitation Department and in the field with the US Marine Corp.

While in school, I had opportunities to go home to Pittsburgh, Pa. at various times on weekends. There was a Naval Air Station at Glenview, Illinois. Some reserve naval pilots performed obligated duty flying to Willow Grove Naval Air Station in Pennsylvania to log flying hours. I made one trip from Glenview Naval Air Station to Toledo, Ohio in a training aircraft and took a greyhound bus from Ohio to Pittsburgh. This experience made me reflect back to my reason for joining the military. These trips were available to military personnel at various times.

The class graduated the first week of October and the graduates were to be transferred to various naval medical facilities in the United States and a few International duty stations. The top graduates academically had first choices of the available billets. I had second choice based on graduating number two in class. The top graduate chose the Naval Air Station at Corpus Christi, Texas. I had a difficult decision in my choice. I had the opportunity to choose the Embassy in London, England, the National

Naval Medical Center in Bethesda, Maryland or the US Naval Hospital, Philadelphia, Pennsylvania. I wanted to stay near home so I chose the Naval Hospital in Philadelphia.

I started my duties at the Naval Hospital working on Ward 3B, an Orthopedic Ward. My duties encompassed patient treatment such as taking of vital signs, administration of medications and other duties relating to patient care. The work on this ward was very difficult because most of the patients were amputees and elderly veterans. Most of the ward population was patients with diabetes, osteomyelitis, Buerger's disease and Raynaud's disease. One of my patients was an extraordinary person. His name was Simon Rappaport. He was a victim of Buerger's disease (thromboangitis obliterans). He had numerous operations due to his medical condition. Both legs had been amputated above the knees and all fingers had been amputated except part of his right thumb. Despite the danger of smoking, he continued to smoke using the partial digit to hold the cigarette. He was able to wash and bath himself with no help from the ward staff. The mystery of this disease is that only smokers are afflicted.

I was fortunate for the opportunity to work in the Orthopedic Department, because in September 1945, three Naval Hospitals appeared on the Council of Medical Education's list of approved residency programs. The Philadelphia Naval Hospital was approved for Orthopedic Surgery and Pediatrics. This allowed me to observe much of the training given to young physicians in the residency programs. I had the opportunity to observe many surgical procedures.

I observed all of the young sailors who were amputees on the ward. Most of them sustained their injuries due to motorcycle accidents. Normally these amputees would have been on Ward 3A because their wounds were non-infectious. Ward 3B was assigned to patients having infections or potential infections. We referred to these wards as clean surgical wards and dirty surgical wards. When space was available on Ward 3A, the young amputees were transferred. They required less direct patient care than the older patients.

The Orthopedic Department had three surgeons. The Chief of Surgery was Captain Richard Morrison. Commander Herbert A. Markowicz was assigned to Ward 3A and Lieutenant Commander Warren D. Bundens was assigned to Ward 3B.

Commander Markowicz had a traumatic experience during the early years of his military career. He was a prisoner of war of the Japanese during a period of World War II. As a young surgeon he was forced to operate on Japanese soldiers, sometimes with crude instruments. He stated that at times he had to use butcher knives and bent forks as retractors. I noticed that Commander Markowicz had a large scar on his forehead. This injury was the result of being hit with the butt of a rifle. He shared this information with the young corpsmen on the wards because at some time in the future, we may be required to serve in the field with the Marine Corp.

In addition to our work on the ward, we had to stand Special watches in other areas of the hospital. About twice a week we were required to stand these watches of four hours after our normal eight hour shift. These watches could be assigned for duties on medical, surgical, neuro-psychiatric wards or in the nursery. We had to work every other weekend. We called it port and starboard liberty. These special watches expanded my overall knowledge in the medical field.

While serving at this hospital, I was a member of the basketball team. I sustained a knee injury when I tore my medial meniscus in my left knee. I decided I would not have a knee operation because of the method used at the time. By working on an Orthopedic Ward I had observed the results of many knee operations. I decided to wait and see if my mobility was adversely affected. I was young at the time and it didn't affect my ability in the athletic arena. Our basketball team competed against other military teams and additionally, we played exhibition games against the University of Pennsylvania, Villanova University and Temple University. One of the most frustrating seasons we had was during my second season. During our schedule in the military league, we lost five games in a row by a margin of two points. We finally got back on the winning side of close games.

The patients on the ward were frequently visited by members of the entertainment industry. In a period of two months, the patients met and talked with Hollywood actresses Jennifer Jones and Virginia Mayo. The patients looked forward to events planned by the Recreation Department.

The Hospital Corpsmen looked forward to the Army/Navy game each year which was played at the Municipal Stadium in Philadelphia. The stadium was located on South Broad Street, very close to the Naval Hospital which was located about two blocks away on Pattison Avenue. Many of us received tickets to attend the game. I always enjoyed being a spectator at the game.

I traveled to downtown Philadelphia by taking a bus from Broad and Pattison Avenue to Snyder Avenue where the Broad Street subway started. The subway route traveled to the northern sector of the city. I frequently made visits to Lombard and South Streets. When I was transferred from

Hospital Corp School to Philadelphia, I was very interested in visiting the area where my father was born. He was born in Philadelphia at 2310 South Street on April 13th 1907. I was able to see the old house where my father was born forty one years earlier. This will always be a very significant event in my life.

I had been in Philadelphia for less than a month when I received a message on October 29th 1948 that my mother had died. I was at the Hospital Recreation Center playing table tennis when I received the notification. I left the next day for Pittsburgh and attended the funeral. It came as a shock because I joined the Navy on May 2nd and she appeared in good health. I found out she had died in childbirth delivering her 13th child. My thought at this time was not taking the billet at the Embassy in London was a good choice. I knew my father would have a difficult challenge bringing up the ten children left at home.

My father loved his children and vowed to keep them all together. It was suggested that aunts and uncles could help him take care of the children but he declined. My father was an orphan early in life. His father died when he was two years old and his mother died when he was six years old.

His Uncle Benjamin, his father's brother took care of him and also his paternal grandmother who was blind. He returned to Philadelphia with his mother's brother Johnny Palmer and worked in a sugar factory when he was twelve years old. There were no child labor laws at the time. This is the primary reason he valued his family with all the young children. I felt relieved and optimistic when I left after the funeral.

I returned back to work after my mother's funeral and got immersed back in my duties. Dr. Warren D. Bundens, our Orthopedic surgeon asked if I wanted to work in the cast/dressing room in order to gain more experience and I accepted. My new duties involved changing the dressings of patients after the surgical removal of an extremity due to diabetes, circulatory problems and infections resulting in osteomyelitis, which is an infectious inflammatory disease of the bone marked by local death and separation of tissues. Changing dressings of patients with osteomyelitis required the debridement of necrotic tissue. During this period of time in 1948 it was proposed that insect fly larvae could be used to remove necrotic tissue. Some hospitals used this procedure. As recent as April of 2004, an article appeared in the New England Journal of Medicine advocating the use of insect fly larvae to debride necrotic tissue in some inflammatory diseases. I also applied casts on patients with certain fractures. I had the privilege of observing lumbar punctures to collect spinal fluid and various operations conducted in the operating room by the orthopedic surgeon.

I received significant encouragement from two of the nurses assigned to our ward. Miss Catherine Marcinko and Miss Anne Barton knew that my plans for the future were to attend medical school. They asked the surgeon to allow me to be in the operating room in order to observe various operations. Dr. Bundens agreed to their request. I will always remember the help and encouragement given to me by many of my co-workers.

While working on Ward 3B, we had a patient who had osteomeylitis of his lumbar spine. Mr. James was in a full body cast and required extensive care each day relative to normal body functions, bathing etc. A section of the cast covering the lumbar spine was cut out to facilitate the day to day dressing of the infected areas. I recall after cleaning the infected area, I had to pack the wound with sterile vasoline gauze approximately twice per week. This helped the tissue to granulate and heal from the bottom to the top.

During one of my special watches, I had the task of caring for an elderly patient on a general surgery ward. The patient required an extra unit of O positive blood. The Blood Bank was low on this type of blood despite the fact this is the most common blood type. I volunteered to donate a pint of blood but the patient's wife refused to accept blood from a Negro. The nurse tried to explain to the wife that all blood is the same however the wife turned a deaf ear. The unit of blood was donated by one of the white corpsmen on an adjacent ward. Apparently this couple had been indoctrinated relative to the "One drop rule" which was a dark event in American History. It was an unfortunate event because many of the corpsmen including myself donated blood on a continuous basis because we were paid $25.00 per pint. There was no indication of the race of the donor. The important issue was the compatibility of the donor and the recipient after type and cross-match procedures were completed.

I was able to maintain a social life despite the demands of my duties. Frequently members of some of the patients' families invited me to their homes for dinner. One of the first families I became close to was the Desphy family. Mr. Julio Desphy was a veteran of World War II. He frequently talked about his time in the Pacific during the war. He was born and brought up in the Phillipine Islands and joined the United States Navy as a stewards mate. Filipinos who joined the Navy at that time could only enter as a steward. His wife Anna was born and brought up in Philadelphia, she was Polish-American. Mr. and Mrs. Desphy had two daughters, Gloria Desphy and Sarah. On occasions I went to the movies with Sarah. We also went duckpin bowling some evenings after work. I enjoyed bowling and eventually started bowling on a regular basis. This friendship with Sarah was only of a social nature. I was not interested in getting into a serious relationship. I was nineteen at the time and she was seventeen. The Desphy family members were very nice people and always made me feel comfortable in their presence.

In April of 1949 I purchased my first automobile, a 1947 Packard. I used my automobile around town and not on extended trips. One of the corpsmen stationed at this facility, Joseph Gaul frequently drove to Pittsburgh. On some weekends I made the trip to Pittsburgh with Joe and shared expenses and helped with the driving. I kept my automobile for approximately fifteen months and sold it because I was hoping I would be selected to attend Clinical Laboratory School.

I met another nice family when I attended a high school basketball game. Mrs. Freda Brown's daughter (Barbara) was a cheerleader at West Philadelphia High School. Mrs. Brown had been divorced from Barbara's father for about four years. Mr. Brown moved to Florida but still stayed in contact with his daughter.

Mrs. Brown enjoyed all sporting activities and I frequently went to West Philadelphia High School basketball games. Mrs. Brown and Barbara attended many of my basketball games. The last game I recall Barbara and her mother attending on my schedule was an exhibition game against the University of Pennsylvania at the Palestra Complex in Philadelphia. Barbara was a junior in high school at this time. Her plans were to attend the University of Pennsylvania after graduation and study accounting. I stayed in contact with the Brown family long after I left Philadelphia.

After working in the cast and dressing rooms for a considerable period of time, I decided to expand my knowledge of medicine. I applied for Clinical Laboratory Technician and Blood Bank School at the National Naval Medical Center. The course of instruction would be for a period of fourteen months.

In the meantime, I started to work in the laboratory as an apprentice while awaiting my orders to the school. I was assigned to the section responsible for blood drawing on patients (active duty, retired and dependents) for tests to determine the diagnosis of medical or surgical conditions. During this time syringes and non-disposable needles were used to draw blood. After normal working hours, I would wash the syringes, needles, test tubes and other glassware prior to sterilization for use the following day. The bevels on the needles had to be sharpened and washed prior to sterilization.

I also volunteered to assist the Pathologist during post-mortem examinations. This activity allowed me to gain additional knowledge relative to the anatomy of the human body. I was able to observe first hand exposed organs, tissue, bones, nerves etc. I was instructed on how to open the skull, expose the brain and inspect the brain stem. This information coupled with my time in the operating room observing orthopedic surgery was very important in my search for additional medical knowledge.

On June 25, 1950 we went to work as usual. Later that day we were alerted that the Democratic People's Republic of Korea (North Korea) had invaded the Republic of Korea (South Korea) and the United States as a member of the United Nations was at war. This event would be a turning point in my life. My enlistment was for a period of three years from 1948 to 1951. We were given assurance this turmoil in the Far East was considered a "police action" rather than an outright war.

In mid July there was a request in the Personnel Office for a draft of twenty Hospital Corpsmen to be transferred to the FMF (Fleet Marine Force) at Camp Pendleton California for duty with the First Marine Division on the Korean Peninsula. I was one of the twenty in the draft, but my orders were modified because orders had just been received for me to attend Clinical Laboratory School.

I packed my belongings and went to the personnel office to obtain orders. A bus departed for Bethesda, Maryland via Washington, D.C. I noticed immediately upon arrival in the District of Columbia that this city was segregated. I took a second bus from Washington, D.C. to the Greyhound terminal in Bethesda, Maryland. I was picked up by a Navy van and traveled down Wisconsin Avenue to the Naval Medical Center.

It is remarkable that while I was writing part of my autobiography I reflected on my history when I left Philadelphia. I watched television while Barack Obama prepared for his inauguration as the 44th president of the United States. A CNN correspondent interviewed the president elect while the two were in Ohio.

Mr. John King, the news correspondent asked Mr. Obama how he felt about taking the oath of office on the west front of the Capital Building which was built on the back of slaves and live in the White House built by slave labor. The president elect replied we only have to go back fifty or sixty years to see a segregated city. The school system was rigidly segregated.

My thoughts went back fifty nine years ago when I was transferred to the Washington, D.C. area (Bethesda, Maryland). My Greyhound bus ticket read from Philadelphia to Washington, D.C. The date was September

9th 1950. Harry S. Truman was the 33rd president of the United States. I had previously mentioned President Truman signed the executive order de-segregating the military. I was feeling a lot of apprehension about my adjustment to the segregation laws of the South.

My plans were upon arrival in the Washington, D.C. area, I would spend much of my free time studying the history of this historic area of our nation. I have always been a student of history. This would be the first time I would be living in a segregated area of the nation.

I enjoyed my tour of duty in Philadelphia and valued the friendship of the many people I had the privilege to know. I promised the Desphy and Brown families I would keep in touch and come to see them when I have the opportunity.

I arrived at the National Naval Medical Center in Bethesda, Maryland on September 9, 1950 for my course of instruction in clinical laboratory procedures and blood bank training. The duration of this course would be fourteen months. During our indoctrination session I noticed there were two African Americans in the incoming class. I was one of the two. During this time in the Navy there were very few African-American corpsmen. In my basic Hospital Corp School class, I was one of two African-American students and finished number two academically in class standing.

When I arrived at this facility to attend school, the incoming class received a brief history of this institution. I learned at this time Secretary of Defense James Forrestal had committed suicide by jumping out of the window of the diet kitchen on the 16th floor of the hospital on May 22nd, 1949. Mr. Forrestal had previously agreed with President Harry S. Truman that "there should be equal treatment in government service for everyone regardless of his race, creed or color". The military had been de-segregated at this time for approximately two years. I recall the important event that occurred in 1948. President Harry S. Truman signed a historic Executive Order 9981 de-segregating the military. My father's five sons served in the military. Ironically, my father died on the thirtieth anniversary of the day of the signing. I felt no overt discrimination at any of my previous duty stations.

I had to make a major adjustment in my life because I was now stationed in the state of Maryland where segregation was the law. Washington DC was less than ten miles away however, the District of Columbia was also segregated. This was the first time I had ever lived in an area that was overtly segregated. Once you left the military facility, you had to comply with the laws of the new society you had to interact with as a citizen.

I knew I had to condition myself mentally for a new reality in my life. I had always known many areas of our nation exhibit covert racism but now I must experience overt racism. Many restaurants and movie theaters were strictly segregated. Some restaurants did not serve African-Americans. I had to learn the areas that were off limits to African-Americans.

I cannot think of any downtown areas of Bethesda, Maryland that I felt comfortable visiting after leaving the Naval facility. If I wanted to get a haircut or go to a movie, I went to Washington D.C. which was only a few miles away. It frustrated me when I had to get a haircut. Despite the fact the Navy facility had a barbershop, there were no African-American barbers. I will never forget the first time I went to the barbershop. The sailors waiting to get their haircut looked at me in an odd way. One of the barbers came over to me and said "we don't know how to cut colored hair". I left and knew I had to go to Washington D.C. in order to get my hair cut. I felt very self conscious in situations such as this.

The price of a haircut at the Navy facility at the time was twenty-five cents. The price of a haircut at a barber shop in Washington D.C. in the "colored area" was two dollars. It is easy to see the disparity relative to economic reality.

I decided to immerse myself fully in my studies and concentrate on my future goals. I knew my academic performance was to be closely scrutinized but I felt up to the task.

This school was very important to my future as a potential medical student. My plan was to obtain an undergraduate degree in Microbiology prior to my entrance into a medical school in the future.

The curriculum for this course consisted of Hematology, Serology, Biochemistry, Bacteriology, Parasitology, Virology, Histology and Blood Bank procedures (typing, cross-matching, titration etc). This course consisted of theoretical as well as practical application of the disciplines studied. During practical work in Hematology, I was very interested in reading bone marrow specimens from patients suffering from various types of leukemia. It was very ironic because my son born six years later would at age twenty-one be diagnosed with myeloid leukemia.

There was an incident that occurred during my practical training that made a permanent imprint on my life. Occasionally students from our class had to travel to various wards and rooms to collect blood specimens for the hospital laboratory. I frequently was assigned to a pediatric ward. There was a small girl about three years old from whom I collected blood on a frequent basis. This small child was suffering with lymphatic leukemia.

When I walked into the ward wearing a white laboratory coat and carrying my blood collecting tray, the small girl named Elizabeth would start to cry because she knew I was there to collect blood. One week I bought her a small doll as a present. The following week when I was scheduled to make my trip to the ward, I was notified that Elizabeth had died over the weekend. Her parents thanked me for my kindness to their daughter. I stayed in touch with them until the father was transferred to a new duty station.

My training was progressing well and I was earning very good grades. My exposure to a variety of scenarios was very educational. During our study of Parasitology, I volunteered to work on a special project as a student with the National Institutes of Health (NIH). This project was to determine the percentage of elementary school students who suffered with pinworm infestation in the Washington DC area. The parasite Enterobius Vermicularis is a common parasitic condition with young children living in impoverished areas. Upon conclusion of the study, it was determined that approximately 40% of the subjects tested turned out positive for pinworm. I learned the proper method of collecting and examining specimens. The National Institutes of Health (NIH) developed a specific methodology for this project. The procedure used for the collection of specimens for microscopic examination was known as the "NIH swab". The swabs were cotton tipped applicators wrapped with scotch tape. The parents were instructed how to obtain the specimens. When the child was asleep at night, the parents would obtain the specimens outside of the anal area. The parasite lays eggs in this area. A courier would pick up the specimens. This was a significant learning experience for me. This experience could also help parents gain knowledge relative to children with this disorder.

Additionally, during our study of Parasitology we investigated the life cycles of malaria, nematodes(roundworms), trematodes (flatworms or tapeworms), flukes (intestinal, liver, and blood).During my time working in the laboratory at the Naval Hospital in Philadelphia, I observed some cases of malaria. The cases observed were Plasmodium vivax and Plasmodium malariae. I have never seen a case of Plasmodium falcipirum. Blood samples were taken at the time during the cycle when the red blood cells ruptured. This was a major learning experience for me in understanding this parasitic disorder.

I knew Plasmodium vivax episodes occur about every 48 hours. Plasmodium malariae episodes occur about every 72 hours. The most important human parasite among the sporozoa is Plasmodium, the causative agent of malaria. I became extremely interested in this parasitic condition that occurs to people primarily in the developing world.

When the individual infested with this parasite experiences the chills and fevers, the red blood cells are rupturing as part of the life cycle of the sporozoa that had been injected by the bite of a female anopheles mosquito.

I have observed a few cases of nematode and trematode infestations. The case I will never forget was an infestation of the tapeworm, Diphyllobothrium latum. The patient was a sailor stationed at the Patuxent River Naval Air Station in Maryland. He was admitted and came under the treatment of a staff physician. During treatment, the stool was examined for ova and parasites. Over a period of a few days, proglottids (segments) were in the stool. It was estimated that the tapeworm was approximately twenty feet in length. The scolex (head) was never recovered. This fish tapeworm infestation occurs in Europe particularly Scandinavia. Japan, Africa, South America, Canada, and the United States especially Alaska and the Great Lakes region are also affected. Infestation often is caused by eating raw or undercooked freshwater fish. The adult worm has several thousand egg-containing sections (proglottids) and is generally fifteen to thirty feet in length. Eggs are released from the proglottids inside the intestine and are expelled in the stool. The egg hatches in freshwater and releases the embryo, which is eaten by small crustaceans. Crustaceans in turn are eaten by fish. People are infected or infested when they eat the fish.

I enjoyed my study of Parasitology. We were at the point in our course when evaluations were being made relative to our academic progress.

An academic board was convened every six weeks in order to determine the academic progress of the students. After three months of school, the other African-American in the class failed the academic board and was dropped from the course. Later that evening in the dormitory, I overheard a conversation about the result of the academic board. One of my classmates stated "one down and one to go". I understood what the discussion was all about. I had enough confidence in myself to know that I would complete the course. Naturally I was upset about the negative feelings.

Some of my classmates had negative feelings about race relative to learning. The group making these comments never knew I was aware of their conversation. I never let emotions dictate my actions in the decisions I make relative to my journey in life.

During our study of Blood Bank Procedures, the name of Dr. Charles R. Drew was mentioned. The instructor stated Dr. Drew was a pioneer in the processing of blood for transfusions, particularly during war time operations. Under Dr. Drew's leadership, blood plasma was used as a blood volume expander thereby saving many lives in the battle field environment.

Dr. Drew died in the emergency room of a hospital in Burlington, North Carolina of severe injuries sustained in an automobile accident. He was on his way to Tuskegee, Alabama along with three other physicians. The other passengers suffered only minor injuries. This event occurred five months prior to my arrival in Bethesda, Maryland.

I felt a sense of pride during our study of blood banking procedures because, an African-American physician was the pioneer in establishing a landmark process that saved many lives during World War II.

When our class was studying serology, I understood antigen-antibody reactions were necessary in the technique of blood grouping. I immediately thought about Dr. Charles R. Drew. In addition to blood grouping, typing and cross-matching using antigen-antibody reaction is necessary prior to blood transfusions. I understood the accuracy during the cross matching of the donor and recipient's blood was very critical to the welfare of the patient receiving the transfusion.

Serology is often used in a limited sense to denote laboratory diagnostic tests. We discussed the various serological tests for syphilis. One of the most specific tests to reduce the number of false positives was the Hinton Test named after Dr. William A. Hinton. I found out later Dr. Hinton was an African-American physician. He became the first of his race to be named a professor at Harvard University Medical School. This was a long journey for a man whose father was a slave. My love of history re-kindled my curiosity relative to pioneers in the field of medicine and science.

It is remarkable that during our studies in Blood Bank Procedures and Serology, the ethnicity of the pioneers in these fields were never revealed to the students. During this period of our studies, I was the only African-American student in the class. We all know the racial climate that was prevalent in the District of Columbia and the state of Maryland in 1950.

I kept myself busy after classes being involved in athletics. I was a member of the varsity basketball and softball teams. The coaches were very interested in the academic progress of the players who were students in the various schools.

The basketball coach, Commander Frank Frates wanted to talk to me after practice one day. He wanted to know why I never went to college based upon my current grades in school. At this time I was carrying a 4.0 grade point average. I informed him I joined the Navy to attend flight school but failed the dental examination because my teeth did not "occlude properly". Coach Frates was a dentist. He wanted to see me in his office the next morning. After the dental examination I was told there was nothing wrong with my teeth and I should re-apply. I felt at this time that I should move on because I believed the incident that occurred two years earlier was racially motivated. I understood that covert racism still existed.

My main focus at this time was academics and athletics. During the summer months I was a member of the varsity fast pitch softball team. During my time as a member of the softball team we played a team from the USS Williamsburg in the summer of 1951. The USS Williamsburg was the presidential yacht. After the game we were invited to dinner aboard the yacht. We had a very enjoyable time. This was an event in my life I will always remember. During the winter I played on the varsity basketball team. Our basketball team, the NNMC (National Naval Medical Center) Admirals competed against very good competition. Our participation in various exhibition games gave us experience when competing against military teams in various tournaments, such as the Potomac River Naval championships etc. Our team played an exhibition game against some members of the Washington Capitals which was a member of the NBA at the time. We also played against the Capital Bisons. This team was composed of many local high school and college players. I recall this team had an outstanding high school player named Elgin Baylor. He later attended Seattle University. He received All American honors during his years at this school and later played for the Minneapolis and Los Angeles Lakers. Upon his retirement from basketball, he was inducted into the Basketball Hall of Fame in Springfield, Massachusetts and coached an NBA team.

I enjoyed my time at this facility which was the National Naval Medical Center. The medical staff at the hospital complex was responsible for treating members of the Executive, Legislative and Judicial branches of government. Additionally, high ranking military officers were also treated and given annual physical examinations. I recall the day President Harry S. Truman was there for his annual physical examination. Another event I was involved in occurred during my time when I had the duty of drawing blood from patients in various areas of the hospital. I previously explained how I was assigned at one time to the pediatric wards for the duty of collecting blood specimens. One day I was sent to draw blood from a patient. To my amazement, the patient was Mrs. Shirley Temple Black. Her husband was

Lieutenant Commander Charles L. Black who was a naval officer. I found out later she delivered a son in 1952 which was about six months after I graduated from school and was transferred to Norfolk, Virginia. These are memories I frequently **recall that happened during my military service.**

I was informed that my youngest sister Marvina was admitted to the hospital because of possible brain seizures. She was born the day my mother died. She was admitted early in 1951. The early diagnosis was an abnormality of the parietal suture in the skull.

My father visited the baby for a few hours before he went to work and was back at the hospital for an hour or so after work. He met a Nurse assistant who was taking care of the baby and they became friends. He hired her as a housekeeper to assist him and my older sister Alma in taking care of the many young children at home. Alma was married and could only spend a specified period of time with her younger siblings.

The baby died on June 15, 1951 as the result of a seizure. The housekeeper Irene continued to take care of the young children still at home.

Prior to graduation from Clinical Laboratory School, I bought a 1950 Chevrolet Deluxe from a General Motors dealership on Bladensburg Road. It was a very nice looking vehicle with low mileage. I knew after graduation I would be transferred to Norfolk, Virginia or San Diego, California for sea duty. When I purchased the vehicle, I didn't stop to think about my impending sea duty and where my vehicle would be parked or stored while I was at sea. Some ships were away from their home ports for six months at a time. I was hoping I would not be assigned to an aircraft carrier because these ships were generally deployed for six months at a time. The aircraft carriers in the Atlantic Fleet were assigned to the Sixth Fleet in the Mediterranean while the aircraft carriers in the Pacific Fleet were assigned to the Seventh Fleet in the Western Pacific. I had to wait until I received my orders to make plans for the future. My class graduated October 12th, 1951.

CHAPTER 6

I received my transfer orders to report to the USS Cadmus AR-14 in Norfolk, Virginia. I was relieved because repair ships spend a considerable amount of time in port. I felt in the future I would be assigned to a ship that traveled to various parts of the world.

I decided to leave my car at the National Naval Medical Center until I became settled at my new duty station in Virginia. I would then return to Maryland to pick up my car and drive back to Virginia.

When I started my journey to Virginia, I had to sit in the back of the greyhound bus due to the segregation laws in the South. This was an odd feeling because I had never been forced to abide by segregation laws. I knew I had to condition myself to live in a segregated society.

The bus made rest stops during the trip to Virginia. African-American passengers were not served at the Howard Johnson Motor Lodges and separate restrooms were made available for white and colored passengers. When the bus reached the city of Newport News, I had to take a ferry boat to the city of Norfolk. The restrooms on the ferry boat were also segregated. I resented the situation I found myself in however I had to comply with the rules and laws that were prevalent in this area.

I arrived at the Norfolk Naval Base and reported on board the USS Cadmus AR-14. This ship was attached to the Service Force, US Atlantic Fleet. This duty station was my first shipboard experience.

I reported to the personnel office and turned in my transfer orders prior to reporting to the Medical Department. I was given my indoctrination by the Chief Petty Officer (HMC) after meeting with the medical officer. The following personnel comprised the Medical Department. The medical officer was Lieutenant Kaufman, the Department Head. We had one Chief Petty Officer (HMC), one First Class Petty Officer (HM1), two Second

Class Petty Officers (HM2), five Third Class Petty Officers (HM3) and five Hospital Men (HN) on board. I was a Third Class Petty Officer (HM3) at the time. One of the Second Class Petty Officers was being transferred to a new duty station.

This ship had a small Clinical Laboratory, Pharmacy, Record Office, Sick Call area, Sanitation office and a small Ward.

My duties involved operating the laboratory, assisting in the Pharmacy and Record Office, treating of patient illnesses, first aid training of the crew and distribution of emergency medical supplies throughout the ship.

I immersed myself in this new assignment and was determined to learn as much as possible. This ship had a crew of approximately 900 personnel. My first day aboard I was taken on a tour of the ship, including the machine shops and stowage areas for emergency medical supplies.

When I left the ship after working hours, I had to remember the city of Norfolk was segregated. It didn't take long to understand that some areas were off limits to African-Americans. This was a situation whereby I knew I had to adjust.

I joined the ship's basketball team and we competed against other ships in the area. This activity kept me busy and focused. Between practice and games I kept busy most of the time.

It was difficult getting accustomed to the segregation laws in the South while competing in athletic events. Overall I had no problems with segregation laws, when I played on military bases however, when our team played civilian teams in the city leagues or minor league teams in some cities, problems occurred. It was very stressful at times because I was the only African-American on the baseball team. I will never forget an instance prior to one of our baseball games. We had a game against a civilian team in the City of Norfolk. Our team manager was informed I could not play because of a city ordinance relative to segregation laws. I felt this event was just a bump in the road of life. I admit however, it was a strange feeling to be self conscious about being in this situation. I also recall not seeing any African-Americans in the baseball stands.

One weekend I found out a civil rights attorney was in Norfolk for a speech relative to school de-segregation. I decided to go to the auditorium to hear the speech. The speaker was the NAACP attorney Thurgood Marshall. I found out at a later date that four de-segregation cases weaved their way to the high court by the fall of the following year. The Brown case (Kansas) would be combined with the other three cases from Delaware, Virginia and South Carolina.

Thurgood Marshall left Virginia to give another speech in Lumberton, North Carolina. It was discovered later that the Klu Klux Klan was planning to harm Mr. Marshall. He was smuggled out of North Carolina.

During this period of time, I was very interested in the mindset of African-Americans living in this area of the country. I felt awkward living in the South where segregation was rampant and the law was strictly enforced.

I received a pleasant surprise at the end of November 1951. My older brother Mervin Jr. was transferred from a ship operating with the Amphibious Force, US Atlantic Fleet to a new duty station. The new duty station was the Tactical Air Control Squadron Six at the Norfolk Naval Air Station. Mervin Jr. had a rating of Second Class Petty Officer (YN2). The yeoman rating was record keeping for the crew other than medical records.

It was nice having my brother stationed in the area. We decided to spend some of our weekends visiting our grandparents. They lived wests of Norfolk in a small town of Valentines. We made the trip to visit our grandparents on many weekends. Our uncle and aunt, Linwood and Sallie Taylor lived in Valentines also. Linwood and Sallie had nine children, six girls and three boys. Mervin and I had the opportunity to get to know and interact with our cousins who were teenagers and pre-teens.

There was an incident which occurred during one of our trips to Valentines that reinforced my feeling about being in this area of the country. My brother and I accompanied our grandmother to a small store. She shopped at this store for many years. The store was owned by the Clary family. The current proprietor was Robert Clary who had grown up with my mother. My grandmother introduced us to Mr. Clary as the sons of her daughter Vashti. My brother and I were both in uniform and Mr. Clary remarked, "I was a good friend of your mother". I purchased some candy for Uncle Linwood's small children and my grandmother purchased a bag of flour. Mr. Clary handed me my change and when my grandmother reached for her change, he slid it to her over the counter. On the way back to the house I asked my grandmother why Mr. Clary did not place the change in her hand. She said the white people always treat colored people in that manner. I asked her why he didn't treat me the same way, she responded I didn't live in the area and was only a visitor.

The African-Americans living in segregated areas such as this become accustomed to this type of treatment.

My uncle warned me and my brother to be careful driving on Highway 58 East to Norfolk, Va. because African-Americans are stopped by the highway patrol more often than whites. I made an effort to drive at the posted speed or slower. Racial profiling was rampant during this period however this is a new term that is used today. Racism is dressed up and to make it more palatable, it is called profiling.

Mervin and I enjoyed the time spent visiting our maternal grandparents in addition to our uncle Linwood Taylor, our mother's brother, his wife Sallie and their nine children.

I recall discussing with my grandfather his life in North Carolina when he was a young boy. He talked proudly about his grandpa Nick and his father James Sr. who was a minister. Being the son of a minister, he was introduced to the church early in life. A considerable amount of time was spent reading the Bible and he was a deacon at Bethany Baptist Church in Valentines, Va. after moving from North Carolina in 1922 at the age of fifty two years. My grandmother Fannie was thirty eight years of age.

As a student of history, I frequently engaged in a period of dialogue with my grandfather, uncles, etc. to attain any information of historical significance in my search for knowledge relative to my family history.

My grandfather's favorite book of the Bible was Ecclesiastes. He told me and Mervin to make a habit of searching the scriptures daily. At the age of eighty one years he was an avid reader. I was amazed that during all of his public reading, I never saw him wearing a pair of eyeglasses. I considered him to be an amazing person. He was born five years after the Civil War was over and the Thirteenth Amendment to the United States Constitution was ratified. I frequently asked him how his father, grandfather and their families faired during the period of slavery. He never liked to talk about the past. He only told me that it was a very difficult time and they did the best they could under the circumstances that were present at the time. I assumed they conditioned themselves to the reality of living in a society whereby they were reduced to the desire of just existing. The period of slavery in our nation's history was an awful blemish on our image throughout the world. I observed many African-American families while I was stationed in Virginia, still sharecropping to eke out a living. I always looked at sharecropping as one step above slavery.

In the summer of 1952, Mervin was released from his reserve duty and went back to Pittsburgh, Pa. I drove him to the Greyhound Bus Station in Norfolk, Va. I waited until he had obtained his ticket. The bus left on time and I drove back to my ship at the Norfolk Naval Base. I found Mervin's Bible on the rear seat of my car. When he arrived back home, I called and informed my brother he had left his Bible in the car. His response to me was to keep it, read it, and use it as a blueprint of life. I still have this bible today with all the written notations placed years ago by my brother.

A few months later in October of 1952, I received transfer orders to the United States Naval Hospital at Portsmouth, Va. I went to the personnel office of the USS Cadmus AR-14 to question my transfer orders. I had been a crew member for approximately one year on this ship. I was transferred to the USN Hospital, Portsmouth, Virginia. At that time, this hospital had a shortage of laboratory and blood bank technicians. During this period of time, the hospital was under staffed and had a large patient load. I had been there for approximately one month when I was informed I would be transferred temporarily for thirty days to the USN Training Center, Bainbridge, Maryland to help organize an Epidemiology Research Unit to investigate the outbreak of a strep throat infectious epidemic at this recruit training center.

I arrived at this new temporary duty station in November 1952. This team consisted of a medical officer and three laboratory technicians. We set up a bacteriology laboratory and started to examine, obtain throat cultures and administer antibiotics to many of the infected recruits. This was a large military establishment with approximately 10% of the recruits infected with bacterial throat infections. We worked approximately eight hours a day initially and then twelve hours per day obtaining throat samples and inoculating blood agar plates to incubate for growth, reproduction and identification of the specific beta hemolytic streptococcal bacteria. With this information, the appropriate dose of an antibiotic could be administered.

The culture media used could be enriched and its composition could vary within wide limits to conform to the requirements of particular problems. The problem facing our team was to isolate, identify and determine the appropriate treatment for personnel infected. One of the commonest means of enrichment was the addition of 10% de-fibrinated blood usually from sheep. After we had been here for approximately three weeks, we were informed this temporary duty will become permanent and we would be getting a permanent change of station order. It appeared this project would take a considerable period of time.

Our laboratory was in the first regiment dispensary. We were given the major part of the building for our offices and berthing spaces because we spent a major part of the day working in the laboratory.

Our group spent New Years Eve and New Years Day working in the laboratory. The first week of the New Year we finally got the opportunity to leave the base and enjoy a little rest and recreation. I had an unfortunate situation happen to me on one of my trips to Baltimore, Maryland. I was stopped by the police while driving through Druid Hill Park after midnight. I went to a party with three other people from our military base. When we left to return back to Bainbridge, Maryland, we were told to go through Druid Hill Park because it was a short cut to Route 40 which was the main thoroughfare going north. When I was stopped, I was told to get out of the car. I noticed one of the officers was talking directly to me and the other officer was about six feet away with his hand on his weapon. The officer questioning me stated "you have been in this park before. I told you two weeks ago not to drive through this park after midnight".

This was not true because I had never been in this park before. The officer insisted I had been in the park before because he remembered the license plate number LU-213, Pennsylvania. Two week earlier my car was registered in Virginia. I knew they were looking for trouble so I remained silent. I was allowed to leave when I showed the officers my military identification card. This was a very demeaning moment in my life. I was a member of the military and was treated as a common criminal.

In March of 1953, I met my future wife in Wilmington, Delaware. We went to Philadelphia, Pennsylvania on April 3rd 1953 to attend a movie. I asked Lillie when was her birthday and she told me today was her birthday.

I kept myself busy competing in athletics and visiting Lillie who lived in Wilmington, Delaware. During the baseball season our schedule included games with many Army bases in addition to other military bases and minor league teams affiliated with major league baseball. When we played Fort Eustis, Virginia, Willie Mays was in centerfield for the "Wheels". Fort Eustis was the Transportation Division. Fort Belvoir, Virginia had a major league player in Dick Groat of the Pittsburgh Pirates. Fort Lee had Wes Covington of the Milwaukee Braves and Vernon Law of the Pittsburgh Pirates.

Fort Meyer had Johnny Antonelli of the New York Giants. We had Johnny Podres of the Brooklyn Dodgers as one of our pitchers. In addition, we had two AAA pitchers and a catcher who was in the farm system of the Cincinnati Reds. I enjoyed playing and competing against this type of talent.

After the baseball season ended, we started gearing up for the upcoming football season. We had a difficult schedule to play this season.

During this period of the Korean War, there were many college and professional athletes in the military to fulfill their military obligations. I knew it would be difficult to make the roster of players however, I was confident I had the ability to compete with anyone. We had two members of the Chicago Bears, a player from the Washington Redskins and many players from major college programs. Near the end of the season, I became a starter. For the 1953 season, I was selected to the third All-Navy team and honorable mention on the All-Armed Forces team.

I had an outstanding football coach. I learned from him that proper nutrition and exercise were important to prevent injuries. I was fully aware of the importance of proper warm up procedures prior to a game. When I played football at the Naval Training Center in Maryland, I was fortunate to have a coach with extensive experience and a trainer from the University of Tennessee. This coach became the head coach at the University of Arizona and an assistant coach in the National Football League. I was contacted by Kansas State University however I had obligated duty to perform in the military.

During the 1953 football season, we played an exhibition game against the University of Maryland. Byrd Stadium was a new facility on this college campus. There were four African-Americans on our team and we became the first of our race to play football on this campus. No negative events occurred and we were treated with respect. African-Americans were not accepted at this University during this time in our history.

In November 1953 we played our final game of the season against the Pensacola Naval Air Station. When we were leaving the field at halftime, I was approached by a gentleman who asked me where I was from. I replied Pennsylvania. His next comment was "too bad you are colored". I did not think that he was trying to insult me by stating his feelings. I assumed he was from a southern school. I found out later this individual was Paul "Bear" Bryant who was the football coach at the University of Kentucky. He later became the football coach at the University of Alabama and recruited the first African-American to play football at that institution.

After my final game of the 1953 season in Florida, I asked Lillie to marry me and she said yes. We decided to get married on her 21st birthday which was April 3rd 1954.

Lillie had a son, Ernest Greene Jr. age four, from a previous relationship. He was living with his maternal grandmother in Cartersville, South Carolina. Lillie and her mother decided that Ernest Jr. should stay with his grandmother. I was hoping that he could stay with us as my stepson.

Lillie was working as a domestic for Dr. S. Ward Cascells Jr. an orthopedic surgeon in Wilmington, Delaware. His wife Oleda was an attorney and they had two sons, S. Ward Cascells III and his younger brother Christopher. Dr. Cascells Jr. developed the procedure of arthroscopic surgery.

Lillie and I were married at the chapel on the base by a Navy Chaplin. A shipmate of mine, Hymie Howell and his wife Juanita along with Jake Harris and his girlfriend Vastine Livingston attended the ceremony. We stayed in Wilmington, Delaware for approximately one week as the guest of Mrs. Corks who knew Lillie since she arrived in Delaware from South Carolina.

I applied to Navy Housing for an apartment and after two weeks I was notified that a unit was available. On April 18th 1954 we moved into the trailer park on the base. Our new address was Trailer #31 Bainbridge Village. We traveled to South Carolina to visit with Lillie's parents after our marriage.

The next month brought turmoil to the nation, state, city and to this military establishment. The US Supreme Court ruled in the Brown v. Board of Education of Topeka, Kansas landmark school de-segregation lawsuit case on May 17th 1954. The court ruled that separate but equal facilities was unequal therefore, un-constitutional. Many problems erupted on this military facility at this time. The African-American servicemen attached to this base were not allowed to send their children to the elementary school on this military facility. It was explained to the African-American parents, the laws of the state of Maryland prevails. Although I had no children at the time, I was involved in petitioning the military to remedy this situation. One of the parents circulated a petition for the African-Americans to sign and to forward a copy to the US Congress and to President Eisenhower. The Commanding Officer of this military installation became aware of the petition and the African-American students were allowed to attend the school.

I had observed the deplorable conditions of the school the African-American elementary school children attended. It was easy to see that these students were denied equal facilities. Additionally, they were made to feel inferior to their white friends who attended the school on the base. The children were all members of the military community. All students were dependents of white and African-American servicemen.

I found out at a later date that President Eisenhower was not happy with the court's decision because he would be up for re-election in 1956 and needed the support of many Southern members of the Congress.

He made a statement in his second term that he made a miserable mistake by appointing Governor Earl Warren of California to the Supreme Court as the Chief Justice. Most people assumed his statement reflected on the school desegregation opinion which was unanimous with no dissenter.

This Supreme Court decision overturned the Plessy v. Ferguson landmark US Supreme Court decision which was decided on May 18, 1896. Despite the Brown v. Board of Education decision, public accommodations were still denied to African-Americans because of rigid segregation laws in the South where I was stationed as a member of the military. I was living in the state of Maryland at the time however I was denied public accommodations in many areas. When my wife and I went to Baltimore on weekends, we had to return to our home on the Naval Base because we could not rent a motel or hotel room in the city or any small towns nearby. When we went to the movies off base, we had to sit in the balcony because we were not allowed to sit on the main floor of the theater because of the segregation laws. This was an emotional situation whereby we had to endure.

I became interested in the Plessy v. Ferguson decision and read the story of the upholding of the constitutionality of racial segregation even in public accommodations. It was ironic that the Supreme Court Justice who wrote the majority opinion was Henry B. Brown on a seven to one vote with one Justice not participating in the case.

Fifty eight years later, the plaintiff was Oliver Brown v. Board of Education of Topeka, Kansas. I looked at this case not only about children and education but also about public accommodations for all people. I felt uncomfortable about the lack of public accommodations despite the court rulings. I was in the military and this decision relative to public accommodations was null and void when African-American military personnel received change of station orders. For the next decade I followed the enforcement of this landmark decision. It was very interesting how the states in the South circumvented this decision because of the clause inserted by Justice Felix Frankfurter. The clause was "all deliberate speed". This was an invitation for the school districts of the South to drag their feet in the implementation of the court order to desegregate the public schools. The District Court and the Fifth Circuit Appellate Court used this clause to insist that plans were being made to abide by the Supreme Court decision. After fifteen years, pressure was applied to the national school districts that were not in compliance with the Supreme Court ruling. I followed this issue for many years because of its historical significance.

For the remainder of my time stationed in the South as a member of the United States military, I felt the sting of discrimination in many instances.

A strange scenario occurred after the children were allowed to attend the school on the base. The military member whose wife circulated the petition was transferred. This was a way to mute the complaints of this woman.

After the issues relative to the schools subsided, everybody settled down to some normalcy in the community. I continued to work in the Epidemiology Research Unit until the threat of new strep throat cases was over, and reports were submitted to the Naval Research Laboratory and the Bureau of Medicine and Surgery.

In August of 1954 the Research Unit was closed and I was transferred to Dispensary 506 to supervise the Clinical Laboratory. This Dispensary was a satellite unit to the Naval Hospital on the base.

One of my major assignments was the responsibility to perform the blood alcohol tests. Military personnel brought to the base by the State Police or the Shore Patrol, who were suspected of being intoxicated while driving or engaged in other illegal activity such as disturbing the peace were subjected to a sobriety test. The results of the blood tests were turned over to the Duty Officer of the base and the Administration Officer of the hospital.

Occasionally the specific individual who was determined to be driving under the influence or other offenses would be subject to a court-martial. This judicial act could determine the career of a military member in many instances therefore, it was necessary to make accurate determinations as to the level of alcohol in the blood stream of the individual tested. I was aware of the importance relative to results of any tests that I had the responsibility to conduct.

In one case, the military person charged with disturbing the peace and driving under the influence was to receive a summary court-martial because the Shore Patrol Officer determined that he may have been under the influence of alcohol. During my initial and subsequent testing on the individual, the blood alcohol concentration exceeded the legal limit therefore, he was charged with both counts.

The defense attorney requested that I be called as an expert witness relative to errors that may occur during the Bogan alcohol test. I was required to explain how the test was conducted and how errors could be made. I was required to explain the entire procedure.

I explained the principle used in this procedure is based on the fact that the alcohol is volatilized from the substance to be tested, whether blood or urine. It is drawn with aeration by means of a suction pump into

Anstie's reagent, a solution of potassium dichromate and sulfuric acid. The quantitative reduction of the potassium dichromate in the presence of the sulfuric acid produces a blue color which is compared with a set of known standards.

I started the test by arranging an aeration apparatus consisting of five test tubes 25 by 200 millimeters. In the first tube five cubic centimeters of Anstie's reagent is placed. This tube acts as a filter to remove any trace of alcohol or reducing substances in the air. Its use is optional if the air is free of reducing substances. In my opinion, this tube should always be used because there is always the possibility of unknown substances. I consider this a safety factor.

With a pipette, I transfer one cubic centimeter of the specimen to be tested into the second tube. Then one cubic centimeter of the Scott-Wilson reagent, three to four cubic centimeters of distilled water and five to ten drops of liquid petrolatum is added to prevent foaming.

The third and fourth tubes are left empty and act as safety tubes in the aeration system to prevent foam from reaching the fifth tube. These tubes can be eliminated if a loose plug of glass wool is used in the second tube to avoid foaming. In the fifth tube five cubic centimeters of Anstie's reagent is placed by pipette. All the tubes are connected in their proper place in the aeration system. All the tubing and rubber stoppers are checked for leaks. The outlet of the fifth tube is connected to the suction pump for aeration. The speed of aeration is controlled so that a constant stream of air is always flowing through the apparatus as evidenced by two to four bubbles per second passing through the Anstie's reagent of the fifth tube. This is a very important step in the procedure prior to immersing the apparatus into the boiling water bath. The aeration process in the boiling water takes a period of ten minutes. If material from the second tube containing the sample enters the fifth tube containing the Anstie's reagent, the test must be repeated from the beginning because of a potential error in the test result.

After aeration for ten minutes, the fifth tube is removed from the unit and cooled in a cold water bath. The contents are transferred to a clean test tube identical in size and color to that containing the standard. The unknown is compared with a known set of standards read against a white background. Alcohol is reported as milligrams per cubic centimeter of whole blood. If the alcohol content is 4.0 milligrams per cubic centimeter, the test is repeated using again one cubic centimeter sample of the unknown but ten cubic centimeters of Anstie's reagent in the fifth tube instead of five cubic centimeters. When ten cubic centimeters of Anstie's reagent and one cubic centimeter of the sample are used, the result is multiplied by two.

The validity of the test is based on accuracy while doing the procedure and cleanliness of the equipment. Cleanliness of glassware as well as care in performing the test is essential for accurate determination. Many non-volatile substances of an organic nature such as proteins, sugars, or soap left on the glassware from improper cleansing or handling will interfere with the test. Additionally, certain substances such as glycerol, phenol, cresol, anesthesia ether, formaldehyde, methyl alcohol, ketones and acetone will produce a color in Anstie's reagent similar to ethyl alcohol.

The Scott-Wilson reagent will unite with most ketones and prevent their interference in the test unless the ketone content is high. If the Scott-Wilson reagent has deteriorated from age, a person with ketosis as from diabetes, dehydration or starvation will show a color change with Anstie's reagent without alcohol in the blood. This information is just to inform you that certain medical conditions can also affect the results of this test.

I previously stated that I was called as a witness to explain to the court briefly how the blood alcohol test was conducted and possible errors that can occur during the procedure. Some instances of error could occur if an alcohol sponge is used to cleanse the skin at the site of the needle penetration to obtain the blood sample. The person could be a diabetic with ketosis or ketones in the blood stream. Many years ago in the United States and Canada, people were picked up off the streets that appeared to be intoxicated because of the smell of alcohol on their breath. They were taken to jail and placed in a cell overnight. The next morning they were found dead in their cell. They died overnight in a diabetic coma complicated by keto-acidosis. At that time, the authorities were not trained to recognize that a serious medical problem existed. This condition is usually fatal.

The charged individual is probably not a diabetic however I wanted the court to understand how ketones affect the body. I particularly wanted the court to understand how critical it is to prepare the alcohol standards properly. These standards would keep for periods of four months or longer. The Anstie's reagent is stable and keeps indefinitely. The Scott-Wilson reagent keeps for about two months.

I generally made new standards and Scott-Wilson reagent every two months and stored the distilled water for these tests in tight stopper bottles and a blank determination was run on the distilled water to prove that it was free of any volatile reducing substances.

My qualifications for conducting these tests were based on the fact that I was a member of the American Medical Technologist Association Inc. which is incorporated in the State of New Jersey and registered in Washington, D.C. After graduation from the Clinical Laboratory and Blood Bank School at the National Naval Medical Center in 1951, I passed the examination to be a certified member of the AMT with a major qualification in Biochemistry. This organization is also known as the American Society of Clinical Pathology. After the explanation to the court of the procedure of conducting the test, the individual was convicted because his blood alcohol test was above the legal limit and he received a summary court marshal. I felt I had detailed my job fully, explaining the test sequence and possible errors that may occur while the test is being conducted.

My first child was born at this military facility on February 12th 1955. We named her Ellen Theresa. I was fortunate to have been in the delivery room to witness the birth of our first child. We enjoyed the period of time we spent on this base after the birth of our daughter. We were able to visit my in-laws in South Carolina and my family in Pennsylvania.

The following month after our daughter was born my mother-in law in South Carolina called to inform us that her father Frank Wheeler had died of a heart attack. I had been looking forward to taking my daughter to spend time with her great-grandfather Frank.

I spent the prior two years playing varsity sports for this facility. We played major level competition in all sports. Our football team played major level college programs such as the University of Maryland, Temple University and other programs. Our team was composed of National Football League players and major college players who were in the military to fulfill their military obligations during the Korean War. Our basketball team competed against the University of Pennsylvania and Villanova University. Our baseball team competed against minor league baseball teams. Our sports schedules were primarily against military teams from all branches of the Armed Forces.

In June 1955, I received orders to report to the Advanced Hospital Corps School in Portsmouth, Virginia to attend school for future duty as a Medical Department Representative, independent of a medical officer. This school was also known as Independent Duty School. The graduates would be assigned to various duty stations, primarily ships without a medical officer.

My wife looked forward to moving to another state, meeting new people, and also being closer to her parents who lived in South Carolina. It was very difficult to locate housing in areas of the town where African-Americans were allowed to live.

I thought it would be better to take my wife and daughter to South Carolina to stay with her parents until I finished my six months course, because of the difficulty of finding housing. I was told at the USO (United Service Organization) to get in touch with Mrs. Churchill, a school teacher who would probably rent my family a room in her house with the use of the kitchen and laundry room. I felt that I could tolerate this arrangement for the period of time I would be in school.

I was wrong because one day when I returned from school, my wife (Lillie) and Mrs. Churchill were arguing about washing on Sunday. Lillie told Mrs. Churchill that the baby's diapers had to be washed regardless of the day of the week. At this point, I knew I had to find another place to live. Fortunately, we met a widow, Mrs. DeBerry who offered to rent our family the upstairs apartment. It was a two family home. We moved in the following week. Mrs. DeBerry and Lillie got along very well. I will always remember Mrs. DeBerry for her kindness and Christian values.

During this period, African-American medical corpsmen were being admitted to Class (B) School as potential Medical Department Representatives. If there was any discrimination as a student, I never noticed. Once aboard ship, I was responsible for the health and welfare of the crew which I took very seriously. We received extensive medical training to respond to potential medical emergencies. In some instances, we were trained to institute heroic measures that might be required in life and death situations. Under very unusual circumstances, a Medical Department Representative may be required to perform an emergency appendectomy. A few of these operations were performed aboard submarines during patrols in World War II.

In December 1955, upon graduation from school, I had the choice to attend the Navy Deep Sea Diving School for Hospital Corpsmen or the Navy Submarine School after finishing third academically in the class. I chose the Submarine School and was transferred to the US Naval Submarine Base in Groton, Connecticut for instruction in basic submarine training and submarine medicine techniques.

While I was in Portsmouth, Virginia, my father asked me to try to locate his Uncle Benjamin who lived in the area. I was unsuccessful in finding his uncle. This was the uncle who raised him as an orphan after his parents died. My father stated his uncle would be approximately eighty years of age at the time.

When we left Portsmouth, Virginia, the weather was nice however, when we reached Washington D.C., a snow storm developed and we drove to Connecticut in a major snow storm. After arriving in the area, I rented a cottage, 12 Ledge Road in Poquonnock Bridge, which is a part of the Town of Groton. This was a very cold winter and the cottages were temporary units brought from Puerto Rico. These cottages were initially built for warm climate and not for the climate of the northeast portion of the United States. The heating bill of our unit during the winter cost us more than the monthly rent. In April of the following year, I was able to obtain military housing at 30 Nereus Avenue in Groton, Connecticut. This was a unit of the Dolphin Garden housing complex.

Basic submarine school trains students to learn and operate various systems necessary for the safe operation of the submarine. I learned how to operate equipment in each compartment. In the submarine I studied, there were two Torpedo Rooms, two Battery Compartments, Control Room, Conning Tower, Pump Room, two Engine Rooms and the Maneuvering Room.

Additionally, I had to trace out sketches of the Trim and Drain Systems, Fuel and Transfer Compensating System, Vent System for the Hull and Battery, Hydraulic Systems, High Pressure Air System, 600 psi Air System, Service Air System, Low Pressure Air System, Magazine Flooding System, Sanitary Tank Drain and Blow System, Fresh Water System, Escape Trunk, Anchor Control System, Snorkel System and Topside Arrangement.

This school was very intense because when you become a member of the crew aboard a submarine, you must qualify on each system and each compartment in order to be awarded your "dolphins".

When you join the fleet as a submariner for the first time, you may be assigned to a submarine built by a manufacturer different from the submarine that was studied in school. The submarine I studied in school was the USS Becuna (SS-319) built by General Dynamics, Electric Boat Division. If I was assigned to a submarine built by the Portsmouth Naval Shipyard, the systems would be the same however the valves for certain systems may be in different locations within a compartment. After completing this school, I started the medical part of my training.

The submarine medical technician's school would give me additional training as a Medical Department Representative. Much of our training would come from medical doctors. Diagnostic procedures, treatment etc. would be stressed. It would be possible that in some scenarios, a medical doctor and hospital facilities would not be available. In situations such as this, our training would be paramount to the treatment of crew members.

Our class was instructed in how to auscultate in order to identify sounds in the chest and abdomen, so as to determine the condition of the heart, lungs etc. We were told this skill takes experience and time but it can be an important step in diagnosing an illness. When a potential basic submarine school student is rejected because of a heart murmur, we were allowed to listen to his heart beat and attempt to identify whether the malfunction was due to stenosis or regurgitation of the mitral valve or the aortic valves based on sound. We also were instructed in identifying respiratory problems such as pleurisy, bronchitis, asthma, pneumonia and others. Overall, this school was a good preparation for duty as a Medical Department Representative, independent of a medical officer. I had a burning desire to learn as much as possible about the art of medicine because I always wanted to be a physician.

I was not aware that my class had African-Americans for the first time. There were twenty-eight students of which three were African-Americans. The class graduated in June 1956 and I finished number one academically in the class. I requested duty in the Pacific Fleet. This would be Pearl Harbor, Hawaii or San Diego, California. I was transferred in June 1956 to the Mare Island Naval Shipyard in Vallejo, California for assignment and further transfer to a submarine either in San Diego, California or Pearl Harbor, Hawaii.

CHAPTER 7

We decided to spend a few days in Pittsburgh prior to heading to California. My father was excited about seeing my daughter for the first time. Ellen was sixteen months old. My brother Harold Lloyd and his wife Marian had a son Harold Lloyd Jr. who was approximately the same age as our daughter. We had pictures taken in front of my sister Alma's house. My father and my older brother Mervin Jr. were holding the babies.

Present at the time was my father, Mervin Sr., Mervin Jr., Alma, sisters-in law Marian and Emiko, my wife Lillie and the two babies. I will never forget the happiness and pride on the face of my father. This was a happy day for him, he loved his family.

The trip across country in an automobile was interesting and inspiring. We obtained military housing on the base, 86 Guadalcanal Village, Vallejo, California. I was informed that I was being assigned to a submarine in Pearl Harbor, Hawaii. My wife was pregnant with our second child. I decided to request a change in my next duty station to a submarine in San Diego, California. My request was approved and on July 1st I was transferred to the USS Nereus (AS-17), a submarine tender for further transfer to the USS Volador (SS-490) a submarine attached to Squadron Five in San Diego, California. Our second child, a son, James M. Mosley Jr. was born in Coronado, California on November 1, 1956. Two weeks later, the submarine I was attached to was scheduled to be overhauled at the Hunter's Point Naval Shipyard in San Francisco, California. After completion, the ship was to be deployed to the Western Pacific for approximately seven months.

When I received this information, I knew I had to make many trips from San Francisco to Coronado on weekends. With a new born son and the post overhaul deployment, I was determined to visit my family as often as possible. When our ship left for San Francisco for overhaul, our newborn son was two weeks old. We lived at 1734 Mullinix Drive in Coronado, across the bay from San Diego.

The ship was due to leave the shipyard in April of 1957, return to San Diego and leave for the Western Pacific in July. From November of 1956 until April of 1957, I commuted between San Francisco and Coronado. The overhaul was completed on schedule. Prior to our return to San Diego, we were invited to visit the city of Portland, Oregon by the Mayor of the city. This visit was a historical event. We entered the mouth of the Columbia River at the city of Astoria and moved up the river on the surface until we entered the city of Portland. The river was very narrow and the shorelines appeared very close to our ship. One of the crewmembers lived in Portland. Apparently, the Captain of our ship had made arrangements with a political leader in the city to have the crewmember board a small boat alongside of our ship and take him into the city of Portland. This event was to publicize our entry into the city of Portland. We were greeted enthusiastically by the political members of the city. We had a nice visit to the Rose City and then departed for our home port of San Diego on April 10th 1957.

In 1957, I was eligible for the first time to take the examination for Chief Petty Officer (E-7). I had been a Hospital Corpsman first class (E-6) for four years. In order to be advanced to Chief Petty Officer (E-7), I would need a final multiple of 120 points. The multiple is based upon time in service, time in rate, medals awarded and the examination grade.

I was informed, despite the fact that I had four years in rate I couldn't reach the final multiple of 120 unless I had at least twelve years in service. I had nine years in service at this time. I decided to take the examination to gain the experience.

When the results of the examination were released, I was informed I would not be advanced because I had not attained a final multiple of 120 or better. I expected this result. The ship's yeoman (typist-record keeper) informed me I had an outstanding examination grade. Based upon my final multiple, I probably missed two of the one hundred fifty questions. I knew I would have to go through this same process for the next two years.

My hope at this time was to be selected for one of the officer programs. I felt I was well qualified for these programs. I was interviewed and completed a written examination, had pictures taken, which was a part of the package to be submitted to the Bureau of Naval Personnel. When the results came back from the Bureau, I was not selected however a few of my shipmates were selected. I was informed by a yeoman (typist-record keeper) who worked in Washington that when a picture was received of an African-American in a submitted package, he observed instances in which the entire application was put in the trash. I am sure this was not a practice of the review committee however some individuals were capable of these practices. I decided to move on and continue to learn and enhance my capability to improve myself. I will never say that I was not selected because of my race, only God knows. I felt my opportunities for advancement were being muted by individuals in positions of responsibility. Events such as this just compounded my frustrations in the fact that others were controlling the circumstances of my life.

Our family moved from Coronado to National City, a suburb of San Diego. This house in National City was our first purchase of real estate. The purchase price was $9000.00 with a down payment of $600.00. I felt this purchase was a good investment in our future as a family. This house was located approximately sixteen miles north of Tijuana, Mexico. I was able to enjoy my family until July 25th 1957 when our ship departed for a seven month deployment. Our new address was 2736 Newton Avenue, National City, California, a nice three bedroom house.

Our first stop after leaving San Diego was the US Naval Base at Pearl Harbor, Hawaii. While at the base, I had to schedule all crew members for submarine escape training. This is an annual requirement for all submariners. The US Navy had two training towers, one on the east coast at the US Naval Submarine Base New London/Groton Connecticut and one at the US Naval Base Pearl Harbor, Hawaii. The crew members were familiar with the training because it was an operation during basic submarine school as part of the course. During school, if a student was claustrophobic, he was dropped from the course. If a person had claustrophobic tendencies, it would generally show during submarine escape training. These escape towers were filled with about 110ft of water. Seven or eight people would be put in a locked compartment at the base of the tower with a flood valve and a pressure gauge. The flood valve is opened and the compartment starts to flood. When the pressure in the compartment reaches 50 psi (pounds per square inch) the water stops and the door that had been "dogged down" can be opened. Once out of the door, you ascend toward the surface at a controlled rate. You must continually blow air out of your mouth to relieve the expansion of air in your lungs. The air in your lungs is compressed therefore, blowing air out acts as a relief valve for your lungs. During shipboard training I explained Boyle's Law of gases. It is a law in physics to the effect that the volume of a gas at a constant temperature will vary inversely as the pressure to which it is subjected. A given volume of gas under a pressure of two pounds to the square inch will occupy twice the space it will under a pressure of four pounds to the square inch.

When you ascend to the surface, as pressure in your lungs decrease, the volume of air in you lungs increase. You must get rid of the air expansion in your lungs. Divers are at various levels in the tank to observe each person as he ascends to make sure he is blowing air out. Divers are usually stationed at the 50, 30, and 18 Foot levels.

During this deployment, many historical events happened. When our submarine left San Diego, our itinerary was not classified. We were to visit Hawaii, Tahiti and Australia prior to arriving at the Naval Base at Yokosuka, Japan and receive our orders of operation from the Commander of the US Seventh Fleet. Our orders were modified after we left Pearl Harbor, Hawaii. Our ship arrived at the 180th meridian on August 11th, 1957. My birthday is August 12th therefore I missed my birthday because the next day was August 13th. We never got to visit Australia because we received an urgent message to proceed to the US Naval Base at Yokosuka, Japan. Very few individuals get the opportunity to cross the International Date Line and miss a birthday. I received a certificate documenting this fact and was given a birthday cake to commemorate this event.

When we arrived in Japan in September, the big news coming from the States was the turmoil in Little Rock, Arkansas relative to the attempt to integrate Central High School. One day on board, I was passing the wardroom on my way to the Torpedo Room and I heard a discussion about the Little Rock High School problem. One of the officers stated "what do they want"? My response was they want the same opportunities that others take for granted. I never heard any more discussions concerning the Central High School integration problems on board.

Prior to going on an extended deployment, we developed a problem in the propulsion system. Despite the fact our ship was overhauled prior to our Western Pacific deployment, we developed a problem with the port side main motor. We had the problem corrected by the Yokosuka Naval Shipyard electrical workers.

When we arrived at the Yokosuka Naval Base, the submarine we were relieving was still at sea. We received operational orders from the US Seventh Fleet to conduct anti-submarine warfare operations with ships attached to Carrier Division 15.

We proceeded to the Philippines along with the USS Razorback (SS-394). One of the most beautiful sights you will ever see is the entrance to Manila Bay. We were docked in the city of Manila for two days prior to leaving for the Subic Bay Naval Base to the South.

While at Subic Bay, I was notified I had been selected to attend the Nuclear Power School at the US Naval Submarine Base in Groton, Connecticut. My class would be starting in April of 1958. This was an honor for me because the Navy was in its infancy relative to nuclear powered submarines.

Prior to our deployment I checked all of my medical supplies. I used the after battery compartment as a sick bay area and had emergency supplies disbursed in the bow and stern compartments. The Bureau of Medicine and Surgery gives each ship an allotment annually to purchase medical supplies and equipment. I picked up my autoclaved surgical packs and suture kits from the Yokosuka Naval Hospital prior to the ship's departure.

Despite the fact I was the Medical Department Representative, my duties were very diverse. Prior to going to sea on extended tours aboard submarines, all of the crew members were required to visit the dentist and any potential medical problems are referred to medical officers. While at sea I was eager to learn as much as possible about submarine operations.

While I was with the ship during overhaul at Hunters Point Naval Shipyard, I attended school on standing radar, sonar and electronic countermeasure watches. After I had completed my submarine qualification requirements and was awarded my dolphins, I strived to learn more. When we were underway some of my duties were the bridge phone talker during the Maneuvering watch, the helmsman during battle stations, operated the radar system and the active sonar system (SQS-4), the passive sonar system (BQR-7) and the electronic countermeasure system (BLR). Additionally, I was responsible for the Atmosphere Control System aboard our ship.

When I was not on watch, I would observe the Chief of the Watch in his performance of duty at the Ballast Control Panel. I learned how to prepare the submarine for submerged and surface operations. Prior to submerged operations, the ship was "rigged for dive". The Variable Ballast Tanks were prepared for the proper trim and the Main Ballast Tanks were flooded to obtain negative buoyancy. After the completion of submerged operations, the Main Ballast Tanks were blown with high pressure air from the 3000 psi air banks. In many instances the Forward and After Main Ballast Tanks must be blown in a special sequence with the Bow Buoyancy Tank. The Bow Buoyancy Tank gives the ship an up angle when high pressure air displaces the water. The ascent to the surface must be controlled. Once on the surface, the Low Pressure Blower is started to obtain list control i.e. to keep the ship from rolling side to side. Before diving again, the ship must be "rigged for dive" for submerged operations.

On diesel submarines there were oxygen bottles in each compartment to be used on extended submerged operations, in addition to perchlorate candles for oxygen generation. I kept records of carbon dioxide concentration by using a Dwyer indicator. The concentration of oxygen had to be estimated based upon the carbon dioxide level at atmospheric pressure. There were many instances whereby crew members were alarmed because they had difficulty lighting matches. During this period, there was no restriction on smoking on board. I estimated when the carbon dioxide level was approximately 3%, the oxygen concentration was close to 12%, which would explain the lack of rapid oxidation. During my lectures to the crew about atmosphere control I explained that combustion is a function of the percent of oxygen in the atmosphere but human respiration is the function of the partial pressure of a gas. I also had containers of Lithium Hydroxide to be used as a carbon dioxide absorber.

When it becomes necessary to use the Lithium Hydroxide for an absorber, the powder is spread on the sheets of the lower bunks. This technique allows a larger surface area for the powder to react with the carbon dioxide. I instructed members of the crew in the proper use of atmosphere control supplies.

The ship's crew was divided into three sections for under-way watch standing. I was responsible for giving first aid training to all members of the crew and how to use the emergency medical supplies that were distributed throughout the ship. This shipboard training was conducted on a monthly basis. Crew training was a very important part of my duties as a Medical Department Representative.

We left Subic Bay Naval Base the first week of November, 1957 after weeks of operations with Carrier Division 15. Our orders were to proceed back to the Yokosuka Naval Base to relieve the USS Blackfin (SS-322).

We departed on our "Northern Run" on the last week of November, 1957. Our first stop after leaving the Yokosuka Naval Base was the Island of Okinawa prior to proceeding on a course due North. Once at sea we were informed relative to our destination and our operational orders.

We had been at sea for approximately three weeks when our first medical emergency occurred. I had finished my sonar watch standing and was asleep in my bunk when I was awaken at 2:00 AM and was informed that the cook had amputated his finger and it was in the sugar bin. I recovered the segment of his index finger. It was a clean cut through the first row shaft of the right index finger. I cleaned the finger with a solution of saline and re-attached the finger, sutured around the periphery and applied a flexible splint to immobilize the finger.

Approximately two weeks later, we were in an area where we could not surface to charge batteries or get fresh air through our Snorkel System. This was a major challenge to our Atmosphere Control System. After the first twenty four hours, we started to get concerned because of the inability to charge the storage batteries. I started to make recommendations to the Commanding Officer relative to the conservation of the oxygen on board. Each compartment has a bottle of oxygen. I estimated that each person utilizes approximately 0.9 cubic foot of oxygen per hour during normal activities. The Commanding Officer issued instructions that all off duty watch personnel stay in their bunks as much as necessary and limit their activity in order to conserve the limited oxygen on board, which included the perchlorate candles. I investigated the theories of these candles. The principles of these candles are based on the decomposition of sodium chlorate and oxygen. The heat for this decomposition is supplied by the oxidation of iron powder mixed with the chlorate. Of course this consumes some of the oxygen, so the quantity of iron is kept at a minimum. Since there is a tendency toward liberation of a small amount of chloride, barium peroxide is above the chlorate melting point. Barium chloride is added to provide an alkaline medium for removing the chloride ion.

After a period of forty-eight hours had passed, we had expended a considerable amount of our oxygen supply. The carbon dioxide level in the atmosphere was increasing. I started to take carbon dioxide readings every four hours with the Dwyer indicator. It was necessary to use the lithium hydroxide to absorb the rising increase of carbon dioxide. In the After Battery Compartment where most of the crew slept, bottom bunks were use to spread the lithium hydroxide absorber. I had previously studied the history and effect of Lithium hydroxide as a carbon dioxide absorber in submerged submarines. The results of studies conducted by the Naval Research Laboratory showed that the rate of production of carbon dioxide per man was determined to be three quarters or nine hundredth of a pound of carbon dioxide per man hour which required lithium hydroxide at a rate of one tenth of a pound per man hour. This criterion was based upon the activity of each individual on board. I had to make recommendations to the Commanding Officer relative to activity on board.

After the carbon dioxide absorber was spread, I continued to take readings on the Dwyer indicator. Contingency plans were made to address the decrease of oxygen in the atmosphere. If necessary, high pressure air from the air banks could slowly be released into the atmosphere. This air system was normally used to surface the submarine after submerged operations. It must be taken into consideration that air contains approximately 20% oxygen and 78% nitrogen. I previously explained the importance of the partial pressure of a gas relative to human respiration. I was hoping this operation would not be necessary.

The next twenty hours would be a critical period for oxygen depletion and carbon dioxide buildup. Every effort was made to conserve oxygen.

We were fortunate after about seventy two hours, we had enough reserve in our storage batteries to get to an area where we could ascend to a depth where we could raise the snorkel mast, start the diesel engines and start charging the batteries. The waves started to get choppy at times. The snorkel head valve has electrodes that close the valve temporarily when a wave hit the valve. When this event occurs, the diesel engines draw air from the submarine compartments, i.e., creates a vacuum. We eventually had to surface because the weather was deteriorating.

The batteries were finally charged and we started our transit back to Japan. We received orders to return to Okinawa prior to our ultimate destination at the Yokosuka Naval Base on the mainland. We remained on the island of Okinawa for about one week before we departed for the Yokosuka Naval Base. When we arrived at the Naval Base, I took the individual who had amputated his finger to the Naval Hospital to have his finger x-rayed. The splint was still on his finger. I had removed it only to apply a fresh dressing. It was x-rayed and the bone had fused properly.

After loading provisions and diesel fuel, we departed Japan and headed to our home port of San Diego, California on January 10, 1958. We arrived at Squadron five on January 27, 1958 and berthed alongside the USS Nereus AS-17.

It felt good to be home after six months away from my family. My youngest child was now fourteen months old. I had been away for over half of his life. During his first five months after birth, I was in San Francisco for the submarine overhaul. I was able to visit my family on weekends by driving and carpooling back to the San Diego area. My daughter was turning three the following month after my return from overseas.

I was awaiting my orders to be transferred back to the US Naval Submarine Base in Connecticut to attend the Nuclear Power Engineering School. My standard transfer orders were issued on February 24, 1958. I was allowed thirty days leave and was to report to my new duty station no later than April 16, 1958.

We made arrangements to rent our house while we would be on the East Coast. A family of eight, two adults and six children wanted to rent our house. They had difficulties finding a house for rent because most landlords refused to rent to large families. We agreed to rent the house to this family because both my wife and I are products of large families. A one year lease was signed and the family was to move in once the house was vacated.

My wife was excited about returning back to Connecticut. We left San Diego the latter part of February and started our journey back East. This involved another automobile trip across country with a wife and two small children. I knew the trip was going to be difficult but interesting because we would see many areas of the country and would enjoy scenery that we would not have otherwise enjoyed. We made plans to visit my wife's parents in South Carolina for a few days and my maternal grandparents in Virginia on our way to Connecticut.

When I was transferred to California after graduation from Basic Submarine School, we traveled the northern route from Connecticut to Vallejo, California and reported to the Mare Island Naval Shipyard for further transfer to Submarine Squadron One in Pearl Harbor or Submarine Squadron Three or Squadron Five in San Diego. We had no problems with motel accommodations or restaurants during our trip across country.

We were traveling the southern route this time and anticipating problems because of segregation laws in the southern states. The further east we traveled, the segregation laws became more rigid. When we traveled through Arizona and New Mexico, we did not experience extreme overt discrimination. When we crossed the border into Texas, we saw the attitude of the people changing. When we stopped for gasoline or to buy groceries, we came face to face with some of the segregation laws of the South. I felt badly for my family because as a member of the United States military, I was subjected to emotional stress during our transit to a new duty station based on military orders. When we arrived in Longview, Texas, my wife was not allowed to take my three year old daughter to the rest room at a gasoline station. The first "colored" restaurant we found was in West Monroe, Louisiana.

We finally arrived in Florence, South Carolina where my wife's parents lived. We stayed a few days and drove north to Valentines, Virginia where my maternal grandparents, two aunts, and one uncle lived. We had a very pleasant visit for a few days. When we arrived in Valentines, Virginia, my grandparents were sick in their daughter's house. My grandparents were elderly and frail. Prior to leaving Virginia, my family stopped in to see my grandparents. My two children got the opportunity to see their great grandparents. I will never forget the statement my grandmother made to me and my wife. She said "I probably will not see you again". We then started on our final leg to Connecticut. My orders read, report no later than 0800 on April 16, 1958. I arrived in March and had several weeks to find housing for my family. I applied to Navy housing and was placed on the waiting list for a two bedroom unit.

It was very difficult finding civilian housing in the area because of covert racism. There was one African-American realtor in the area and he showed me the very limited area where housing was available to African-Americans. The specific area I was taken to, I considered it undesirable for my small children.

I saw an apartment for rent in the newspaper and called the landlord. He asked me if I wanted to see the apartment. I replied I would be right over. When I arrived, there was a startled look on his face and he informed me it had been rented. For the next few months the rent article still appeared in the newspaper.

I was informed Mr. Jeff L. Nelson, who was a crewmember of the USS Croaker (SS-246) owned a home at 13 Thompson Court in New London and was willing to rent my family two rooms with the use of the kitchen until I was able to move into Navy housing. Mr. Nelson and his wife Estelle agreed on the rent etc. My wife and I had two small children and we felt very fortunate to be situated before I started my classes. Mr. Nelson is an African-American who is a friend to this day.

I reported to the Nuclear Power School on April 16, 1958. During student orientation, we were informed of the subjects we would be studying relative to our duties on board nuclear powered submarines. As a Medical Department Representative I had to study the Engineering principles of reactor operations in addition to specialized training relative to crew safety in the environment of ionizing radiation.

The curriculum for Medical Department Representatives was Mathematics, Physics, Electricity (AC theory), Reactor theory and principles, Radiological controls for reactors and testing, water chemistry for reactors and testing, radiac instrument use, testing and calibration, photo-dosimetry (read, interpret and record) film exposures to beta, gamma, and neutron radiation. Additionally, read and record portable dosimeters, calibrate these devices with radioactive isotopes such as Cesium 137, Iodine

131 and Strontium 90. We learned procedures for monitoring the reactor water daily gross activity of radioactive material and buildup, studied the effects of ionizing radiation on the human body, and to perform baseline blood cell counts prior to radiation exposure, and to perform shield surveys and radioactive calculations to determine human health hazards in an enclosed environment. These calculations are all logarithmic functions e.g. the thickness of lead shielding to attenuate beta and gamma radiation and the thickness of borated polyethylene to shield against neutron radiation. The criteria is used to establish a limit of radiation exposure per unit of time on personnel working in a potentially hazardous environment, and to study the importance of Air Particle Detectors to determine the effects of air pollutants such as chemicals, and large radioactive particles such as alpha radiation. This study of Air Particle Detectors would determine how often these units should be calibrated and checked for levels of pollutants.

In addition to radiological controls and water chemistry, we also received intense training in atmosphere controls during the specialized training. Atmosphere control is a major undertaking in submarine operations.

When I was on diesel submarines, a Dwyer carbon dioxide meter, oxygen candles, oxygen bottles and lithium hydroxide were available to me for atmosphere control.

The nuclear submarines have an atmosphere analyzer console in the control room with sensors in each compartment. Additionally, equipment aboard includes carbon dioxide scrubbers, oxygen generators and carbon monoxide burners to enhance atmosphere control aboard a submerged submarine.

The atmosphere analyzer records the percentage of hydrogen, oxygen, carbon monoxide and carbon dioxide. The carbon dioxide in the atmosphere is removed by the scrubbers. The scrubber is a device which absorbs carbon dioxide. This reaction uses monoethanolamine solution to absorb carbon dioxide when cold and to release it when warmed. The system is pressurized and the carbon dioxide is removed from the ambient air and pumped from the ship.

The carbon monoxide hydrogen burner captures the stated gases in an oxidizing catalyst bed. The chemical reaction that occurs creates carbon dioxide and water. The carbon dioxide is pumped into the scrubber system and removed.

This course of instruction was very intense and I believed I would receive a very good education from this school. We started our instruction in Cromwell Hall, a new building recently completed. There were two other African-Americans in class # 58-2. Both of these two individuals were in engineering rates. They would go to the reactor prototype for further training after graduation from the basic nuclear power school and I would remain at the school for specialized training in health physics. The school was notified by the Johnson Publication Company (Ebony and Jet magazines) that upon graduation they wanted to feature the three of us in the November 1958 issue of Jet Magazine.

Our family obtained military housing a few months after arrival in Connecticut. I thanked Mr. Nelson for his generosity in renting to our family at a time when housing was difficult to obtain for African-Americans. We moved into a nice apartment at 17 Lake Street in Groton, Connecticut. This street was parallel to Route 12 about 500 feet from the Clam Bar Restaurant. My family enjoyed living in this area despite the drastic change in climate conditions.

We were notified by my uncle that my grandmother died at the age of seventy four in July and my grandfather died two months later at the age of eighty eight. My mother, who was one of their daughters, died ten years prior to their death. I will always cherish the opportunity I had to spend time with my maternal grandparents, particularly when I was stationed in Virginia during the 1950s. My father's parents died years before I was born.

At this point my wife heard from her friend who lived in National City, California near our rental house. She told us that the tenants were destroying our house. The screen on the front door was hanging on one hinge and no effort was made to fix the door. The shrubbery and plants were also being destroyed. The lemon tree we had in the back yard had some limbs broken and many of the roses on the wall in the back yard were being torn up. My wife took her yard work very seriously. This was a headache we had to deal with while 3000 miles away. We were notified in August 1958 that the state of California was buying a large parcel of property which included Newton Avenue to extend Highway 101 to the Mexican border at Tijuana. This turned out to be the saving grace for our family.

I completed school in November, 1958 and was assigned to a nuclear submarine in Pearl Harbor, Hawaii. The USS Sargo (SSN 583) was the only nuclear submarine at the time attached to the US Pacific Fleet.

The three African-Americans in the graduating class had pictures taken and were featured in the November 1958 issue of Jet magazine. I considered this an honor.

This was the second time in about two years I was placed in a special dilemma. I was aware my wife was eight months pregnant with our third child. I thought I would be assigned to a submarine in this area, because most of the nuclear submarines were attached to the US Atlantic Fleet.

After I received my assignment, I was troubled because my wife was due the following month. I talked with some of the Hospital Corpsmen that were in my specialized training graduation class. The graduate assigned to the USS Skipjack (SSN-585) wanted to go to Hawaii. He said if we could have our order changed, he was willing to go to the USS Sargo (SSN-583).

CHAPTER 8

I made a request to have my orders changed and it was approved. I was assigned to the USS Skipjack (SSN-585) stationed in Groton, Connecticut. Our third child, a son was born on December 5th 1958. This was the child I delivered in our automobile on the way to the hospital.

It was a very cold day however I had blankets, a first aid kit and clean towels in my gym bag. By having these items in my vehicle, the emergency was handled more effectively. The birth occurred on Crystal Lake Road in Groton approximately one hundred yards from the Main Gate of the USN Submarine Base. I brought my wife and son to the hospital. Our son was placed in isolation for a short period of time because he was not born in the hospital. Everything worked out fine. We named him Thomas Robert Mosley.

While I was attached to the USS Skipjack (SSN-585), I knew at the time we would spend a considerable amount of time in this area because with the exception of one nuclear submarine in Hawaii, the USS Sargo (SSN-583), the rest of the nuclear submarines were stationed in Groton, Connecticut. We were living in military housing at the time. Our unit was in the Dolphin Gardens complex. We lived on an end unit at 71 Orion Avenue.

I was a member of the pre-commissioning crew and we spent long hours in training and getting prepared for the commissioning ceremony which would be April 15th 1959. We spent a considerable amount of time conducting builder's trials. The tests included a range of propulsion plant operations as well as high speed surface and submerged runs. They were all completed successfully.

The statistics of our ship were the overall length of 252 feet, the extreme beam of 31 feet seven inches, mean draft of 26 feet, standard displacement of 3075 tons, submerged displacement of 3513 tons, design depth in excess of 400 feet, designed surface speed of 20 knots, designed submerged speed, in excess of 20 knots. The crew consisted of twelve officers and eighty eight enlisted men. The armament was six 21 inch diameter torpedo tubes. As part of our submarine qualification, some of these statistics had to be committed to memory.

We were commissioned on schedule and joined the Submarine Force, US Atlantic Fleet and immediately started work to prove the soundness of her radical design. The results are best exemplified by the fact that most follow-on nuclear submarines including the Polaris/Poseidon SSBN Trident, and fast attack submarines have all retained the basic design.

The first major trip after commissioning was to the United Kingdom, La Spezia, Italy and Gibraltar. This was our shakedown cruise. After a fast transit through the North Atlantic, we docked in Weymouth, England after operating at sea for a few days. I recall the headlines in the newspaper when we arrived, "world's fastest submarine one hour late".

We had five members of the British Royal Navy embarked on board in order to obtain experience operating a S5W reactor plant which powered the USS Skipjack (SSN-585). During our pre-commissioning, the ship was visited by Lord Mountbatten of Burma, the Admiral of the British Fleet. The first British nuclear submarine, the Dreadnought would be powered by the Westinghouse S5W reactor plant. This ship was originally designed to use a British reactor, but in order to accelerate the completion, an agreement was made to use a Westinghouse reactor built in association with Rolls Royce. To accommodate the reactor, the after end of the submarine was based on the Skipjack design. The rest of the hull was British.

I worked with three members of the British Royal Navy in reactor plant monitoring of the primary and secondary water chemistry in addition to radiological controls. The radiological controls included dosimeter readings, calibration and film badge development and reading of beta-gamma and neutron film.

We left the British Isles and proceeded to Gibraltar to enter the Mediterranean Sea. We became the first nuclear ship to pass through the Straits of Gibraltar into the Mediterranean Sea. We visited La Spezia, Italy and Gibraltar during this trip. I was able to visit the cities of Pisa and Florence while in Italy.

During this trip, there were two incidents that occurred in which I was directly involved. In La Spezia, one of the crew members became involved in an altercation at a drinking establishment and was hit on the head with a heavy glass ashtray. It took fourteen stitches to close his scalp. I then took him to an Italian hospital to be examined. The crewmember was cleared to return to the ship.

After leaving La Spezia, Italy, we docked in Gibraltar for a few days before our transit back to the states. A second incident occurred involving the same crewmember. An American diesel submarine from Key West, Florida was also in port. The ship challenged our softball team to a game. We defeated them seven to five. After the game I went back to the ship. An hour or so later, the ship received a call for me to go back to the ball field because of an emergency. When I arrived back to the ball field, our crewmember had been severely beaten. His nose was completely gone and his right eye was out of the socket. I took him to the British hospital and he was airlifted to Germany. I was told disciplinary action would be taken against the crewmember from the Key West based submarine. Our crewmember lost an eye and was medically discharged from the US Navy. This was a very informative trip for the crew in operating the ship in an extended operation.

We returned to the states and docked at the Electric Boat Division of General Dynamics Corporation for a Post Shakedown Availability (PSA).

This availability was to examine any problems or potential problems that were observed and encountered during the operation of the ship during this shakedown cruise.

The latter part of the year 1959 was spent operating with anti-submarine units of the Atlantic Fleet in Norfolk, Virginia. Because we were the first class of an advanced submarine incorporating the marriage of a "tear drop" hull with a nuclear power plant, most units of the Atlantic Fleet wanted to operate with this type of submarine because of sonar potential implications. We spent a considerable amount of time at sea involved in anti-submarine warfare training.

Near the end of the year 1959 our family had to relocate from our housing unit in order for the units to be renovated. I found a house for sale in Waterford, Connecticut, and this was a major event in the life of our family.

I found out that purchasing a house at this time in this area would be a difficult task. I requested a mortgage at the Savings Bank of New London and was informed by the loan officer that my income was insufficient.

The individual I was purchasing the house from and also the next door neighbor were both in the Navy and my income at the time exceeded both their individual incomes. In addition to my base pay, I was also receiving submarine duty pay (hazardous) and proficiency compensation.

I requested the realtor intercede on my behalf. The agent was Mr. Louis Massad. The price for the house was $13,500. I had a down payment of $2000. I needed a mortgage of $11,500. After the loan officer was contacted by Mr. Louis Massad, I received a call from the loan officer requesting that I make an appointment to discuss my application for a mortgage. During our subsequent meeting, I was informed I was not eligible because I owed a financial institution for an automobile. This statement shocked me because I owed one final payment of $89.71. My wife and I tolerated all the red tape and the various obstacles placed in our path to deprive us of owning a home. We finally were approved for the mortgage in December of 1959. We refused to give up on our dream of getting this house.

In January 1960, Code 1500 of the Bureau of Ships (Nuclear Reactors) issued a directive to the Commanding Officers of all nuclear submarines stating that water chemistry (primary and secondary) would in the future be conducted by engineering laboratory technicians (ELT) instead of nuclear trained hospital corpsmen. This directive was issued because of a shortage of nuclear trained hospital corpsmen. My job was to develop lesson plans to instruct and train engineering personnel to assume the duties of water chemistry testing on board nuclear submarines.

The first few months of 1960, our ship conducted Bureau of Ships special trials to evaluate speed and maneuverability. Most of these trials were conducted off the coast of Bermuda, B.W.I.

Type training and services were conducted for the surface front line defense units, task Group Alfa and Bravo. These operations demonstrated the speed, endurance, flexibility and maneuverability of the USS Skipjack and our ship was acclaimed to be one of the best fighting weapons available in the Navy.

We returned back to Connecticut after our operations with surface units of the US Atlantic Fleet. We started to prepare for our next deployment. I was notified that our family could move into our new home in the first week of March. We moved in on March 6th 1960.

We encountered a very difficult transition after we moved into our new home. There were signs placed on the front of our home that stated "nigger move out." I felt very uncomfortable about this scenario because I was in the military and expected to be away from my family for extended periods of time. At the time I had a wife, a daughter age four, a son age three and a new born son.

I was informed our ship was assigned an extended operation commencing on May 16th 1960. I purchased a Dictograph Fire Alarm System that would give me peace of mind while I was deployed overseas away from my family. The fire alarm unit cost $475.00 which I knew I could not afford at the time however, I knew it was necessary.

I was selected for promotion to Chief Petty Officer the same day we left on our extended operation. We departed and knew we would be away from our families for a few months. We transited the North Atlantic and headed toward the British Submarine Base at Faslane, Scotland. Our ship conducted sound trials and other sonar operations in the area. The water in this area was very deep with various temperature gradients. After a few days, we left Faslane, Scotland and headed north into the Norwegian Sea past the North Cape of Norway into the Barents Sea. We operated in a vast area just below the Artic Circle.

The Naval Research Laboratory was interested in various pollutants in the air of submerged submarines during extended operations. Air samples were collected during this operation from the Electrostatic Precipitators which were installed during the construction of the ship. These samples were tested and showed that the majority of the pollutants were from cigarette smoke.

The operation in this area was completed after six weeks and we left our station and headed back to the States. We arrived back in Connecticut on July 16th, 1960. This operation we had just completed was called an advanced Atlantic Submarine Exercise. For the fiscal year 1960, the USS Skipjack received the Battle Efficiency "E" award for Submarine Squadron Ten. We had a nice period in port before our next assignment. Our ship was to proceed to Port Everglades, Florida and operate in the area testing a new missile.

The crew of our ship was invited to a party at a hotel in Fort Lauderdale, Florida. There were three African-American crewmembers on board. We decided not to attempt to attend the party because of the segregation laws of the South.

The new missile to be test fired was the SUBROC. This new weapon was fired while the ship was submerged from one of the torpedo tubes and the operation was successful.

Prior to returning to Connecticut, we operated off the coast of Key West, Florida for a few weeks. Upon our return we docked at the Electric

Boat shipyard to have some work conducted in the reactor compartment. When the reactor compartment was open, I had to be on board the ship. This was a ship's instruction. Due to the extended work to be done I was allowed to go home and be on a phone watch. One night I was called and had to go back to the ship because a major repair had to be accomplished on one of the heat exchangers in the reactor compartment. I returned to the ship at about 1:00 AM and went into the reactor compartment tunnel. The duty officer of the watch, my-self and three Electric Boat employees went into the reactor compartment. The discussion was how the freeze seal would be applied prior to cutting the line. It was determined the work would be done on the first shift in the morning. I went back home and knew I had to be back on board prior to 7:00 AM.

About 5:00AM, I received a frantic call from the ship to report back on board immediately. When I arrived back on board, I found out the Electric Boat employees went back into the reactor compartment and cut the wrong heat exchanger line which was pressurized. This event contaminated the entire reactor compartment.

The Commanding Officer was called and he met with members of Electric Boat Management. It was determined a major decontamination process was necessary. Three shifts of cleaners were required to start the decontamination process.

The objective was to get the level of contamination down to what I considered an acceptable level. Based upon multiple half lives of many of the radioactive elements, I had to set limits on acceptable levels. I knew the safety of personnel working in this compartment in the future would be based upon levels of contamination. This was an area I would spend a considerable amount of time doing surveys after reactor shutdowns. I had to do swipe surveys to determine the level of contamination exposure by shipboard personnel approximately one hour after reactor shutdown. The swipe is measured in micro-curies per gram. The major potential problem was the ionizing radiation from this contamination. Based upon medical knowledge, a maximum permissible expose (MPE) was established along with the radiation biological effect (RBE). Each type of radiation, e.g., alpha, beta, gamma, fast neutrons and thermal neutrons has destructive effects, particularly on the areas of the body which is exposed.

I learned during my medical training that human cells that regenerate rapidly are more sensitive to ionizing radiation. Bone and nerve cells are more resistant. The (RBE) was calculated based upon the biological effects of radiation. Radiation equivalent man (REM) was used as a factor to determine the lifetime dose of an individual. The formula used is $D=5(N-18)$. The dosage is 5 REM times the age of the individual minus 18 years of age.

There was an effort to decrease the level of contamination in the reactor compartment to 100 micro curies per gram. I was pessimistic this level could ever be achieved. My objective was to have the reactor compartment decontaminated to a realistic level. After approximately one month of decontamination, the level never went below 250 micro curies per gram. We felt the level of contamination would never go below this level. The United States Navy accepted this level of contamination.

The next potential problem was a decision that had to be made whether to change the demineralizer resin bed which would cost hundred of thousands of dollars. The primary system demineralizer serves three functions. It picks up dissolved solids by ion exchange, it physically filters suspended solids and it establishes an alkaline PH in the primary system. The first two maintain the radioactivity of the primary system within reasonable limits for reactor compartment accessibility. In my duties as a Health Physics Technician, I spent a considerable amount of time in the reactor compartment during shutdown. It's filtering action causes many long ½ lived radioactive corrosion products to collect near the top of the demineralizer and therefore the shielding on the upper portion of the demineralizer was thicker than on the lower portion. If the resin bed channels, these suspended long lived radioactive solids will appear in the effluent. Therefore, channeling would be indicative by an increase in the effluent 120 hour gross activity over what it had been running in the past. Due to a break in the continuity of the primary system, I had to recommend a new charge of resin. The capacity of the demineralizer was seven cubic feet.

This experience became a vast learning and educational opportunity for my future duties on board this submarine. I passed this knowledge on to individuals at other duty stations.

Our ship was notified we had been awarded the citation for the Navy Commendation Ribbon for one of our extended operations. The Secretary of the Navy, John B. Connally stated "for exceptionally meritorious service during operations from May through July 1960, the first of a new class of nuclear submarines with advanced characteristics, the USS Skipjack succeeded in making a highly important contribution to the antisubmarine warfare capabilities of the United States Navy. The skill, resourcefulness, and intrepidity of her dedicated officers and men in developing and mastering the unprecedented capabilities of their ship and in utilizing these capabilities to the fullest, reflect great credit upon themselves and the United States Naval Service. All personnel attached to and serving on board the USS Skipjack (SSN 585) during the above period, or any part thereof, are hereby authorized to wear the Navy Unit Commendation Ribbon". This citation was signed by John B. Connally.

In early 1961 our ship conducted many antisubmarine operations while training with various units of the fleet. A considerable period of time was spent at sea which placed a burden on family life.

The Ethan Allen class of Polaris missile submarines was being constructed at Electric Boat. I had been on an attack submarine for over two years and wanted to experience duty on a missile submarine. I applied for pre-commissioning duty.

My request was granted and I received orders to report to the USS Thomas A. Edison (SSBN-610) on May 1st 1961 while the ship was under construction.

I had been on board for about six weeks when the ship was scheduled to be launched. While on the building ways, a Steinway piano was lowered on board into the crew's mess prior to the hull being closed. This was a unique event because this ship was the only submarine with a piano. During this period in the submarine construction industry, major components such as generators, condensers etc. are "top loaded." This means large components are installed into the ship from the top before the hull is closed.

Today, this installation is made by "end loading" whereby, large segments or cylinder are welded in place by automatic welding machines. These individual cylinders are then welded together in the final construction phase. These individual cylinders weigh hundred of tons each.

The piano was donated by the Steinway Company, at the request of Mrs. Joan Eyre Sloane, the daughter of Thomas A. Edison. The piano was located in the crew's mess hall with a picture of Thomas A. Edison above it.

On June 15th1961, the ship was launched from the building ways into the Thames River. This was a milestone in the construction of a ship.

The construction period gave me the opportunity to get acquainted with the ship's systems and compartment equipment. Once the ship was constructed and delivered to the Navy, I had to qualify on the systems for this submarine which had a missile system. The other systems were similar to those on an attack submarine. The Polaris Weapon System installed on this ship provided the technology for the continuous accurate determination of the ship's position and for constant readiness to launch sixteen missiles within minutes after receipt of a launch command. I learned the ballistic Polaris missile is powered by a two stage solid propellant rocket motor and achieves virtually complete invulnerability through its great speed and completely self-contained guidance system.

The inertial navigation system enables the ship's position to be determined with extreme accuracy. The ship was equipped to launch the longer range A-2 Polaris missile. The Polaris Missile Submarines has two crews designated "Blue" and "Gold", each consisting of about twelve officers one hundred enlisted men alternately taking the ship to sea. The use of two crews enabled the ship to remain almost constantly within range of targets and provides the maximum deterrent capability at the minimum expense. I was assigned to the "Blue" crew. After being part of the skeleton crew for approximately ten months, the remainder of the crew reported on board and commissioning was scheduled for March 10th 1962.

I felt fortunate because I was able to spend approximately a year at home with my family during the construction period. After commissioning I knew we would spend a considerable amount of time at sea on deterrent patrols. With two crews, the "Blue" crew would be on patrol for three months and the "Gold" crew for three months.

Now that the ship had been launched and in the water, preparations were made for the commissioning ceremony. Systems were operated and the engineering plant was on line. I was familiar with these operations because I had experienced them on my last nuclear submarine. Energy for propulsion of the ship and for the generation of electricity and other vital services is obtained in the nuclear reactor from the fission process of uranium. Heat resulting from the fission process is transferred through the medium of pressurized pure water to steam generators where the heat is given up to secondary water. Steam produced in the secondary system is used to power the propulsion and electrical generator turbines. As a result of the care with which the engineering plant was designed and constructed, I informed personnel they would receive on the average less radiation exposure than would result from normal exposure to natural cosmic radiation, natural radioactivity present in small quantities in virtually all substances, and routine medical and dental x-rays. Borated polyethylene, lead and water are used as shielding materials on board nuclear submarines. Different types of radiation are attenuated by different materials.

As a Health Physicist, my job was to lecture crew members about the dangers of ionizing radiation and the detection devices such as dosimeters and film badges that all members of the crew were required to wear. I kept records of exposure of all personnel on board. Dosimeters were read and recorded weekly, beta-gamma film was read and recorded monthly and neutron film was read and recorded quarterly.

The ship was commissioned on March 10th, 1962. The Blue Crew was commanded by Captain Charles M. Young and the Gold Crew was commanded by Commander Walter Dedrick.

After shakedown training off the east coast of the United States, our ship was to conduct the standardization trials for a new class of ship. Generally the first ship of a class conducts these trials. We were the third ship of this class. The USS Ethan Allen (SSBN-608) and the USS Sam Houston (SSBN-609) were the first two ships of this class that carried the Polaris A-2 missile. I never found out why the USS Thomas A. Edison (SSBN-610) was selected to conduct the standardization trials.

These trials entailed many operations to test the structural integrity of the ship. The systems of the ship were tested at various depth levels. We started at one hundred feet and checked for leaks. We followed this procedure at deeper depths. When we descended to test depth, all systems were operated including the torpedo tubes. The ship also operated relative to the speed of ascent and descent to various depths. I was relieved when these operations were completed.

The crew was notified we were heading to Norfolk, Virginia to welcome the President of the United States John F. Kennedy and Secretary of Defense Robert S. McNamara on board. The night before the President and Secretary of Defense was to come aboard, our ship was involved in a collision with another ship. During operations about 200 miles east of Norfolk, Virginia while conducting antisubmarine operations, our ship collided with the USS Wadliegh (DD-689), a Destroyer. Our topside rudder was bent and the Destroyer's forward bottom plates were pierced. Our ship was repaired at the Newport News Shipbuilding Company overnight. The USS Wadliegh (DD-689) required more extensive repairs. The next day the President and the Secretary of Defense came aboard our ship.

A special cage was constructed to lower the President through the hatch into the Control Room because of his medical history of back pain. This cage is on display at the Submarine Base Museum at the Submarine Base.

During this period I again applied for consideration under the Limited Duty Officer Program. I had previously applied for a commission and warrant grade. I applied for a commission as a Warrant Officer in 1957, Limited Duty Officer in 1959, 1960 and 1961. I was never selected. I felt optimistic this time I would be selected. Despite my record of performance and positive reviews relative to my leadership qualities and supervisory abilities, I was not selected. This was a major disappointment in my naval career.

The next operational order for the USS Thomas A. Edison was to proceed to Cape Canaveral, Florida to test fire the Polaris A-2 missile. This was to be a test of our major weapon system.

I recall one night while we were there, a missile misfired on one of the launch pads and the ensuing fire drove a large number of rattlesnakes out into the open. The Fire Department had a difficult task fighting the fire and rattlesnakes.

While our ship was at Cape Canaveral in May of 1962, I was able to observe an astronaut entering space aboard a rocket. Scott Carpenter was one of the first astronauts in the Space Program. He flew solo into space aboard Aurora 7. This event was the second American flight into space. I was pleased I observed history being made.

After our operations were completed at Cape Canaveral we returned to Connecticut. We conducted various operations during the summer. In the autumn of 1962 a major international event occurred that put our nation on the brink of war. In October of 1962, the Cuban Missile Crisis put the military on full alert. We received orders to proceed to the Naval Shipyard at Charleston, South Carolina to load missiles and await further orders. We had to load sixteen missiles. It took approximately one day to load and check out each missile.

This was another difficult time for our family because my wife was pregnant and due to deliver in May of 1963. I knew I would be at sea for a major period of time during her pregnancy.

We departed Charleston, South Caroline on November 7th and started our first deterrent patrol with sixteen Polaris A-2 missiles on board. We proceeded to our station and conducted exercises and drills to train the crew, hoping that the drills would never evolve into actual combat operations. We finished our first deterrent patrol and arrived at the USS Submarine Tender in Holy Loch, Scotland. We remained there for a few weeks and turned the ship over to the Gold Crew. Our crew flew back to the States. We landed at the Quonset Point, Rhode Island Naval Air Station and boarded buses for our trip to the USN Submarine Base in Connecticut.

I was happy to be home the latter part of January 1963, because my wife was due a few months later. I was notified I would be transferred in March of 1963 for my tour of shore duty. This news assured me I would be home for the birth of my fourth child.

CHAPTER 9

In March 1963 I was transferred to the Station Hospital at the USN Submarine Base Groton/New London, Connecticut. I was assigned as the supervisor of the Clinical Laboratory.

My first objective as the Laboratory Supervisor was to lobby for the hospital to have a Blood Bank. I established and had approved a plan to have a blood drive to obtain blood donors from each incoming class of the Basic Submarine School.

When we collected blood from military donors, the units of blood were transferred to the local civilian hospital. Despite the fact the Station Hospital was an accredited facility, we had no Blood Bank. The Commanding Officer and many of the medical officers became involved in this issue. It was not long before we had a Blood Bank at this medical facility.

My next objective as the Supervisor of the Clinical Laboratory was to set up a schedule for laboratory samples to be taken on a regular basis in order to monitor different areas of the health care facilities and other areas of the Submarine Base relative to sanitation and preventive medicine.

The main areas of my focus was the Operating Room, Maternity Ward, Labor Rooms, Dental Clinic, Swimming Pool and Shower Rooms in the Gymnasium. Additionally, the Base Commissary Store (groceries) where fresh produce and dairy products were delivered on a daily basis. The dairy products were checked for temperature and samples of different dairy products and juices were taken for laboratory analysis.

One month after I was transferred to this facility, a major submarine disaster occurred on April 10th 1963. The USS Thresher (SSN-593) was lost during sea trials off the coast of New Hampshire. I had many friends on board this ill fated submarine. Many of the electricians on board were transferred from the USS Skipjack (SSN-585) and were previous shipmates of mine. One of my friends I had known for many years in the San Diego area was Roscoe Pennington. We were both attached to Submarine Squadron five. He was a crew member aboard the USS Ronquil (SS-396) and I was a crew member aboard the USS Volador (SS-490). Both submarines were overhauled at the Hunters Point Naval Shipyard in San Francisco, California in the latter months of 1956 and the first quarter of 1957. We both had discussed our plans to eventually attend the Nuclear Power School. After I had completed the school, Roscoe enrolled at a later date and completed the school. He had changed his rate from a Steward to an Electrician. I lost a great friend. There is a building on the USN Submarine Base, Pennington Hall named in his honor.

On May 18th 1963, my wife gave birth to our fourth child, a girl whom we named Patricia Ann at the Station Hospital on the Base. It was a blessing to be on shore duty and able to be home with my family. During this period of time, the Navy was collecting information on the feasibility of building a Naval Hospital at the USN Submarine Base because of an increase in the number of military personnel and their dependents. The current medical facility was designated a Station Hospital in the 1940s.

I was given the task of collecting data relative to total laboratory procedures conducted at the Station Hospital. With limited resources and personnel, our work load compared favorably with other military hospitals on the East Coast.

When all the statistical information from the hospital was submitted to the Defense Department, the decision was made to construct a new hospital.

In addition to my duties at the hospital, I played softball for the Atlantic Fleet Submarine Force Sea Raiders. We were one of the top fast pitch softball teams in the country. I played shortstop or left field for our team from 1963 to 1966. We won many tournaments. In 1963 we won the Atlantic Fleet tournament for the fourth straight year and the tenth time in the twelve years the event had been going. We lost in the All Navy finals in Chicago. The following year, we lost in the All Navy finals in Seattle. We always had a very competitive team.

A few months later while sitting in my office, a report came in over the radio stating President John F. Kennedy had been shot in Dallas, Texas. The date was November 22nd. I remembered the year before on April 10th 1962, President Kennedy and Secretary of Defense McNamara visited our ship in Norfolk, Virginia.

The following year was a very challenging period in my navy career. The Administrative Officer of the Hospital convinced me to apply for a commission in the Medical Service Corps. I received an outstanding recommendation from the Commanding Officer of the Hospital as well as the Commanding Officer of the USN Submarine Base. The application was submitted on May 18th 1964. I felt optimistic because my daughter was one year old on this day.

During this period of time when I had the duty, I was the Administrative Watch Officer for the hospital or Chief of the watch. I was informed later I was on the list of the selected candidates however due to budgetary conditions, the list was cut and I was not selected. This was another major disappointment for me, I knew I was qualified. I was very frustrated and vowed to accept the fact that maybe in the future things would change for the better. A shipmate of mine stated "you are before your time".

In November of 1964, I was selected to be advanced to Senior Chief Petty Officer. I was transferred to the Management and Planning Office at the USN Submarine Base to be the instructor for the Atomic, Biological and Chemical Warfare School and Director of the Submarine Base Disaster Control Branch. My collateral duties were as a lecturer on Civil Defense and Disaster Control for business and industry in the state of Connecticut. Additionally, the lectures were for government prime contractors and other military facilities. I was also the Submarine Base Brig counselor and temporary Chief Master at Arms. The Management and Planning Officer informed me I had been assigned as a member of the Nuclear Accident Team which was the Explosive Ordnance Disposal (EOD) unit at Indian Head, Maryland. The EOD unit stationed west of the Mississippi was at the Sandia Base Nuclear Facility in New Mexico. Training was conducted at the US Army Bases at Fort Detrick, Maryland and Fort McClellan, Alabama.

I continued to be an instructor at the Atomic, Biological and Chemical Warfare School. I had enlisted classes and officer classes. The officer in charge of the Management and Planning Office directed me to have fallout shelter signs placed on various buildings and stock the shelters with emergency supplies.

On March 26th 1965, I received orders to proceed to Pratt and Whitney Aircraft in East Hartford, Connecticut to conduct a presentation and lecture on Disaster Control and Civil Defense. It was interesting to observe how the audience was so attentive to my lecture. This time period was approximately three years after the Cuban Missile Crisis and most citizens were aware how close we as a nation came to an armed conflict with the Soviet Union.

On October 6th 1965, I was directed by the Management and Planning Office of the US Naval Submarine Base to conduct presentations and lectures at the US Navy Underwater Sound Laboratory at Fort Trumbull, New London, Connecticut for all of their employees.

The Commanding Officer of the US Navy Underwater Sound Laboratory put out a memorandum for all employees, military and civilian. He stated "much thought and planning has been predicated upon enemy action involving atomic, biological and chemical warfare. While these forms of attack are major consideration in a Disaster Control Program, it is intended that Disaster Control shall include measures taken to reduce the probability and minimize the effect of damage in peace or war due to natural or man made causes".

The Civil Defense Disaster Control training was held in the Christopher Columbus auditorium. The employees were divided into four groups. The training was conducted on the 11th, 12th, 14th and 15th of October 1965. Each session was conducted from 8:30 AM to 12:00 AM and consisted of lectures, supplemented by film, slides and demonstrations of various radiac instruments. I gave the attendees a ten minute break on the hour. After each session, I accepted questions from the audience.

The first few months of 1966, my wife and I discussed how much longer I intended to remain in the Navy on active duty. We decided I would retire at nineteen years and six months. During this period of time, my retirement date would count as twenty years of service.

In January 1966, I enrolled at Mitchell College as a part time student. My focus was to eventually earn a college degree. I took two classes to start my college career. I attended school twice a week from 6:00 PM to 9:30 PM studying English and Psychology.

I had earlier successfully completed the college level GED equivalency test while in the military. The test included Physics, Mathematics, English, Psychology and other disciplines. My graduation from Nuclear Power School helped me in some areas. I knew this pace pursuing a college degree would take many years, but as the old Chinese proverb states, "a long journey begins with the first step". I intended to pursue my schooling as a full time student when I left active duty and joined the Fleet reserve.

During this period of time, I also obtained a part time job at Sears as a salesman in the men's clothing department. I enjoyed working at this store because it was only about a mile from home. I worked four days a week from 5:00 PM to 9:00 PM.

My wife delivered our fifth child, a son on October 31st 1966 we named him Mervin McKinley Mosley III. It was a joyous feeling to be at home. I was fortunate to be at home for the birth of all five of our children.

I requested to be transferred to the Fleet Reserve in the first quarter of 1968 and be released from active duty. We owned a home locally and were optimistic I would remain at my present duty station, and be released from active duty.

The hospital released my wife and son on November 4th. I took them home and returned to work. I was preparing my lesson plans for a new class when I received a call from the Personnel Office. I was informed that transfer orders had been received and I was being transferred to the West Coast. I immediately went to the Personnel Office to find out the details of my transfer orders. I had previously requested transfer to the Fleet Reserve.

The orders were initiated by the Bureau of Medicine and Surgery on October 28th 1966 and it stated, "you are being nominated for duty to report in March 1967 to Commander, Puget Sound Naval Shipyard, Bremerton, Washington for temporary duty in commissioning and outfitting of the USS Samuel Gompers (AD-37), and on board for duty when commissioned, this ship will be home ported in San Diego, California".

I was to be transferred from my present duty station in January 1967, and to report to my new duty station in March 1967. This was my preliminary orders for planning purposes. I received my final transfer orders from the Bureau of Naval Personnel.

I received orders and planned to leave Connecticut at the end of January. There was a major snow storm in the mid-west. I decided to take the southern route despite the fact we would be covering practically three sides of the country.

CHAPTER 10

We left Connecticut on January 31st 1967 and headed south. The baby was three months of age. We stopped in South Carolina for a few days to visit my wife's parents and the rest of their family. We then headed south toward Georgia. When we arrived in Columbus, Georgia I knew we would be subjected to the segregation laws of the south. I stopped for gasoline and my wife and daughter could not use the restroom. We had to transit a long distance across the south therefore I knew what to expect relative to public accommodations. We could not stop at a restaurant or motel. We planned to buy groceries and eat in our vehicle. My wife and I took turns driving and took naps while the other one was driving. We stopped in safe areas to sleep and rest. I felt the best places to stop overnight was at truck stops. We made very few stops in Alabama and Mississippi. When we arrived in West Monroe, Louisiana, we found a "colored" restaurant and motel. The signs on these two establishments read "colored". This was a rest stop we really needed. We finally were able to get a good night sleep and enjoyed a chance to obtain a shower.

I noticed the further west we traveled the segregation laws were less rigid. When we traveled through Texas, New Mexico and Arizona, we found accommodations better than the southeast. We made an emergency stop in Las Cruces, New Mexico due to a severe wind storm.

When we arrived in San Diego, California, the baby was suffering with diarrhea. We had intended to stay in San Diego for a few days. I had a sister and her family living in the city. We took the baby to the Naval Hospital where he was treated and released. After a few days staying with relatives, we headed north.

I had another sister and her family living in Oakland, California. We arrived in Oakland, California and stayed for two days and then started on our last leg of the trip to Bremerton, Washington.

When we arrived in Eugene, Oregon, there was a major rain storm coming in from the Pacific Ocean. The wind practically tore off the carrier on top of our station wagon. We had household items such as an ironing board, kitchen utensils and other miscellaneous items in the carrier. The carrier was not of a hard shell construction therefore a lot of the items that were packed in the carrier got wet. We stopped for a few hours and proceeded north.

We finally arrived in Bremerton, Washington on February 10th 1967. This was eleven days after we left Connecticut. I checked in at the Personnel Office at the Puget Sound Naval Shipyard. I was directed to report to the officer in charge of the pre-commissioning crew of the USS Samuel Gompers (AD-37). Lieutenant Commander A.G. Hartman, the officer in charge would later become the Repair Officer.

I was given time off to apply for housing and to enroll our children in school. I went to the housing office and applied for a three bedroom unit. I was informed that a unit would be available in about two weeks. We stayed in a motel for four days and then were notified that the unit was available. We moved into our unit. I was surprised the unit was furnished. We had no furniture because our furniture was in storage.

This unit was very nice and not too far from the shipyard. Our new address was 131F Schley Boulevard, Bremerton, Washington. I went back to work and my wife got the children enrolled in school.

Our pre-commissioning crew's offices were on the first floor of Building 50. On the second floor, the pre-commissioning crews of the two surveillance ships, the USS Pueblo (AGER-2) and the USS Palm Beach (AGER-3). After commissioning, one ship would be assigned to the Pacific Fleet and one to the Atlantic Fleet. When I reported for duty, each department had personnel assigned for organizational procedures such as writing department instructions and getting familiar with the ship while under construction. I went aboard the ship to see how the Medical Department was being laid out. The ship had been launched on May 14th 1966. The medical needs of the crew and the tended ships would be ministered to in a modern forty three bed hospital, a well equipped operating room, complete X-Ray and laboratory facilities and the latest in hospital equipment. This was a very large ship and would have a crew of 40 officers and 1200 enlisted. I had to determine how emergency medical supplies would be dispersed around the ship. The last submarine in which I was a crewmember, the length of the ship was 410 feet and the emergency medical supplies were primarily in the forward and after section of the ship. This ship was 643 feet and the emergency medical supplies had to be dispersed at many locations.

The Medical Department would have one Medical Officer, one Division Officer, one Chief Petty Officer and eighteen Hospital Corpsmen. In addition to being the department Chief Petty Officer, I also assumed the duties of the Division Officer. My next major undertaking was to assist the Medical Officer in writing the department's organization and regulation manual.

The manual was composed of eleven sections. The first defined the mission of the Medical Department. The next four sections outlined the duties of the Medical Officer, Division Officer, Leading Petty Officer and the remainder of the medical personnel. The next six defined the emergency medical facilities, emergency bills, training, hygiene/sanitation, health physics and the routine of the Medical Department on the daily, weekly, monthly, quarterly and annual basis.

As the Health Division Officer, I was given the responsibility and authority to take care of the administrative functions of the Medical Department. My first objective was to establish a training program for the Department and crew members. The Department training was for all Hospital Corpsmen and crewmembers who wanted to change their rate to Hospital Corpsmen. We called them strikers.

The senior Hospital Corpsman was assigned the responsibility for crew training. The training program for the officers and crew includes first aid, control of hemorrhage, asphyxia, artificial respiration, shock, wound dressing burn treatment, transportation of the wounded, fracture treatment and personal hygiene.

I conducted the training relative to Atomic, Biological and Chemical Warfare Defense. I had extensive experience in teaching this course at the USN Submarine Base in Connecticut.

A ship of this size needed a comprehensive training program in first aid to function in emergencies. When at Battle Stations or General Quarters, each group throughout the ship must have basic first aid training.

Another major responsibility of the Medical and Health Division Officers was the hygiene and sanitation of the ship and its personnel. With a crew of over 1200 officers and enlisted, this would always be a major concern.

I conducted a thorough inspection of the ship once a week on Thursday however I made frequent unannounced inspections during the week. I reported my findings to the Medical Officer who advised the Commanding Officer with respect to hygiene and sanitation affecting the ship. The inspection conducted on Thursday took approximately six hours.

The sanitation inspection of the ship was divided into segments. Inspections were done on food and its preparation, food handlers, mess men, messing spaces, scullery, mess gear, commissary/culinary spaces, butcher shop, living spaces, soda fountain, head/washrooms and the barber shop. Additionally, garbage disposal and the Brig. Personnel for confinement to the Brig must be examined by the Medical Officer or the Senior Hospital Corpsman in the absence of the Medical Officer. This same procedure applies in the release of a crewmember from the Brig.

The Health Division Officer had appropriate extracts from the Sanitation Bill posted in the galley, laundry, barber shop, coffee messes and messing spaces. This was a major new experience for me after serving on numerous submarines with crews of approximately 100 officers and enlisted personnel.

The Health Physics section was information I was very familiar with because I was a graduate of the Navy's Nuclear Power School and I had the experience of being responsible for radiological controls and water chemistry on nuclear submarines. This was the reason I was assigned to this ship. This manual would go into effect when the ship was to be commissioned on July 1st 1967. The commissioning ceremony marks the acceptance of a ship as a unit of the United States Navy.

The schedule for completion of the ship after commissioning was three months. We were to leave the shipyard on September 30th 1967 and have sufficient load out time prior to deployment. It was estimated that deployment from San Diego would be the first week of November.

The crew was informed when we leave Bremerton for San Diego, some of the families would be able to ride the ship to San Diego and also take their automobiles.

I watched the commissioning of the USS Pueblo (AGER-2) and the USS Palm Beach (AGER-3) on May 13th 1967. The Commanding Officer of the USS Pueblo (AGER-2), Commander Lloyd M. Bucher was the only crew member that wore submarine dolphins and I was the only crew member of our ship wearing submarine dolphins. Commander Lloyd M. Bucher's ship headed for San Diego and the USS Palm Beach (AGER-3) headed for the East Coach via the Panama Canal.

A significant event happened to me at this same period. I was told I would get a staff job in San Diego after our Western Pacific deployment. My record indicated I completed the course for Military Justice in the Navy with a grade of 4.0 and a performance rating of 4.0 relative to professional performance. Additionally, I had completed courses in the Uniform Code of Military Justice, Investigations, Leadership and Instructor school and completed courses in General English, College Algebra and Psychology. I also successfully completed college level GED equivalency tests. The fleet wide examination for pay grade HMCM (E-9) was administered on May 23rd 1967. The examination results would be published in November and approximately six months after the examination and review by the examining board, advancements will be made.

The next few months I was busy helping to get the Medical Department ready for the commissioning ceremony when the ship would be placed in service.

The commissioning date of July 1st 1967 finally arrived. The flag was hoisted from the staff aboard the ship as the 13th Naval District Band played the National Anthem during ceremonies putting this new destroyer tender into commission. Our crew marched aboard to officially man the new ship for the first time. Top national labor and governmental figures were here for the ceremonies held in Drydock Six at the Puget Sound Naval Shipyard.

After commissioning, the Chaplin's office started to order magazine subscriptions for the ship. Two African-American crewmembers requested that the Ebony magazine be ordered along with the other magazines. The Chaplin's office stated that a numerous quantity of subscriptions had already been ordered.

The two crewmembers asked me to intercede on their behalf. I was the senior African-American crewmember on board. I talked to the Chaplin and the Ebony subscription was approved. I felt that the Chaplin's staff was insensitive to the diversity of the crew.

With a crew of 1240, there were approximately 150 African-Americans. There were no African-American commissioned officers, only African-American Chief Petty Officers. I was a Senior Chief Petty Officer (E-8) and three Chief Petty Officers (E-7).

I didn't think the personnel in the Chaplin's office had any negative thoughts about their decision not to subscribe to the Ebony Magazine. I talked to them later and they had never heard of this magazine.

We had sufficient time prior to commissioning to institute our training programs, inspections etc. I felt the crew was ready to go to sea and benefit from the first aid training and other inputs from the Medical Department. We knew our ship would be deployed to the Western Pacific in November 1967.

After commissioning, the shipyard had approximately three months before the completion date. The shipyard schedule was to complete all work and release the ship on September 30th 1967. The crew was very busy in the outfitting and loading of the ship.

After arriving in Bremerton in February, I had a considerable amount of time to spend with my family. We allowed the children to choose where they wanted to go on weekends. The first two areas our oldest children wanted to see were the Space Needle in Seattle and Vancouver, Canada. In March we went to Seattle and toured the Space Needle and took pictures. We spent the remainder of the weekend in Tacoma and Olympia.

In April we decided to take a trip to Vancouver, Canada. This trip was also to celebrate our wedding anniversary and my wife's birthday. We spent an entire day taking pictures and sight seeing. On the trip back to Bremerton, we stayed overnight in Bellingham, Washington. When we got back from our trip, I went back to work on Monday. When I returned home after work my wife informed me our three year old daughter had exposed four rolls of film we had used in our trip to Vancouver. We intended to make another trip to Vancouver before we left Bremerton, but we never seemed to have the time.

We had a nice birthday party for our young daughter Patricia who was four years old on May 18th. A favorite past time for Patricia was to look out the bedroom window and see Mt. Rainer in the distance. It was a beautiful sight to see the snow capped mountain in the spring and summer.

The two older boys wanted to play pee wee football when the practice started in August. I allowed them to play until the ship was scheduled to leave the shipyard. Jim was ten years old and Tom was eight. Jim played on the end and was the kicker and Tom was a running back. They played through the month of September. I was an assistant coach for their team.

The ship was completed on the scheduled date of September 30th 1967. We left the shipyard on October 3rd 1967 and headed for the Keyport Ammunition Facility to load ordnance.

The crew was informed in mid September that the plan for allowing some dependents to board the ship for our transit to San Diego was cancelled because of the danger of ammunition loading.

Some of the crew members were given time off to relocate their dependents. After the ship arrived in San Diego, the next few weeks would be spent outfitting the ship for a seven month deployment to the Western Pacific.

I was fortunate to have a sister in San Diego who was the Assistant Superintendent of Schools for the El Cajon District.

I applied for Navy Housing and we immediately received a three bedroom unit. Our new address was 6027 Boxer Road, San Diego, California. My sister helped us to get the children enrolled in school.

On November 10th 1967 the ship departed San Diego for deployment to the Western Pacific. We stopped at Pearl Harbor, Hawaii for a few days prior to transiting the Pacific.

Our ship received a radio message from the USS Pueblo (AGER-2) on the morning of November 29th requesting assistance to transfer a crew member to our ship which had a medical officer and a large sick bay. The injured crewmember sustained a fractured spinal vertebra. We transferred the injured crew member to our ship. The next morning we arrived at the Yokosuka Naval Base. Our ship received orders to proceed to the Tonkin Gulf in support of the ships operating in that area. Our Repair Division had nine officers and 430 enlisted personnel. The six repair divisions represented a repair capability equaling that found in any Western Pacific shore based Ship Repair Facility. In keeping with the newest generation of skills required to support new modern ships. We were well qualified. One division was charged with the repair of nuclear propulsion plants. Included within this division was an extensive radiochemistry laboratory, equipped with the latest analytical apparatus. I was very familiar with this division's work because I had the responsibility for this work aboard nuclear powered submarines.

I worked closely with the Radiological Control Division. In my duties as the Division Officer of the Medical Department, I had the responsibility for Health Physics and nuclear medicine. I gained my experience and training as a graduate of the Navy's Nuclear Power School and a member of the National Health Physics Society.

During this period of time with the war raging in Vietnam, I often thought about a statement by General Omar N. Bradley, an outstanding flag officer during World War II. "We have too many men of science, too few men of God. We have grasped the mystery of the atom and rejected the Sermon on the Mount—ours is a world of nuclear giants and ethical infants. We know more about war than we know about peace, more about killing than we know about living".

I was notified I had been selected to be advanced to HMCM (E-9). However, I had to extend my enlistment for two years. The Bureau of Naval Personnel had a date for my transfer to the Fleet Reserve as of February 16th 1968. I decided I would like to be transferred to the Fleet Reserve in February. My children were at the age whereby I felt I needed to be at home.

We returned to Japan a few days before Christmas and spent the rest of the holidays in port. There were three ships waiting to tie up along our ship for service.

I was a member of our ship's basketball team. We participated in the Annual 7th Fleet Holiday Tournament. We played well however we lost in the championship game.

I was looking forward to returning to the states and being discharged. I was informed by the ship's Personnel Office that I would be transferred from the ship on January 14th, 1968. I had previously sent resumes to three employers back home in Connecticut, Northeast Utilities, Pfizer Corp. and Electric Boat Co.

The first week of January, the Medical Department had a farewell party for me at a Japanese restaurant in Yokosuka. Some crewmembers from other Departments also attended the party. It was nice to feel appreciated by my shipmates. I had another week on board before I would be transferred.

I left the ship at the Yokosuka Naval Base on January 14th, 1968 for my flight from Tokyo. My orders were to proceed to the USN Submarine Base in Connecticut for transfer to the Fleet Reserve. I had difficulty getting my orders changed to San Diego for transfer to the Fleet Reserve.

When I left Japan, it was aboard a plane that had been chartered by the military. The plane made a stop at Travis Air Force Base north of San Francisco. I then took a flight to San Diego.

My orders made it difficult for planning purposes. I had to get my household effects ready for shipment to Connecticut, move out of Navy housing and get my family ready for the trip across country. When we arrive in Connecticut, I would have to check in with my orders and then be processed for my transfer to the Fleet Reserve.

When I arrived in San Diego, I proceeded to the Naval Station with my orders. I explained to the Assistant Personnel Officer my dilemma. He informed me not to worry because I could be discharged at the Naval

Station. This was a tremendous help for me and my family. Everything worked out fine. I had approximately one month before I was to be discharged. I was able to make plans for my children to leave school and have their records transferred back to Connecticut. My discharge date was scheduled for February 16th 1968.

I got in touch with the minister in Connecticut who had recommended a family that was willing to sign a year's lease to live in our home. I informed the minister that we would be back at the end of February 1968.

The minister informed me that the family had moved out in November 1967 and left the house abandoned. There was no heat in the house and some of the water pipes had ruptured. We found out that the couple that had rented the house was not married. There was nothing I could do until I returned to Connecticut. The rent was paid in November but not in December. I reflected on the fact we had previously been victimized by renters ten years earlier when we were transferred from California to Connecticut. We were only trying to help people however it back fired on us again.

A major international event occurred nine days after arriving in San Diego. The news came in that the Democratic Republic of North Korea had attacked the USS Pueblo (AGER-2) and forced the crew to travel to North Korea. This event occurred on January 23rd 1968. I recall the date this ship left Yokosuka heading out to sea. When this ship left port, it was about three days before I left Japan for San Diego.

There was speculation that all discharges would be frozen. This potential event worried me because of what happened eighteen years earlier when the Korean War started during the Truman Administration.

I had planned to leave the military after my enlistment ended and enter college as a pre-med student. The circumstances prevented me from exercising that Plan.

What surprised many people was there was a large segment of the US 7th Fleet in Yokosuka for the holidays. I guess the Johnson Administration wanted to use diplomacy because our nation was still bogged down in Vietnam. I heard many people in San Diego say the US Government deserted the crew of the USS Pueblo and the crew of the ship should have fought.

The USS Pueblo was attacked by high speed patrol boats and could not flee because of a maximum speed of 12 knots and carrying only two 50 caliber Browning machine guns. I felt sorry for the crew because I knew most of them.

There was another ironic incident that occurred. Each of the two surveillance ships carried a first class Hospital Corpsman. I was told that these two Medical Department Representatives decided to change ships while we were in Bremerton prior to commissioning. The Hospital Corpsman attached to the USS Palm Beach wanted to be transferred to the USS Pueblo because he wanted to stay on the West coast. He lived in Chula Vista, California. Both of the Hospital Corpsman agreed to the transfer, and it was approved by both commands.

I was worried that my discharge could be delayed because of the Pueblo incident. I had approximately three weeks before my discharge. February 16th finally arrived and I was transferred into the Fleet Reserve from active service. It was a significant event in my life that I will never forget. The feeling was something I cannot describe.

The vision of my military career passed through my mind. I recalled leaving home for the first time alone and boarded a train heading for Chicago, Illinois. I then headed north to the US Naval Training Center, Great Lakes. I had spent one half of my life on active duty in the US Navy.

When I got home, my wife wanted to take a picture of me with my discharge papers in hand. This was a joyous day for the entire family. We relaxed for a few days and visited members of our family who lived in the area.

My career in the Navy was a real adventure covering education and work experience. When I reflect back on my journey of twenty years on active duty, my shore duty and sea duty was fascinating. My first sea duty was aboard a repair ship, USS Cadmus (AR-14) and my last sea duty was aboard a destroyer tender, USS Samuel Gompers (AD-37). In between these duty stations, I spent aboard submarines. I was qualified aboard diesel, nuclear powered fast attack and nuclear powered missile submarines.

My last sea duty was aboard a destroyer tender that serviced nuclear powered surface ships. I was nominated for that billet because of my experience serving aboard nuclear powered submarines as a Chief Petty Officer. In addition to my primary duties as the senior enlisted person in the Medical Department, I was also the Assistant Radiological Control Officer for the Engineering Department. I will always remember my duty aboard this ship, which happened to be my last sea duty in the Navy.

We started to get everything in order to leave San Diego. Jim our eldest son wanted to visit Tombstone, Arizona and Carlsbad Caverns in New Mexico. I felt we were in no hurry to get back to Connecticut so we decided to take our time traveling.

We left San Diego on February 19th 1968 and knew we would face the same segregation laws when we arrive in the southeastern states that we encountered on our trip west in 1967. We traveled east at a leisurely pace and stopped in Tombstone, Arizona for the day and remained overnight. We left Arizona and stopped again in Hobbs, New Mexico. We headed south to Carlsbad, New Mexico and toured the caverns and took pictures and enjoyed a lot of sight seeing.

When we traveled through Texas going east, we stopped infrequently at truck stops. When we arrived in Georgia, we headed north and stopped in South Carolina to visit relatives. Our next stop would be Connecticut.

We arrived in Connecticut on March 2nd 1968. I knew we would face problems with the house. The problems were greater than I anticipated. Apparently it was a very cold winter and the water pipes under the living room had ruptured. The refrigerator and washing machine I left in the house were gone. The glass inserts for the front and back storm doors were also missing.

I had the pipe repaired and we tried to settle down to a post military career. We had to purchase a new washing machine and refrigerator. I found out later what happened to our refrigerator. We visited a family that we knew and when I saw their refrigerator which was a Sears Kelvinator, I asked them where they got their refrigerator. They replied it was purchased from a friend. I knew it was our refrigerator because the children had scratched it with their tricycle and I had painted the area. When I found out his friend's name, I told him this individual had rented our home while we were in California and took our washing machine and refrigerator. They wanted to return the refrigerator to us but I told them we had purchased a refrigerator and washing machine from Sears.

My next project was to get a job. I wanted to go to school but I felt my number one priority was to get a job and spend more time with my family. I planned to start school again at Mitchell College later. I had previously taken two courses at this school in 1966.

I decided to contact the three employers who received my resumes. Northeast Utilities was interested in my experience in Health Physics. There were no positions available at the time however, I would be contacted soon. I was informed that I would have to go to Chicago for an indoctrination course for new land based reactors. I was not interested in leaving my family again after a twenty year military career.

I contacted Pfizer and was offered a position working in their Research Laboratory. I would enjoy this type of work but was informed I would be working in rotating shifts. I had always had sleep problems so despite the fact of enjoying this work, I decided to wait and have my interview with Electric Boat Division of General Dynamics Corp.

During this period of time, I had a part time job as a salesman for a furniture store in Groton, Connecticut. This was just a temporary place of employment until I was able to obtain a full time job.

CHAPTER 11

I was notified by a Professional Placement Representative from the Electric Boat Division to come in for an interview. The interview was conducted on April 2nd 1968. I was informed no positions were available in the Radiological Control Department at this time but a position was available in the Procurement Department for a Buyer position. A transfer to the Radiological Control Department could be made at a later date when a position becomes available.

I asked the interviewer when I could start. He stated I could report the next day to the Procurement Department. The starting salary would be $7,000 dollars per year. I was excited because this would be the most money I ever received during my working career.

I went home and informed my wife that I had been hired and could start the next day. This would be a significant event in our life because my first day of work would be my wife's birthday and our 14th wedding anniversary. I felt very optimistic about my future with this company based upon my familiarity with submarines.

I reported to the Procurement Department on April 3rd 1968. This Department was located at a satellite site away from the main shipyard. The building was a leased roller skating rink. There were many desks for Buyers and Expediters on the main floor of the building. The Managers had offices on the periphery of the main floor. I will never forget the strange reaction when I was escorted from the lobby to the office of the Assistant Manger of Procurement. One hundred pairs of eyes focused on me as I entered the Manager's office. I was asked if I had any buying experience, my answer was, I spent twenty years in the military and was transferred to the Fleet Reserve in February therefore I had no buying experience. His response to me was it will be very difficult to transit to purchasing material from a military career. A philosopher once stated, "80% of questions are statements in disguise." I was compelled to respond to his statement. I said nobody was born having the skills to be a Buyer. I am confident in myself and I feel if other people can learn a skill, so can I, if given the opportunity. If I can't do my job, I demand to be fired. I was also informed I was the first African-American hired as a Buyer in the Procurement Department at Electric Boat Division. I noticed there were no other African-Americans in the Department. I was surprised there were no African-American clerks or typists in a Department of this size.

I felt many of the people assumed I had been hired and placed in the Procurement Department because of the company's Affirmative Action Program. This was not the case. The individual that hired me had previously served in the military and was familiar with my qualifications.

I was informed at a later date by a member of the Department about discussions relative to why I was placed in the Procurement Department.

After my meeting with the Manager, I was introduced to the Buying Group supervisor in the area I would be working. I was amazed at the stares and silence of the people on the floor. One of the Secretaries came to my desk and welcomed me to the Department. I was assigned to the group that purchased MRO (Maintenance Repair and Overhead) material for the shipyard. Most new hires start working in this group initially.

I was given a letter authorizing me to sign contracts for $10,000 per commitment. Each buyer, manager etc, receives signing authorization for various dollar commitments.

I was informed that after gaining experience in this area, I would progress to the Coded Stock Group. This group purchases inventory material to be used on selected contracts as CFE (Contractor Furnished Equipment). An example of this would be purchasing raw material to be used in our Foundry to manufacture selected valves for shipboard use.

The Department Management Manual was divided into approximately seven main sections with approximately thirty four flow-down charts. Buyers and Expediters were assigned relative to the commodities each group purchased. The Department was responsible for purchasing all shipboard material with the exception of the GFE (Government Furnished Equipment).

My first day was basically indoctrination. I learned about the various functions of the Department and how the buyer groups were designated relative to commodities. I recall placing my first two purchase orders with the Hunter Spring Company and Bunting Magnet Company.

When I got home I explained to my wife how the day progressed and how I was happy with having a full time job. I was looking forward for my next day at work. I was determined to study and gain as much knowledge as possible about my job. I took home a copy of the terms and conditions that the Government imposed on Prime Contractors, which in many instances flow down to subcontractors.

My second day was a complete day of placing purchase orders and learning the functions of sending out RFQs (Request for Quotations). When I send these requests out to potential suppliers, in many instances, I solicit at lease three potential suppliers in order to foster competition. I stayed pretty busy for the entire day. Many orders that had no specifications invoked were awarded over the phone. When an order was over $5000.00, an acknowledgment copy was sent to the supplier and their reply had to be returned in a specific period of time. I had to learn the legal ramifications for failure to follow this policy. Once a subcontract was awarded to a supplier, the Expediter had the responsibility of following the progress of the order. This is a very important function because in the terms and conditions, the supplier agrees to a contract delivery date that must be met. If I place a subcontract with a supplier, I felt that I should also be responsible to follow up on the progress of the order to meet the contract delivery date.

I was at home working on my car when my wife called and told me to come inside. She had the television on the news report. Reverend Martin Luther King Jr. had been shot in Memphis, Tennessee at about 6:00 PM on the balcony outside of his room at the Lorraine Motel. He was taken to a local hospital and underwent emergency surgery. He died approximately one hour after being shot.

The next morning I went back to work. The Department personnel observed a moment of silence in respect for the slain civil rights leader. This was my third day on the job and I immersed myself into reading the Department Instructions, manuals and learning the functions of the various buying groups. I felt very comfortable and looked forward to the challenges I knew lay ahead.

My family scheduled a trip to Pittsburgh to visit my father for a few days over a weekend. I had been out of the military a few months and most of my brothers and sisters would be present. We met at the house of my brother Donald and his wife Shirley. This was the first time in years that all my brothers were present together. We had all served in the military but I was the only one that made the military a career. My sisters Franciene and

Madge were present. Five of my sisters were absent, Norma Jean, Yvonne, Lorraine and Alma. My brother William Roger and his family who lived in New York accompanied us on our trip from Connecticut.

My father was happy to be in the presence of most of his children. We talked about the death of Martin Luther King Jr. and what would happen in the country in the aftermath of this tragedy.

We returned to Connecticut and I enjoyed and reflected on my time visiting my father and many of my siblings. My focus now was my job and how I could best perform my duties as a Buyer in the Procurement Department.

I studied department instructions and how the different buying groups were organized. After three months, I started to purchase construction material to build submarines. Much of this material required strict government and company specifications. I was informed in a joking manner that you are probably the only one in your group that understands what you are buying, based upon your experience and time in the U.S. Navy serving aboard submarines. Despite the fact that technical information is irrelevant in purchasing a product, it is also an advantage to know the use of the product relative to shipboard application.

Each buying group had an EDP (electronic data processing) printout of suppliers used by our Procurement Department. This listing included the supplier's product, person to contact etc, and a copy of the Thomas Register for commercial products. I noticed this listing did not contain the telephone numbers of this long list of suppliers. Each buyer had a rolodex file with phone numbers of their suppliers. I submitted an unofficial employee suggestion that the suppliers' phone numbers should be incorporated in the printout. This action would save time and increase productivity in the Department. The suggestion was not adopted however, approximately six months later it was adopted when it was submitted by a member of the Administrative staff.

A few months later, an African-American female was hired as a clerk. I over heard an individual make the comment, "we are being invaded". I understood what he meant by that statement.

I received a purchase requisition to purchase approximately $8000.00 worth of venetian blinds for buildings in the shipyard. I solicited three suppliers on my request for quotation. After the bids were received, I did my bid comparison and determined the lowest competitive bidder. After the order was awarded, I received a call from one of the unsuccessful bidders asking me how close were they to the successful bidder's pricing? My response was your bid was competitive. I thought this would be the end of this issue.

Apparently this supplier called the Second District Congressman, Robert Steele informing him of their protest of this purchase order and requested an investigation of the bid process relative to this order. The Congressman sent a letter to the General Manager of Electric Boat Division requesting an investigation.

I received a call from the Director of Procurement asking me to bring the disputed purchase order to his office. After the order was reviewed, the Director stated that I made the proper decision. I informed the Director that the supplier protesting the award was basically asking me to divulge the successful bidder's pricing.

During my study of economics, I was informed by one of my professors that there are ten pillars of economic wisdom. The fifth pillar stated that "a company cannot remain in business and meet its payroll unless it first meets its competition". I was determined to be fair to all suppliers and be ethical in my duties as a Buyer. I noticed at a later date that this supplier's representative was very friendly with members of our Maintenance Department.

It was important for me to follow the Department Instructions closely on the placement of purchase orders because I would be carefully scrutinized as a new buyer. I was very confident in my work ethic, knowledge and ability.

I was shocked when I was on a telephone call to a supplier in California at 4:30 in the afternoon. One of my co-workers informed me that "you are making us look bad". I didn't understand what he was saying by that statement. I asked him to explain himself. He said that salaried people left the building at 4:30 PM.

I stated that time in California is three hours earlier and I needed some information on one of my particular purchase orders. I had previously noted that many of the Buyers took their phone off the hook at about 4:15 PM.

I could easily see the difference between civilian and military work ethics. In the military when you had a job to accomplish, you did not look at a clock but accomplished the task regardless of the time.

A considerable amount of contact with suppliers was via the telephone. The Buyers at this time had to place their calls with switchboard operators. The Buyers received a printout monthly detailing their phone calls. I noticed many calls that appeared on my printout were not made by me.

It appeared someone was giving the operator my number and making unauthorized calls. One of the switchboard operators notified me that an investigation was being conducted. I was informed later the guilty person was identified but I was never given his name. Despite these low points, I felt optimistic about my future as a Buyer.

I was transferred into the Coded Stock area which was a little more challenging than my previous buying group. I was in a position to negotiate pricing and enhance competition. I learned to determine if adequate price competition existed when I purchased many commodities. This was an important concept when you determine if a price was reasonable. I felt if I made a determination that adequate price competition exists, then by definition, the price is fair and reasonable, as defined by federal auditors.

During this period of time, the workload was increasing due to prime contracts being awarded to Electric Boat Division. Our entire group was very busy. One morning, my Manager wanted to see me in his office. When I arrived in his office, he informed me that one of my co-workers was out with an illness and he wanted me to take over his desk because the orders he had to place was for material that was urgently required in the shipyard to meet scheduled dates. I informed him I had a heavy workload on my desk and it would be difficult for me to adequately cover both desks. He ordered me to do the best I could for the time being until another Buyer could be transferred into our group.

I was surprised when one of the typists informed me that you are not getting credit for covering the other Buyer's desk. When the evaluation period arrived, I was penalized because my desk was not current and up to date. I protested my evaluation and it was corrected stating I was given the responsibility of covering two desks and thereby two major sets of accounts.

This was another wake up call for me early in my duties as a Buyer. I started seeing a pattern evolving to discredit me in my duties and this would be a bitter pill to swallow.

After I had been in this buying group for about two years, I was transferred to a special buying group that worked on a special contract for the US Navy. This group would purchase material for the overhaul of a class of missile submarines. We were prohibited from working on any other project or contract. Our labor hours would be charged only to this contract.

This was a major opportunity for me because I gained experience buying major components relative to a class of missile submarines. The contract was for the overhaul of the USS Lafayette (SSBN-616) class.

I attended a seminar and workshops on cost/price analysis and how to conduct audits when determining the reasonableness of a quoted price. This was necessary training because many of the suppliers of the components we were purchasing were manufactured by a single or sole source company, where competition did not exist. I was also required to complete a course on Armed Service Procurement Regulations (ASPR). This course also included the Federal Truth in Negotiation Act that flows down from the US Government to the Prime Contractor.

The Truth in Negotiation Act requires contractors to disclose accurate, current and complete cost and pricing data. The question most frequently subject to differing interpretations and litigation is what constitutes cost or pricing data under this Act. I learned that one of the most difficult issues in any analysis of defective pricing is the need to disclose data relating to business judgments. The regulations state that cost and pricing data are factual, not judgmental and are therefore verifiable. The instructor informed our group that business judgments are not subject to disclosure. While that may be correct, this analysis has not provided adequate guidelines on which contractors can base their actions. The regulations state that the data underlying the judgment do constitute cost and pricing data.

The cost price analysis course was very important to me as I approached my first major negotiation with a single source supplier.

I purchased many major components which included electrical and mechanical pumps, switchboards, controllers, valves, fittings etc. If competition was not available for certain items that were single or sole source, a cost breakdown was required by government contract law, if the potential award is $100,000 or greater. This action was necessary to justify the price. A contract pricing proposal on a Department of Defense form (DD-633) must be submitted and an audit conducted by the government or the prime contractor. Amazingly, my first subcontract audit was conducted at a vendor's plant in Rochester, N.Y. (Dynalec Corp.)I was given a quotation for an electrical switchboard for a price of $79,000. This vendor was a single source supplier. The government required this supplier to manufacture the unit based upon mutual specifications.

Dynalec Corp. submitted a contract pricing proposal form (DD-633). This submittal was not necessary because the award was to be less than $100,000. Once this form is submitted, an audit must be performed.

It took two days to perform the audit. This was a major learning experience in my two years at General Dynamics. After a thorough review of my audit and negotiations, a price of $64,000 was agreed upon. I had to make adjustments in the vendor's manufacturing labor, overhead, inspection and quality assurance costs. This was a very important experience for me because in the future, I would be negotiating million dollar contracts.

While purchasing material for the overall, I questioned why the Copper Nickel (CuNi) alloy material for the missile tubes had to be seamless at a price approximately double that for seam welded parts. My rationale was that the pressure forces acting on the applicable surfaces were equal. As a result of my questioning, the nomenclature was changed to seam welded parts. This resulted in considerable savings.

I also requested that Engineering look into changing the military specification for the missile tube locking rings. These large rings of Nickel Aluminum Bronze (NiAlBr) were forged. I felt that these rings could be centrifugally cast at a fraction of the cost relative to the cost to open frame forge these rings. I noticed that at a later date, the specification was changed and the rings were cast and machined at a major savings that ran in the millions of dollars for the next generations of missile submarines. All future missile submarines had centrifugally cast locking rings.

During this period of time, I had my second protest of a purchase order I had awarded. A company in Three Rivers, Wisconsin (Kalenberg Brothers) requested that I place them on the bidders list for the air whistle valve requirements for the submarines to be overhauled. This company had been in contact with the US Navy in Washington, D.C. and had their design approved for the air whistle valve. The request for quotation would be for ship-sets of material. This item had previously been purchased as a single source from the Leslie Company of Parsippany, New Jersey.

Both potential suppliers were placed on the bidders list. Upon receipt of the bids, I made a comparison and determined that the Leslie Company was the lowest competitive bidder. After the purchase order was awarded, I received a call from a representative of Kalenberg Brothers Company asking me if their research and development costs that were submitted can be subtracted from the hardware price. My response was I had to evaluate the total price of the quotation. I informed their representative that I had awarded the order to the Leslie Company.

I was notified by a principal of their company that they were protesting the award of this order. Senator William Proxmire of Wisconsin requested that an investigation be conducted relative to the award of this order. After the investigation was conducted, it was determined that the research and development costs were an integral part of the submitted pricing. I had made the proper decision to award the contract to the Leslie Company. I informed the unsuccessful bidder they would have the opportunity to bid on future requirements for this item.

I was fortunate for the training I received in Cost/Price analysis and Truth in Negotiations by the Sterling Institute and the American Graduate University. I learned many valuable concepts during my training such as the relationship between price and cost. Additionally, how cost and efficiency impacts the outcome of a contract and whether a penalty or incentive clause could be negotiated and contract type determined. The contract type could be Fixed Price, Fixed Price Incentive or Cost Plus with a Fixed Fee.

I felt very optimistic at this point because of the trust placed in me and the advanced training I received as a Buyer in contract negotiations. I knew this training would be an important part of my future in the Procurement Department.

I was happy with my job as a Buyer and enjoying my experiences and exposure to manufacturing of major components at some vendor's plants. Many of these parts I observed being manufactured were familiar to me because of my experience in the US Navy as a crew member on board submarines.

I had been a member of the Procurement Department for about three years when I was notified by the Human Resource Department that a position was available for me in the Radiological Control Department as a Health Physicist. The resume I submitted to the company was for this position which was not available at the time. I was a member of the National Health Physics Society.

I talked it over with my wife (Lillie) and we decided I would remain in the Procurement Department because I loved my work. I was looking forward to a long career in negotiating and awarding subcontracts. In hindsight, I should have accepted the new position in the Radiological Control Department.

I purchased a 1970 Datsun station wagon in the spring of 1971. About one week later when I left the building to go home after work, I found many scratches on the driver's door and the hood had been dented. I went back into the building and reported the incident to my Manager.

The next day after work, I was unable to start my vehicle. I had it towed to the dealer's facility. I was informed that sand had been put in my gas tank and the fuel pump was inoperative. The gas tank had to be taken down and the carburetor and fuel pump had to be replaced.

The Security Department started to investigate these incidents. I previously stated that our department was a satellite operation away from the shipyard. The investigator asked me questions about my interactions with other members of the department. I explained that some members of the department were not happy with the fact that I was a co-worker. The investigator stated that maybe the perpetrator was upset over Japanese automobiles. My response was I believe I was intentionally targeted.

I felt violated and my emotions internally were very high at the time of these incidents. My property was being destroyed and I was very angry. If I caught the perpetrator while my property was being vandalized, I would have become violent. I did not want this to happen because I had a wife and five children to support. After three years in this department, very few people spoke to me during the day. This lack of interaction with my co-workers was not a major concern of mine because I was absorbed in my work with the objective of supporting my family.

To my knowledge, the Security Department never was able to identify the person or persons who vandalized my vehicle. For a considerable period of time, I watched for any future attempts of vandalism.

A major event occurred on June 30th, 1972 that changed the direction of my life in this department and ultimately destroyed my civilian career after a military career of twenty years. I took a purchase order into the office of my Manager. He was not there and I placed it on his desk. I noticed a memorandum on his desk signed by the Director of Procurement stating I had accepted a position as the Minority Business Enterprise Administrator. I will never forget that date. I was hired as a Buyer and I didn't expect this sudden change in my life without being consulted. I thought it was a lack of respect for me as an individual. The following people were notified about this change, the US Small Business Administration, General Dynamics Corporate Office, Department of Defense (Pentagon) and the US Navy Department.

I asked my Manager why I was not consulted about this event that affects my life. His reply was "you were the only minority in the Department". I said you didn't allow me the dignity of turning down the position. You just forced the job down my throat. I knew this was a political job and I am not a politician. I informed my Manager that if he wanted the job done correctly, I needed the tools and authority to accomplish the job.

I was determined to do the job to the best of my ability. I knew this position was just "window dressing". I was to continue working eight hours a day as a Buyer. What time would I have to implement a program for the company? I knew this new position would be very challenging with the extra burden of being a Buyer at the same time.

I was sure the objective was to have an African-American in the position as a token to comply with US Government contract requirements. I would never compromise my principles or be a pawn in the hands of others who had their own agenda. I have always been committed to performing at the best of my ability and refuse to be directed for political reasons.

I knew this federal program would be highly resisted in the Purchasing Department. If I performed my duties in a professional manner, this would make me the target of some members of the Department management. I was correct because for the next four years, I was resented because I was committed to doing my job.

I called the Small Business Administration's regional district in Boston, Mass. I requested information on this new program. The Small Business Administration's representative informed me that the first Director of the Office of Minority Business Enterprise would be in Colchester, Ct. along with Second District Congressman Robert Steele to explain the program and its genesis on August 8th, 1972. This would be all new information to me and would help me set up a program in the Procurement Department.

In the meantime, I searched for information on this program and how to implement a viable program at our company. I knew it would be a major challenge because of buyer resistance to change. It would be very difficult to implement without the support of senior management through out the company. I strongly felt this position I was placed in was another penalty for me being an African-American.

When the date arrived for the visit of the Director of the Office of Minority Business Enterprise and the Second District Congressman, I was directed to attend the meeting along with another employee whom I considered a "monitor" to report back to management about the meeting even though I would write an official trip report. I felt like a pawn in a chest game. This individual had no knowledge of the program or my job. I knew this was a precursor to a politicized program I was being saddled with only a few weeks into the new job.

While the stresses of this job were building, less than two days earlier, problems evolved in my home life. On a Friday afternoon while at work, I received a telephone call from the Police Department in my home town informing me that my wife (Lillie) was arrested for assaulting a neighbor.

I left work and went to the Police Department. When I arrived, I asked to see my wife. The person on the desk stated that she was being processed. When the officer came out with my wife, I asked him, what was the problem? He replied that my wife struck our neighbor in an altercation about a dog knocking over a garbage can. My wife stated the woman hit her also, and assumed that our dog had upset her garbage can.

The officer stated that my wife had been fingerprinted, photographed and was given a court date of August 2nd 1972. She was charged with section a-61 assault in the third degree with a case no. of 72-604 and released on a $500.00 non-surety bond.

When we got home, my wife stated that when the officer arrived at our house, he had already questioned the neighbor, parked his cruiser in the woman's driveway, arrested her and walked with her to get into the cruiser in the woman's driveway.

We had a five year old son that had to stay with our next door neighbor while my wife was being taken to the Police Department. This was an incident I will never forget. The officer wrote his report only on information the other woman supplied. You can imagine how upset I was to learn how the police handled this incident.

The next day which was a Saturday, I went back to the Police Department with my wife and made a complaint against our neighbor who was a principal in this incident. I was told I had to wait until Monday. My reply was I would be notifying the State and National Chapters of the NAACP to voice my complaint. The neighbor was notified that she had to appear in court along with my wife in order for the judge to hear both sides of the story.

When the court date arrived, the presiding judge of the Family Court dismissed the charge and stated that this was a waste of the court's time. When we returned home, I decided to go back to the Police Department and ask about the disposition of my wife's fingerprint and photograph records. To my knowledge, the other woman was never fingerprinted or photographed. I was told by a person in law enforcement that copies of the fingerprints and photograph records are sent to other agencies other than the local Police Department.

My wife asked me not to return to the Police Department. I will never forget that she feared someone would turn their frustrations onto our children. I honored her request and when she died, to my knowledge, this blot remained on her record.

These events at work and at home placed an enormous degree of stress on me during this period of time. I was determined to not allow these incidents to control my life.

My objective at work was to research the history of the Minority Business Enterprise Program and to make a concerted effort to establish a viable program at Electric Boat Division.

In 1968, the Small Business Administration 8(a) program was established, to enhance federal purchases from socially or economically disadvantaged owners of small businesses. This program worked well for most small businesses but not for minority owners of small businesses. This problem was directed to members of Congress and the Executive branch of the government.

The following year, President Richard M. Nixon signed Executive Order 11458 establishing the Office of Minority Business Enterprise within the Department of Commerce. The first Director of this new office was John L. Jenkins.

In 1971, Title 41, Federal Procurement Regulations required all federal contracts exceeding $500,000 to contain a clause encouraging contractors to utilize minority businesses as subcontractors on a "best effort basis".

In the fourth quarter of 1971, another Executive Order was issued to assist the Minority Business Enterprises in technical and management areas. Many of these businesses were technically sound however they were denied access in many instances.

When I started to put our program in place at Electric Boat Division, indoctrination and training were my main concerns. I knew a defense contractor had a more difficult road to follow than a commercial organization, especially in areas of set-asides. Many orders placed by our Department invoked government and company specifications. The government invoked a quality control system (MIL-Q-9858) on many items used in submarine construction in addition to an inspection system (MIL-I-45208A) which flows down to subcontractors.

I put together a source manual of minority businesses detailing their capabilities etc. Many of the suppliers were sent vendor capability forms to complete and return to my attention. Some of these potential suppliers had experience working and supplying components to other major defense contractors, and had their quality assurance and inspection programs approved by government inspectors.

I informed all potential suppliers who would be manufacturing or distributing items for submarine construction, that a quality assurance inspection would be required before their company would be approved and become a valid member of our Vendor Capability Listing. I also informed the potential suppliers that destructive and non-destructive procedures which includes, welding, brazing, x-ray, magna-flux, liquid penetrant and ultrasonic testing must be approved by our Material Engineering Department. Our technical people would give assistance if necessary. I also informed these suppliers that many items of a nuclear or non-nuclear specification would require either government source inspection or our company source inspection prior to shipment from their plant.

The suppliers were instructed on how to submit their procedures for approval on a vendor procedure approval request (VPAR) and additionally, our vendor information request (VIR) for non-conforming materials during manufacture.

Some of the minority suppliers had satisfactorily performed contracts with the Small Business Administration under Section 8(a) of the Small Business Act. The Small Business Administration provides direct contract assistance to small and minority business concerns owned and operated by economically or socially disadvantaged persons. Through cooperation between the Small Business Administration and Government procurement agencies, prime contracts are awarded to the Small Business Administration and this permits negotiated non-competitive subcontracts to be awarded to small and minority firms.

During the period of contract performance, the small or minority business gains expertise that would benefit them later on bids for competitive procurements. Construction procurements in particular should present many opportunities with the potential for follow on work.

I found that the set-aside programs work very well with organizations and corporations that deal primarily with commercial contracts. It was very difficult to explain to some potential suppliers that defense contractors had a difficult time with set-aside programs. I referred many of the suppliers to other divisions of General Dynamics that had significant commercial contracts. I continued to work with suppliers that had potential to supply contract material with various invoked government and company specifications.

My main focus to buying personnel relative to the objective of the Minority Business Enterprise Program is to expand the market and broaden our base of suppliers and become a good corporate citizen. Many minority businesses had capital and the know how to compete for contracts.

What they needed was access to the huge untapped market of American Corporations.

I explained to the buying groups that one of the many problems facing minority firms is establishing a market for their products. Access to the general market place is a necessary prerequisite to business growth. This seemingly obvious fact of business life has special significance for the minority firms whose markets traditionally had been limited to its immediate community because of social and economic discrimination. Minority firms had been mostly isolated from the inter-corporate market. Unlike majority owned small businesses, minority firms had little experience in dealing with large corporate buyers and almost no opportunity to demonstrate their capabilities. I wanted all buying personnel to understand the significance of this program and how to broaden our base of capable suppliers.

I understood the frustration of some minority firms. One of the first individuals interviewed was a manufacturer from Bridgeport, Ct. His products were printed circuit boards, electro-mechanical assemblies, cable and wire harnesses. He informed me he had made trips to Electric Boat Division in the past but never got beyond the lobby.

When I started interviewing suppliers, they were surprised at the fact I did not have an office for privacy during our discussions. If you recall, our Department was in a leased roller skating rink with desks a few feet apart. I felt embarrassed facing principals from some of these firms that were nationally known for their products.

This scenario gave the appearance that our program was not a serious undertaking. A few of the potential suppliers informed me their visits and interviews by other Corporate Small and Minority Business Administrators were conducted in private offices. It felt demeaning to me doing interviews in the middle of the floor of a roller skating rink surrounded by buyers.

In order to make buyers aware of potential suppliers, as requisitions come into the Department, I reviewed them and recommended to the buyers potential suppliers. I recommended small businesses, minority businesses and labor surplus firms to be considered. Labor surplus areas are towns and cities with high unemployment statistics. I attached referral forms to the requisitions prior to buyer assignment.

Many of the requisitions for submarine construction components are single or sole source and in that case, no referral sheets were attached. One of the major problems in buyer solicitation of minority suppliers was to overcome inertia. To do this, I had to educate the buyers relative to the history of many minority suppliers. It was believed by many buyers that all minority business enterprises were start up companies. I felt that my first full year of administering the program would be a challenging task unless I had the support of senior management.

The word minority means different things to different people. Some people interpret the term to mean a minority group relative to the general population. Others look at the term to mean an inferior position relative to supplying goods and services. I tried to convince some of the buyers that most potential vendors are only asking for an opportunity to compete in the competitive marketplace. My focus for the upcoming year was to get more opportunities for minority and small businesses.

The statistics for the first six months for Minority Business Enterprises were dismal. There was a total dollar award of $40,000. This represented thirty purchase order transactions, seventy solicitations with three awards.

My objective for the first full year administering the Minority Business Enterprise Subcontracting Program was to get a significant number of Minority businesses on our bidder lists. A distributor for fasteners (nuts and bolts) was very competitive on many solicitations. This company was All-Stainless Inc of Hingham, Ma. This minority supplier won a significant contract of approximately $60,000. Their Quality Assurance and Inspection systems were found to be in compliance with government specifications. I was sure that this supplier would be successful in future solicitations.

On March 12th 1973, I issued a memorandum to all buying personnel that stated the backbone of the entire program is the buyer. If you are unlucky and have a bad experience with a minority supplier, try another one. After all, I am sure you haven't stopped patronizing majority firms just because you had troubles with a few.

On March 20th 1973 I issued my first revision to the Minority Business Enterprise Source List. A few firms were added in addition to changes to our conditions of purchase for prime contractors as outlined by our Legal Department. The Minority Business subcontracting requirements paralleled the Small Business Program requirements with a "best effort" utilization clause in contracts between $5,000 and $500,000, and the subcontracting clause (with flow-down) in contracts exceeding $500,000 as required by Revision 10 of the Armed Service Procurement Regulations.

The Defense Small Business Subcontracting Program required me to submit a quarterly report to the applicable military agency (NAVSHIPS), the Small Business Administration and the Office of the Supervisor of Shipbuilding here at the shipyard. This report included the number of dollars committed to small, large businesses and labor surplus areas. This data was reported on Department of Defense form 1140-1. This form was revised to require data from prime contractors on subcontracts and purchase commitments to minority owned concerns. This revision was optional for quarterly reporting period October 1st, 1972 through December 31st 1972 and mandatory thereafter.

It was difficult to reconcile or accommodate socio-economic objectives with the exigencies of Electric Boat Division's procurement functions. I stressed that we are called upon to give increased support to these programs that contribute much to the attainment of future goals.

I stressed to the buyers that a stated objective of the Government in the procurement policies was to enhance the possibilities of implementations of the socio-economic policy represented by the Small Business, Labor Surplus areas and the Minority Business Subcontracting Program. I expected to revise this listing of potential suppliers or issue supplements as our base of potential suppliers continued to increase.

I was officially given the task of administering the Small Business Subcontracting Program and submitting the quarterly reports of dollar commitments to Small Business, Minority Business and Labor Surplus Areas to various government agencies. It was clear to me that the buyers and management in the Procurement Department did not take these programs seriously. It was very frustrating however I made a vow that I would aggressively attack the negative responses of the buyers.

I received a call from the Corporate Office in St. Louis, Mo. requesting a copy of my Minority Business Enterprise list of suppliers, vendor capability forms and my source selection file to all operating divisions of General Dynamics Corporation, with copies to the Corporate Manager of Purchasing. Copies were sent to Stromberg Carlson Division in Rochester, New York, Electro Dynamics Division in Pomona, California, Convair Aerospace Division in San Diego, California, Convair Aerospace Division in Fort Worth, Texas, Electro Dynamic Division in San Diego, California, Stromberg Datagraphics Division in San Diego, California and the Quincy Shipbuilding Division in Quincy, Massachusetts.

During the period from June 1972 to June 1973, I had been administrating the Minority Business Enterprise Subcontracting Program. Additionally, a majority of this time I was a buyer negotiating and placing Blanket Purchase orders and Blanket Purchase Agreements. Later in the year I was appointed as the Company's Small Business Administrator.

Annually the salaried personnel are evaluated by the Department supervision and management relative to performance. The form used was the Salaried Personnel Accomplishment and Development Review (SPADR).

My evaluation period from March 31st 1972 to March 31st 1973 didn't mention the fact that I had been administrating the Minority Business Program for nine months. I was evaluated as a part time Buyer. This was a major insult to me relative to my performance. This was the first evidence shown that my management was using me as a pawn in a political game. I was being manipulated to fill a position to satisfy a federal government contract requirement. I was also administering the Small Business Program, submitting reports to the federal government.

It was amazing that I was never evaluated for administering the Small or Minority Business Programs. I was evaluated for the next few years as a part time Buyer. I objected to the way I was being evaluated but nothing changed. I was still listed on the Organization Chart in a management position.

I was later told by my manager to write a job description relative to my duties and responsibilities. It appeared that my supervision and manager had no knowledge of the intricacies of my job function. This request was a major frustration to me because I felt the responsibility to write job descriptions were not my responsibility. I typed a five page description of my duties and responsibilities.

The management of our Procurement Department finally came to the realization that I could not possibly do the job of administering these programs and being a buyer at the same time. This information was pointed out to our management by the Department of the Navy and the Small Business Administration. The Navy representative stated that I should use all of my time managing these programs. These recommendations were the result of the first quarter review of 1973.

It was also interesting that my personnel record in the Human Resource Department classified me in the same pay grade as a Procurement Representative which was basically a clerk, and was never changed by the Procurement Department despite the fact that I was listed in the Management Chart for the Department and the company.

A letter was sent to the Naval Ship Systems Command, Small Business Administration, Supervisor of Shipbuilding, Pentagon and the Corporate Office that I had been appointed as the Small Business Administrator in addition to my duties as the Minority Business Enterprise Administrator. This letter changed nothing. Our Procurement Management assigned a Purchasing Agent whose total job was to issue blanket purchase orders as the Small Business Administrator despite the fact I alone administered these programs and submitted reports and maintained records. This was an irrational way to handle this issue but I understood the motivation.

It was also interesting to note that I was listed in the Management Manual for the Company. I always received a copy of the chart from the Manager of Management Services for the Company which stated "attached for your information is a copy of Organization Chart No. 15.0. You will be provided with a copy of each future organizational chart on which your name appears. A file of these can serve as a personal record of the management positions you have held at Electric Boat". The Procurement Department used this as "window dressing". My job description was equivalent to that of a Procurement Representative with a salary of Pay Grade 9. My position on the Department Organization Chart was Pay Grade 18. I was not evaluated for my duties as the Small Business Administrator for the company. I was evaluated as a basic Buyer which was a farce. My entry level position as a Buyer was assigned to me on the date of my hire in 1968. I had been with the company over three years, prior to my assignment to this new position with the company.

I was anxious to find out how the Navy Representative and the Small Business Administration Representative would view this change during the next quarterly review. I am sure they can only make comments about the direction of the various programs.

During this turbulent period for me, on April 17th 1973, I received a phone call from Pittsburgh, Pa., stating that my younger brother Harold Lloyd died of asphyxiation. He choked on food during a meal.

My brother was a veteran of the Korean War and had received a purple heart for injuries received in action. After leaving the military, he was employed by the Nabisco Company. My father was devastated by the death of Harold Lloyd who was his second child to die after the death of their mother. Marvina was born the day my mother died. She lived two years before dying of a seizure. I will never forget what my father said "You always assume your children would out live you".

I attended the funeral and returned to Connecticut and assumed my duties in the Procurement Department. I was looking forward to our next review of the Programs in June.

When our next quarterly report and review arrived in June 1973 the Navy Representative and the Small Business Representative only questioned and reviewed dollars committed to small and minority businesses, and whether the buyers were making a concerted effort to increase the supplier base. The Purchasing Agent that Procurement Management assigned as the Small Business Administrator was never mentioned. The report did mention that I had a lot of responsibility but no authority to administer these programs. Prior to being appointed as the Minority Business Enterprise Administrator in 1972, the Small Business Administrator had a private office to conduct business and I am sure he was compensated differently than I was when I was appointed as the Company's Small Business Administrator. I was the first African-American to hold this position in the company.

I received a call from the Maritime Administration requesting a meeting between some minority vendors and our procurement personnel. The Maritime Administration is a division of the U.S. Department of Commerce. Their objective was to get more minority enterprises involved in the shipbuilding industry. Representatives of the Maritime Administration from New York and Connecticut attended this meeting. They were very impressed with our face to face meeting with potential suppliers. We studied their brochures and allowed them to present their capabilities. Nineteen representatives were in attendance from business, industry and government agencies. Mr. William L. Bush, the President of the NAACP in Connecticut asked what responsibilities the prime contractor assumes to ensure that our subcontractors are in compliance with the Federal and Armed Forces Procurement Regulations. I informed Mr. Bush that clauses 1-703.3 and 1-703.4 of ASPR outlines responsibilities in this area and we must undergo a review of our Small and Minority Business Subcontracting Programs by the government on a quarterly basis.

I sent a personal letter to the general and specialty contractors thanking them for their attendance and input during the meeting. I explained the purpose of the meeting was to assemble the minority contractors together with large general contractors in order to exchange information that would be mutually beneficial. Minority contractors needed business opportunities in order to expand their operations and maintain sell sufficiency in the marketplace.

The Minority contractors had been one of the big disappointments in the Minority Subcontracting Program nationally. The refusal of the surety companies to bond inner city builders is adamant. In many cases the bond of course is essential to obtaining the contract, especially if it is a public contract. The construction industry is the largest business in the country, about 100 billion dollars in volume and headed for 150 billion dollars in a few years.

It was critical to bring about many more successes in the construction business. We could contribute our small share by giving minority firms the opportunity to perform if it is within their capabilities. I hoped that meaningful progress would result from all our meetings at the time and in the future. I felt optimistic about our progress and the future direction of our programs.

In addition, in my position as the company's Minority and Small Business Administrator, General Dynamics Corporation was on the distribution list from the U.S. Senate and U.S. House of Representatives on all matters that come up before the Senate and House Select Committees on Small Business. All Administrators throughout General Dynamics were given copies of the Congressional proceedings. Federal Procurement Regulations were specific in outlining that the Minority Business Subcontracting Program obligations were in addition to those required by the Small Business Act. I emphasized to my management these were federal programs for prime contractors.

In our next meeting, I was given a new listing of the Small Business Administration's 8(a) contract assistance Companies. This meeting happened at an opportune time because within the next year, there would be major construction work to be done in the shipyard. I was hopeful that some of the minority specialty contractors would have an opportunity to bid on some of the work. A multi-million dollar project would be awarded to construct a graving dock (Land Level Facility) to launch Trident Submarines and in addition, another multi-million dollar project to construct a support building. The upcoming contract awards would be an exceptional opportunity for many minority specialty contractors. I made sure that the general contractors were aware of potential subcontractors. Morrison-Knudsen Co. Of Boise, Idaho was awarded the contract for the Graving Dock (Land Level Facility). I had a meeting with the Project Manager (Mr. George Swanson) He informed me that a Project Office was being set up locally for the offshore project and purchasing people would be opening an office in the area. I received a request to furnish a list of potential minority contractors to Morrison-Knudsen's purchasing personnel. I asked Mr. Swanson if minority contractors had been subcontractors in the past by his company, and he replied, "Not to my knowledge". The Gilbane Building Company of Providence, Rhode Island was awarded the contract to construct the Support Building. I met with the Project Manager, Mr. Frank Totonelly and supplied his company with a list of potential minority contractors. I felt that only good things would happen because every one at the meeting appeared to have a positive attitude about these socio-economic programs.

Another important milestone in my life occurred at this time. My eldest child would be graduating from high school in June of this year. She received her diploma from Waterford High School and decided to look for a job and further her education in the future.

My sister and her husband owned a medical practice in Oakland, California. They offered my daughter Ellen a job working in their practice and promised to have her enrolled as a student at Merritt College in the Oakland Bay area.

Ellen became homesick and decided to return to the East Coast. She moved to New York and obtained employment in the city.

I was seriously thinking about looking for employment with another company. I saw no opportunity for any advancement as an employee with this organization. I decided to stay with the company because I loved the work.

I was looking forward to the NAVSHIPS representative and the Small Business Representative's review of our programs for the third quarter of 1973. This review would answer many questions relevant to the effort being placed on these socio-economic programs by the Electric Boat Division of General Dynamics Corp.

The review was conducted on the first two days of October 1973 and the report from NAVSHIPS was issued on November 7th, 1973. The report was in accordance with the Armed Service Procurement Regulations 1-707.

The Navy Representative stated that during the early period of the subject review, the enthusiasm toward the programs did not appear to be energetic. The attitude was explained by the Purchasing Agent that was assigned as the Small Business Administrator and myself who was the Minority Business Enterprise Administrator for the company.

The Small Business Representative (SBA), the Representative from the Supervisor of Shipbuilding (SUPSHIPS, and the Navy Representative (NAVSHIPS) attributed the lack of enthusiasm to the accelerated procurement program, the hiring of many new buyers, shifting of personnel and the consequential learning curve.

The Purchasing Agent that the management had assigned to administer the program stated that his workload placing purchase orders prohibited him from administering this program. It was ironic because I was the

Administrator responsible for submitting reports, maintaining records, and meeting with business and industry representatives.

I explained to the Government representatives that I would submit a memorandum to the General Manager of Electric Boat Division via my Department Management to issue a company statement of policy for these socio-economic programs and the establishment of a method of implementation of these programs. The buyers would be made aware of the company policy to broaden the competitive base by solicitation of minority business enterprises as well as small businesses. In the past, very few minority businesses were solicited despite the solicitation sheet I attached to many purchase requisitions.

I explained to the review board that I requested the solicitation of small businesses and labor surplus areas and the Vendor Capability List (VCL) should indicate the size and ownership of these businesses. I knew it was beneficial to list the previous supplier however, I had to be careful of restrictive solicitations.

With my buying experience, I understood that many subcontracts were single or sole source based upon government or company specifications. I explained that every effort to place orders with small business, minority business and labor surplus areas would be aggressively pursued.

I knew the Company and our Parent Corporation were determined to be good corporate citizens. I had numerous conversations with our corporate office and always received positive feedback.

The Review Board's exit interview was conducted with the Director of Procurement. It was suggested by the Board that an administrator be assigned whose primary duties would allow sufficient time to perform the necessary functions. Give the assigned administrator the "authority" required to enable the proper compliance and for the buyers to seriously consider his recommendations. Small and Minority business firms should be solicited on a continuous basis and should be documented. It was also recommended to revise the solicitation form to include the size and ownership and to de-emphasize the previous supplier. Additionally, institute a training program to indoctrinate new buyers and to re-kindle the enthusiasm of the veteran buyers.

The Director of Procurement advised that the Administrator would have the needed "swat" and "authority" to effectively administer these socio-economic programs. This never happened.

An official letter was sent to the Department of the Navy (NAVSHIPS) Code 02, 05, and 07. A copy was also sent to the Supervisor of Shipbuilding in Groton, Ct. and the Small Business Administration Regional Office in Boston, Ma.

The following month I sent a memorandum to my Manager requesting a company statement of policy relevant to the Minority Business Enterprise Subcontracting Program. The solicitation of minority firms was progressing slowly. I also referenced Volume 36, Title 41 of the Federal Register relative to Public Contracts and Property Management and the Armed Service Procurement Regulations 1-332. The policy statement must be signed by the President of the company and distributed to all Departments.

I was asked by my Manager to explain to him the part of the Federal Register that applies to Minority Business Enterprises and how it is to be implemented by a defense contractor.

My reply was that many corporations were involved in minority purchasing programs, some were successful and some were not. There is a consensus that two requisites were prevalent in any successful Minority Purchasing Programs. The adoption of a corporate or company statement of policy and the establishment of a method of program implementation must be addressed.

The Federal Register prescribes subcontracting policies, procedures and contract clauses designed to foster and encourage the participation of minority business enterprises, in the subcontracts awarded by Government Prime Contractors. I wanted to make certain that all management personnel understood our contract obligations. The Armed Service Procurement Regulations details provisions and procedures that would be required of prime contractors in the implementation of a Minority Business Enterprise Program. This was my response to my Manager.

I wanted to emphasize that the success of any corporate or company program is totally dependent upon the support of senior management. It is not sufficient for this support to be assumed by members of the organization nor is it enough for top management to verbally communicate its desire to staff members. The expectations of top management must be documented in a company statement of policy and distributed throughout the company. Dissemination of such a directive signifies that the Minority Business Enterprise Subcontracting Program has or will become an integral part of company operations.

The same principles should be applied that resulted in effective programs in equal employment opportunity. A successful Minority Purchasing Program must become a function of normal purchasing procedures as equal employment became an integral part of normal personnel policy and procedures.

I requested that my comments be forwarded to the company's top management for evaluation. A policy statement from the company would inform buying personnel and Purchasing Management that compliance is necessary. Despite the fact that I reviewed incoming purchase requisitions, and requested that buyers solicit various minority and small business firms on a continuous basis, very few minority firms were given the opportunity to bid on a requirement.

It came to my attention that some minority suppliers had difficulty obtaining a reasonable line of credit at some financial institutions. This problem prevented some potential suppliers from bidding on major subcontracts because raw material had to be purchased before manufacturing could be started. This information was also given to our top management. It may be possible for our company to give an assist to potential suppliers in the areas of technological and managerial assistance.

We had previously given assistance to potential suppliers relative to quality assurance. Our Procurement Quality Assurance Department had previously assisted some potential suppliers in the qualification of their quality and inspection systems to meet our company and government specifications.

Many Departments at Electric Boat Division were eager to help potential suppliers but, it was necessary for these suppliers to be solicited and win awards on a competitive basis.

In the first week of January 1974, Mr. Joseph D. Pierce, General Manager of Electric Boat Division of General Dynamics Corporation issued a Statement of Policy relative to Minority Business Enterprises. This was a powerful statement by the General Manager and I felt confident that the program would move in a positive direction which would make my job less stressful.

The policy read and I quote, "It is the policy of Electric Boat Division as an equal opportunity employer to ensure that Minority Business Enterprise Programs are carried out by its operating departments in a manner that will enable minority business to be considered fairly as subcontractors and suppliers in conformance with our contractual requirements, and applicable federal regulations. It is the intent of Electric Boat Division to provide assistance to small minority enterprises which can provide both jobs for minorities and useful goods and services at competitive prices.

Equal opportunity as related to minority business enterprises include bid qualification, pre-award competition, contract negotiations, bid award, listing as qualified bidder, and solicitation for quotations. In addition, it is Electric Boat Division policy to encourage the establishment and growth of minority suppliers through both technological and managerial efforts as well as the placement of appropriate business with them.

The Minority Business Enterprise Program as practiced at Electric Boat Division is directed at implementing the provisions of ASPR 1-332 and Title 41-Public Contracts and Property Management (1-1.13). In the implementation of this policy, Electric Boat Division will continue to advise its subcontractors, vendors and suppliers, community organizations and agencies, employment sources and others of its minority affairs policies and will encourage them to adopt similar policies as appropriate. This program is a commitment that such a policy will be consistently applied throughout Electric Boat Division by all appropriate management personnel, with supervisory accountability enforced on a uniform basis".

My next major objective after the company's policy statement was to put together a Minority Business Enterprise Subcontracting Plan. The statistics for the year 1973 for Minority firms was not much better than the 1972 statistics. The dollar awards were $164,266, the number of purchase order transactions was fifty seven, and the number of solicitations was one hundred forty four. The number of awards was twelve. My goal for 1974 was dollar awards of $500,000, one hundred fifty purchase order transactions, five hundred solicitations and forty purchase order awards.

During this period of time, my father was still grieving the loss of his son when he was told that his leg was gangrenous, and had to be amputated. He had medical problems including diabetes and glaucoma. I went to Pittsburgh to visit him in the hospital after his surgery. He was always positive and I stated previously that I never heard any negative statements about him and never heard him make any negative comments about anybody. I have always been extremely proud of him and was fortunate to have him as a father. I returned to work and experienced a surprise.

Electric Boat Division hired an African-American woman as a Buyer in the Procurement Department in the latter part of 1973. I thought she was well qualified for this position. She possessed a post graduate degree. I thought this was a positive move because she would be the second African-American buyer to be hired at our company. I was hired in 1968. I assumed she was to replace me as a buyer because I was to administer the socio-economic programs for the Company.

With this New Year starting with a policy statement from top management, I was very optimistic about the future direction of our socio-economic programs. If I had a crystal ball, I would have seen a turbulent time ahead relative to buyer resistance and management indifference. This would turn out as the most difficult period of my time at Electric Boat Division.

On February 1, 1974, I had to send a report to our Accounts Payable Department on awards to Canadian and foreign sources for the fourth quarter of 1973. All awards were to Canadian Vickers. I submitted a list of awards and/or supplemental changes processed in the fourth quarter of 1973. There were twelve work authorization assignment orders that were supplemented increasing the price by $78,713.

There were five purchase orders ceiling awarded and advance customer (NAVSHIPS) notification was issued. Canadian Vickers agreed to accept formal purchase orders subject to downward revision based upon audit findings, negotiations and Electric Boat Division supplied material. The supplied material was from our Foundry. The issuance of the purchase orders would allow Canadian Vickers to continue proper production. After audit and negotiations, supplements would be issued with final fixed prices. These figures would be reflected in the first quarter report of 1974. The five orders had a total price of $3,259,705.

I never received credit or was evaluated about my total duties and responsibilities as Electric Boat Division's Small Business Administrator.

On February 13, 1974, I was invited to attend an award banquet by Region 1 of the Small Business Administration in Boston, who in cooperation with the United States Air Force Electronics Systems Division would present an award to Input-Output Computer Services Inc. This company was selected as the Small Business prime contractor of the year.

The award ceremony was scheduled for February 21, 1974. My manager sent another individual who had no knowledge of my job as the Small Business Administrator. It appeared that I was to be a pawn in a political game that I was unwilling to play.

The African-American woman who was hired as a Buyer started to get frustrated relative to the way she was being treated in our Department. On April 29, 1974, she wrote a letter terminating her employment to the Director of Procurement that stated and I quote, "Please be advised that I will be terminating my employment with Electric Boat on May 10, 1974 for the following reasons. In my initial interview, I was miss-lead as to how long it would take in advance beyond my starting position of Status Seeker-Buyer. My job was in effect a clerk and nothing resembling either an Expediter or a Buyer. I never had a desk and constantly being shifted around was demoralizing and made me feel that my job was not a necessary function of the Department. Finally, I was told that I lacked experience and must start out as a status seeker-Buyer and then move up to an Expediter and a full Buyer. This statement appears to be invalid due to the fact that two men have since entered the Department and have become Expediters, neither of them had buying or expediting experience and one had no business experience whatsoever. Therefore, due to the above reasons, I feel that employment with Electric Boat does no offer me a real opportunity for advancement". She signed the letter and referenced her Procurement Badge # 66020. Copies of her letter were to be sent to the General Manager who had recently issued the Policy Statement for the Minority Business Enterprise Subcontracting Program, the EEO Manager for the company, her manager and supervisor, General Dynamics Corporate Office in St. Louis Missouri, Department of Health and Human Services in Washington, D.C., Department of Labor for the State of Connecticut, Department of the Navy in Washington, D.C. and the Department of Commerce (Maritime Administration) in New York. She gave me a copy of her letter for my records because of the turmoil I was going through in this Department. She decided not to send the letter because it may impact any future African-American buyers in the Procurement Department.

My focus at this time was to help minority suppliers and other small businesses obtain subcontracts with Electric Boat Division and its general contractors.

I stayed in touch with the two general contractors that would be involved with two major projects in our shipyard. I had supplied a list of minority contractors in the state of Connecticut. I had compiled my list from Electric Boat Division's Minority Business Enterprise list, the city of Hartford's Minority Registry of Construction Services and the city of New Haven's Minority Business Directory. These listings identify the companies and their construction specialties.

A representative of Morrison-Knudsen Co. explained the off shore subcontract packages (electrical, mechanical, painting and erection of metal). With the exception of the painting and erection, the other packages had been awarded. The representative stated that being an out of state firm, his company was unaware of local minority contractors during the bidding period. Morris-Knudsen Co. would consider minority contractors on packages still open for bid now that his company had a list of minority specialty contractors that I had supplied.

The other general contractor, Gilbane Building Co. had utilized minority contractors in the past. Gilbane entered into joint ventures with some minority suppliers on some government projects in Washington, D.C., The District of Columbia Courthouse and the Social Security Building. In the Connecticut area, Gilbane Building Co. had minority participation in the Hartford Civic Center project. In fact, one of the minority contractors at our previous meeting (B&T Masonry Co.) completed a $100,000 subcontract for Gilbane Building Co. Performance bonds would be relaxed on a case by case basis to assist some minority suppliers. The Vice President of the Gilbane Building Co. also indicated that Business Opportunities Inc. of Rhode Island could possibly help minority firms in the financial area.

On June 6, 1974, I received a letter from the Director of Purchasing for the Gilbane Co. He informed me that Pep's Electric Co. of Glastonbury, Ct. and C&S Plumbing Co. of Hartford, Ct., would be on their list for a major subcontract package.

It appeared our general contractors were very up beat about using minority contractors. They felt it was good business practice that would help the entire industry. Many minority suppliers had proven themselves to be capable subcontractors.

On June 24, 1974, I met with the regional director of the National Association of Minority Contractors (NAMC) and explained to her the efforts of General Dynamics on behalf of minority and small businesses. The Director would travel in the future to our Corporate Office to discuss our Corporation's Affirmative Action programs in general and minority contractors in particular. The Director stated to me, "I do not envy your task, but am appreciative of your efforts".

During this period of time, I was looking forward to the high school graduation of my eldest son, James Jr. I was happy to hear my son had a plan for his future education. James Jr. aspired to be a broadcaster and journalist. He graduated from high school in June of 1974 and planned to enroll at Mohegan Community College in Norwich, Ct. for the fall semester. His plan was to obtain an Associate Degree and then finish his four year degree at San Diego State University in San Diego, Ca. I was happy to have a positive event on my mind for a short period of time.

A few weeks later on July 15, 1974, I sent another memorandum to my supervisor and asked about my job classification and compensation. My duties were to administer the Small and Minority Business Programs for Electric Boat Division.

My records designated me as a buyer despite the fact that I had been administering these socio-economic programs for over two years. My question was how I was being evaluated as a buyer and how I could ever possibly be upgraded when I was not performing the duties of a buyer. I never received an answer to my memorandum. It appeared my Management was making my job more difficult.

I faced another obstacle at about this time. Some Purchasing personnel were taking classes at a local college and the company would reimburse the student on successful completion of the course. The course of instruction had to have some association with your job.

I was informed by my Supervisor that the company would not reimburse me because Accounting was not part of my job. He knew I was pursuing a degree in Business Administration. This came as a shock to me because one of the clerks was taking the course in basic Accounting. I talked to one of the Cost Analyst in the Department and he informed me that he would take up the issue and talk to the Director of Procurement. I gave him the reimbursement form and he took it into the Director's office. He returned the form signed. My Supervisor knew he had to sign off on the form and grudgingly affixed his signature. I felt I was singled out for this harassment. After this incident, I started to feel this supervisor was making a concerted effort to retaliate against me in many subtle ways.

It was amazing that less than two weeks later, this Supervisor directed me to go to a minority supplier in Brooklyn, New York to conduct an audit. I sarcastically asked him, I thought that accounting was not a part of my job. I received no comment from him.

Due to my workload at this time, I requested permanent clerical help. I had been getting temporary help when requested. I was told by my Supervisor to make a formal request relative to my clerical needs and appropriate justification. One of the Manager's secretaries typed the memorandum.

I outlined a few areas where clerical help was necessary on a permanent basis. I referenced three sections of the Armed Service Procurement Regulations (ASPR) and a letter from the Naval Ships Systems Command (NAVSHIPS). The Minority Business Enterprise Source List must be updated as required by our customer (NAVSHIPS). It took approximately 101 hours of clerical work to make revision #2 to the Source list. Then it took three months after my request for typing support to have the Minority Business Enterprise Source List typed. I had requested help on May 15, 1974 and as of July 22, 1974 no permanent clerical help was given.

I had requested in March of 1974 that in the orientation of new buying personnel, a Minority Business Enterprise Source List be issued to the new employee along with the Procurement Policy Manual, Procurement Department Instructions and a Standard Clause book. The employee should also be made aware of the Small Business and Labor Surplus Area Programs.

Records must be maintained and reporting for Rapid Supply Orders (RSO) activity and minority solicitation and awards. Many of the solicitations and awards to minority firms are rapid supply orders and this is very time consuming when statistics and records are kept manually.

A daily review of incoming requisitions, making copies of forms (minority, small and labor surplus), to attach to requisitions in order to notify buyers of potential sources as suggested by our customer (NAVSHIPS). Making copies of these forms each day is a clerical function.

A clerk must check the weekly form 2980 printout for corrections and errors in order that the monthly and quarterly printouts are correct. This involves checking the applicable purchase orders. Minority vendors who do not respond to our request for quotation were requested to explain the reasons for **no response.**

During the quarterly review of our Small Business Report with (NAVSHIPS), (SBA) and (SUPSHIPS), I had to check all orders issued over $10,000 to large business firms where no small businesses were solicited or small business declined. I then listed the vendor commodity and the reason why no small businesses were solicited or why small businesses declined to quote or bid.

Continuous mailing of letters and vendor capability forms to suppliers referred from our reviewing agencies and mailing capability forms to newly identified minority firms and some selected small business and labor surplus firms were reasons I needed permanent clerical help.

It was ridiculous that I had to explain to my management why I needed clerical help on a permanent basis. I am sure my management did not understand the scope of my responsibilities, or did not care.

My frustration was increasing because I was forced to take this position because it was a prime contract requirement. I will always remember that I was placed in this position because I was the only minority in the Department. The remarkable aspect of this situation was it appeared I was being denied the resources to properly administer these programs.

I finally realized that I was placed in this position for political reasons. Many of the potential minority suppliers felt that my company was not serious about helping them form a business relationship. I felt unfairly scrutinized. I was making a concerted effort to succeed in my job despite the lack of support from my management. I will repeat that the majority of Departments at Electric Boat Division were enthusiastic about the programs. The resistance to my efforts came from my Department.

I overheard a conversation between a Manager and Supervisor in the Procurement Department. The Supervisor said to the Manager, "I don't trust minority companies because they are probably unreliable". This mentality made my job more difficult.

I always knew the Minority Business Subcontracting Program involved all minority and disadvantaged businesses. With my position as the company's Small Business Administrator, I had to consider awards to all small businesses and labor surplus areas throughout the nation.

I attended a business meeting in Massachusetts the previous year and the focus was on the road ahead for Minority Business Enterprises. The host for that meeting was Ken Guscott Associates, a management consulting company. I recall that a representative for a Native American Indian tribe was in attendance. The representative stated that the tribe would be soliciting business in the near future. I advised him to keep me informed of the progress. I was interested in expanding our supplier base. I wondered if the Small Business Administration maintained any contact with the Native American tribe in Montana.

I called the regional office of the Small Business Administration in Boston informing them of my interest in assisting this Native American business enterprise. I was informed that the company was established in 1971 and was only interested at the time in doing business with commercial companies and not with government contractors.

I received a call later from a representative of the tribe in business development. I was informed that the company had its plant in Browning, Montana and was interested in doing business with our company. The name of the company was the Blackfeet Indian Writing Company. This company employs over one hundred tribal members and is 80% tribe-owned.

I was told to contact the sales representative at the factory and get their organization involved with Procurement personnel at all Divisions of General Dynamics Corporation. I contacted the factory in Montana and had a productive conversation with the Sales Manager. I mailed a vendor capability form to the factory and notified the Small Business Administrators at all Divisions of General Dynamics Corporation.

I felt that this potential supplier would be an ideal candidate for a volume purchasing agreement (VPA). An agreement such as this would allow this company to supply writing pens and pencils to all Divisions of General Dynamics for a specific period of time.

I met the representative at a meeting in Cambridge, Massachusetts and informed him about my plan for the Blackfeet Indian Writing Company. They would get the opportunity to bid on a major contract. I found out at a later date that the Blackfeet Indian Writing Company was a successful bidder on a Blanket Purchasing Agreement (BPA).

I was asked to attend a seminar on behalf of the Connecticut Department of Commerce to participate in a Minority Enterprise Sales Contact Center at the Yale Motor Inn in Wallingford, Connecticut. I interviewed potential suppliers and distributed vendor capability forms to be completed and returned to Electric Boat Division's Procurement Department.

The Commissioner of the Connecticut Department of Commerce and the Defense Supply Agency sent a letter to the Vice President/General Manager of Electric Boat Division thanking him for my participation in the seminar. I knew this would be a very busy year for me as the Small Business Administrator for the Company. I later received a personal letter from the Commissioner of the State Department of Commerce thanking me for my participation in the seminar benefiting the business community of Connecticut.

I received a letter from the Corporate Manager of Purchasing in St. Louis, Missouri on August 13th 1974 requesting that I advise the Avenel Division of General Dynamics in broadening their Minority Business Program based upon my accomplishments in that area. I had conversations with the Avenel Division's Procurement Department and forwarded a copy of my Minority Business Enterprise Source List.

I received a second letter from the Corporate Manager of Purchasing on August 27th 1974 expressing his appreciation for my efforts with regards to my assistance to the Avenel Division's Minority Business Program. My experience in this area was a great assistance to the Director of Procurement at the Avenel Division. I was happy to help increase the supplier base on a corporate level.

The Corporate Manager of Purchasing sent an inter-office memorandum to the Director of Procurement at Electric Boat Division and the Corporate Director of Material on August 29th 1974 stating that he had a conversation with Mr. Tatigan of the Navy Department in Washington, D.C. Mr. Tatigan had some fine comments with regards to Electric Boat Division's overall small business participation and in particular the efforts of Jim Mosley.

I was starting to get very frustrated about my treatment in trying to administer these socio-economic programs and my employment compensation. I contacted the Equal Employment Opportunity (EEO) Manager at Electric Boat Division and requested an investigation. I found out that people listed on the Organization chart on my level were compensated at a different level. I also asked why I was listed in Human Resources on the level of a Procurement Representative (Clerk) when I was listed on the Management Organization Chart as the company's Small Business Administrator. The pseudo investigation was a sham. The representatives conducting the investigation from the EEO office only talked to the individuals that were guilty of discriminating against me in this Department. I was never asked any questions by the investigators. This is a good example of how injustices are covered up. I asked the EEO Manager for an independent investigation by the Connecticut Commission on Human Rights and Opportunities. He told me that if I made an outside complaint, "I would be skating on thin ice". I am sure what he meant was that I would face retaliation from agents of the employer. This is exactly what happened.

I refused to be intimidated by what may happen if I voiced a complaint relative to discrimination by a small number of individuals in my Department. Knowing what I would be facing in the future, I decided with much thought and consultation to voice my complaint as a person who was discriminated against. My hope was that I would get a fair internal investigation from the company. I was wrong.

When I think back on the date of my initial hire at Electric Boat Division's Procurement Department as the first African-American, I heard that many of the personnel in this Department were under the impression I was placed in this Department because of affirmative action. I was hired because of my interview and many years of submarine experience.

The memorandum that I typed at home on my personal typewriter was addressed to my supervisor. The subject was Lack of Equal Employment Opportunity in my duties at Electric Boat Division dated September 15th 1974. The file number was JMM/35/74. I referenced my memorandums to Management, the EEO office and the Management Manual Policy Statement—Equal Opportunity. A copy was forwarded to the General Manager of Electric Boat Division, Corporate Office, Maritime Administration and the Equal Employment Opportunity Commission.

I knew retaliation would follow but I accepted this fact as a man that would not compromise my principles. When this memorandum was circulated, I was informed by a Department Manager that as long as I worked in the Department, I would never advance. His next question was whether I typed the memorandum on company time. My answer was I typed the memorandum on a personal manual typewriter in my home. I am sure that my management was hoping I would voluntarily leave the company. I don't run away from problems or faint in times of adversity. My resolve was to continue being a productive employee of the company. I felt that a major part of my management's frustration was based on my memorandum requesting a company statement of policy relative to the Minority Business Enterprise Subcontracting Program. The policy statement was signed by the General Manager of the Electric Boat Division of General Dynamics Corporation in January 1974.

My next initiative was to get a woman owned company (disadvantaged business) as a potential supplier of goods and services to Electric Boat Division. I called the Small Business Administration Regional Office in Boston, Massachusetts to inquire about a potential business entity owned by a woman.

I was given the name of a company in Tonawanda, New York which is a suburb of Buffalo. The company name was American Women Metals. I contacted the President, Mrs. Diane L. Chandler and arranged to have a meeting to discuss her products, quality assurance and inspection systems.

Mrs. Chandler made the trip to our Procurement Department and gave me a history of the company and supplied brochures. In a period of five years, her company became a million-dollar a year business. It was stated that the company name was chosen very deliberately because she felt that women were in the fore-front of so many careers but not really with metals.

The company shares a building with Malyn Machine & Tool Company which is owned by Mrs. Chandler's husband. She informed me that "he has nothing to do with my shop. He buys raw material from my company and I buy material from his shop at times".

Prior to forming the company, Mrs. Chandler worked part time as a Purchasing Agent buying raw material for a machine shop. There were large requirements for specialty raw material and lots of government contracts. It also didn't take long for her to realize that the government both state and federal actually put aside some contracts for women or other minorities who had their own companies.

American Women Metals decided the route to go was to supply raw material straight from suppliers to customers. I informed her that their quality and inspection systems had to be approved by our Procurement Quality Assurance Department.

I made an appointment for the inspection and supplied Mrs. Chandler a copy of our vendor capability form. This form was to be completed and returned to my attention. In the meantime, solicitations would be made.

Our Procurement Department purchases an enormous amount of raw material. American Women Metals could supply orders that range from a specialty cuts three feet long of nickel alloy to 10,000 pounds of metal.

I introduced Mrs. Chandler to the buyers that purchase raw materials and requested that her company be solicited on future requirements. I also informed the buyers that I had scheduled a quality assurance survey.

I found out weeks later that American Women Metals was solicited and their quality assurance and inspection systems were approved and they had been awarded some contracts for raw material.

On September 16, 1974, I received a memorandum from the Manager of Corporate Purchasing in St. Louis, Missouri requesting information about my Minority Business Enterprise Source List and how it was compiled. I replied that I used multiple sources from newspaper clippings to various directories, publications etc. A few potential suppliers forming enterprises notified me direct when their organization was actively soliciting business. I continuously searched for additional Minority as well as Small Business sources to broaden out competitive base of suppliers. Electric Boat and other Divisions of General Dynamics Corporation buys from potential vendors with products geared to the shipbuilding industry.

I kept in close liaison with Newport News Shipbuilding and Drydock Company, Litton Industries/Ingalls Shipbuilding Division and the Maritime Administration in the mutual dissemination of information relative to potential minority vendors e.g., if a vendor wants to supply pipe fittings or other related marine hardware with strict quality assurance standards, a request is made to survey their facilities. I sent a copy of sixteen sources I used to compile my list to the Corporate Office.

The Navy scheduled a review of Electric Boat Division's Small and Minority Business Subcontracting Program for September 27, 1974. Those in attendance represented the Naval Sea Systems Command, Small Business Administration and the Supervisor of Shipbuilding at the Shipyard and I represented Electric Boat Division. The total volume of subcontracting, approximately $241 million for Fiscal Year 1974, is the largest among prime contractors assigned to the Naval Sea Systems Command for surveillance. This figure represents nearly double the volume placed during Fiscal Year 1973. The small business share had declined from 27.78% in Fiscal Year 1973 to 22.56% in Fiscal Year 1974. The Navy representative stated, "it is hoped that increased management attention and direction will arrest and reverse the declining trend which will have a significant impact upon the total small business subcontracting share of Fiscal Year 1975. During the exit interview it was noted that various supervisory personnel over Mr. Mosley, among others, attended the exit interview in the absence of the Director of Procurement. During the interviewing of various Buyers, many were not aware of the responsibilities of the Small Business Administrator for the Company". It was also noted by the review panel that provisions should be made for the evaluation, qualification and utilization of small business/minority business firms nominated by the Small Business Administrator.

It was my responsibility to document and report subcontract dollars committed to large, small, minority businesses and labor surplus areas to the Naval Sea Systems Command, Small Business Administration and the Supervisor of Shipbuilding at the shipyard.

I received a letter from the Acting Director of the Small Business Administration in Boston on September 28, 1974 requesting nominations for the Small Business Subcontractor of the Year. This request was sent to all major defense contractors. The award is made annually by the federal Small Business Administration during Small Business Week in Washington D.C.

Nominations were limited to a maximum of two from each defense contractor. One nomination was to be located in the same region as the prime contractor and the other nomination could be outside the region. The nominations were to be sent to the Small Business Regional Office by February 14, 1975. The award was to be given in the nation's capital in May of 1975. Representatives from all defense prime contractors were expected to attend along with selected members of Congress.

I was wondering how long it would take before I received any feedback relative to my discrimination complaint. On September 30, 1974, I received a letter from the District Director of the Equal Employment Opportunity Commission in Boston, Massachusetts. It stated that we have received your communication alleging unlawful employment practices in violation of Title VII of the Civil Rights Act of 1964, as amended. Under Section 706(b) of Title VII this Commission is unable to accept jurisdiction in your case until the matter has been deferred for 60 days to the Commission on Human Rights and Opportunities in Hartford, Connecticut. The charge number is TB05-0635.

On December 5, 1974, the Electric Boat Division EEO Compliance Officer sent a report to the Civil Rights Officer of the Maritime Administration. The report was a complete cover up. He said that my job classification was changed from Buyer to Minority Business Administrator on November 24, 1974. I had held the title of Minority Business Administrator since June 30, 1972.

The supervisors in Procurement evaluated me as a Buyer which I was doing on a part time basis. I was not evaluated as the Minority and Small Business Administrator for the Company. My supervisors were unaware of my duties and responsibilities. I was placed in this position for "window dressing" purposes.

The company investigators stated they found no evidence of discrimination relative to compensation despite evidence that I was on the Management Organization Chart at pay grade eighteen however, I was compensated at pay grade nine. The investigators never explained this discrepancy.

The report stated that on an organization reporting level, I should not report to a buying group supervisor but to an Administration section. It is remarkable that the Minority Business Enterprise Program was initiated by an executive order signed by President Richard M. Nixon and my supervisors were ignorant of the program or subtlety ignoring the Program.

The report stated that due to a lack of space in the Procurement Department, office space was not available to the Administrator. I was administering the Minority Business Program and the Small Business Program. The previous Small Business Administrator had a private office. My space was a desk and chair in the middle of a roller rink surrounded by many Buyer desks. There was no privacy when I interviewed potential suppliers. This was an insult to many of the representatives from various companies. Many minority suppliers informed me that our Department management was not serious about socio-economics programs. One supplier that I interviewed stated that in the period of time he had been calling on Electric Boat Division, he never got past the lobby.

The answer given in the report relative to the question about educational benefits was ridiculous. It was stated by the investigators that the complaint about tuition reimbursement resulted from a delay in the approval process. My supervisor in the buying group stated Accounting, Economics and Marketing are not related to my job thereby, tuition reimbursement is denied and he would not sign my tuition reimbursement form. I had one of the Department Cost Analyst take my reimbursement form to the

Director of Procurement and he signed the form. My supervisor knew that he had to sign the form and he signed it grudgingly.

To summarize the report from the EEO compliance Officer from Electric Boat Division, it is easy to see how cover ups occur. I was never asked one question about my complaint. The EEO Compliance Officer met with my management only. The entire report was a sham.

I received a letter from the Small Business/Minority Liaison Officer from the Convair Aerospace Division in Fort Worth, Texas on November 12, 1974. A letter also was sent to the Administrators at all General Dynamics Divisions and to the Small Business Manager of Mc Donnell Douglas Corporation.

The subject was that some companies nationally are defined as small business but in reality, they are large businesses. These errors distort the statistics of the federal Small Business Program.

Each General Dynamics Division was advised to be vigilant about suppliers, particularly if they are subsidiaries of large corporations. I stated in my reply that if all the Administrators make the effort to weed out erroneous classifications, it would help avert any possible criticism of "self certification" in the future.

The Small Business Administration had the capability to help prime contractors in the identification of small business concerns. Records of industry size standards are kept by the Small Business Administration for small business concerns who receive government contracts. There are criteria in the proper identification of small business e.g. the number of employees over a period of one year and annual receipts over a three year period. Additionally, size standards vary with the industry. In the case of minority or other disadvantaged business, it must be owned 51% by this group.

Most Small Business Administrators representing Prime Contractors found it very difficult to certify a company as a Small Business, Disadvantaged Business or a Minority Business Enterprise. This was a challenge for me to accurately define some businesses in my quarterly reports. I felt skeptical about a few of our current suppliers.

The federal Small Business Administration investigated and exposed various cases of fraud among some Small Business and Minority Business Enterprises during certifications for government contracts.

Some business enterprises falsified their records in order to obtain government contracts on a set aside basis. This action allowed them to obtain contracts without the competitive bid process. I was aware this happens in many instances and the results distort the overall accuracy of the Small Business, Disadvantaged Business and the Minority Business Enterprise Programs.

With my workload increasing, I finally received a memorandum from the Director of Procurement stating that I would receive permanent clerical help. I had requested permanent clerical help in a memorandum dated May 15, 1974 and it was answered on February 25, 1975.

Prior to the Director's memorandum, I was given temporary clerical help on and off since December 6, 1974. I was notified on February 6, 1975 that my temporary clerical help that I had partially trained was being moved to another area. There was an Industrial Engineering report that listed some recommendations of methods to strengthen our program. Without adequate support, the job was more difficult. The expansion of these programs I was administering and the continuous training of new personnel to assist in my activities, was not a luxury of time I could afford.

During this time our company had multiple ship contracts for 688 Class and Trident Submarines. The Procurement Department was committing multi-million dollar contracts to many of our suppliers therefore the Government was very interested in the amount of dollars committed to Small Business, Disadvantaged Business and Minority Business Enterprises. I had to submit reports on a quarterly basis.

These reports were scrutinized carefully by the Naval Sea System Command and the Small Business Administration. I was informed by my management in no uncertain terms that these socio-economic programs were my responsibility and if the job was not properly accomplished, the blame rests with the person administering the programs. I gladly accepted the challenge however, I should have had more to say about how I performed my functions if the total responsibility rest on my shoulders. The Naval Sea System Command Representative stated succinctly, "You have a lot of responsibility but no authority".

I recalled that during a review in 1973 by the Naval Sea System Command Representative and the Small Business Administration Representative that the Director of Procurement stated during the exit interview that the Small Business Administrator of Electric Boat Division would have the "swat" and "authority" to properly administer the socio-economic programs. The authority was never given to me to properly administer these programs. My supervisors had no knowledge of these programs and made no attempt to learn my responsibilities.

I was notified by the Corporate Office that I would be a member of a delegation of nine people to represent General Dynamics Corporation in Washington, D.C. during Small Business Week on May 20th 1975. I represented the Marine Group of the Corporation. The Aerospace, Commercial Group and the Washington Office would also be represented. Our delegation was seated at Table 29. The award banquet was at the Sheraton Park Hotel in a massive ballroom.

There were members of other major defense contractors including General Electric, Raytheon, Boeing, Lockheed and selected Small Businesses and members of Congress and the Defense Department.

The following day we attended a meeting and luncheon with the Assistant Secretary of Defense for Installation and Logistics at the Golden Ox Restaurant. The agenda for this meeting was to discuss some upcoming defense contracts. When I returned to Connecticut and assumed my duties, I was still treated as a Procurement Clerk.

On May 22nd 1975, Mr. Robert Blackwell, the Assistant Secretary of Commerce for Maritime Affairs requested that our Corporate Director of Material schedule a meeting for the Director of the Office of Minority Business Enterprise, Mr. Alex Armendaris. The purpose of this meeting was for Mr. Armendaris to meet the Director of Procurement and discuss our Minority Business Enterprise Program and to obtain first hand knowledge of the operation of a shipyard and discuss methods to utilize more minority subcontractors. In addition to Mr. Armendaris, also present was Mr. Horace Bohannon who represented the Maritime Administration.

During discussions about the upcoming visit, I overheard a Manager and the Director of Procurement stating that "he has no clout". This was in reference to Mr. Armendaris. Despite the fact that I administered the program, I was not invited to the meeting in our Procurement Department. I often wondered what was discussed during the meeting. The shipyard tour was cancelled due to time constraints.

The Director of Procurement received a memorandum on June 2nd 1975 from the Corporate Director of Material stating a meeting would be held in St. Louis, Mo. The subject was Small Business and Minority Business participation in General Dynamics' ongoing programs.

The meeting was held on June 27th 1975 and my supervisor was sent in my place despite the fact he had no knowledge of the program or my overall duties. It was easy to see the politics of this job.

I started to think seriously about requesting that another individual be appointed to this job and I return to buying. I was initially hired as a Buyer and enjoyed my duties and expected to be treated fairly.

I knew when I made the complaint on September 15th 1974 I would be demonized and denied opportunities for advancement as long as I worked at Electric Boat Division. I knew there were laws in the State of Connecticut commonly know as "retaliation" statues that prohibit an employer or their agents to discipline an employee for filing a discrimination suit. I knew there were individuals in the Procurement Department who were violating these statues in the name of General Dynamics, Electric Boat Division. I knew the major disadvantage I would be facing.

I received an inter-office memorandum from the Corporate Manager of Material on September 8th 1975 requesting that I submit to his office an outline of potentially effective activities which could be undertaken to achieve an end objective of "the finest socio-economic program within the industry" for General Dynamics Corporation. This memorandum was also sent to the Small Business Administrators at other Divisions. The subject was Reassessment of General Dynamics' Socio-Economic Procurement Activities.

When input was received from all Divisions, a proposed program incorporating the consensus of opinions and elements of successful programs developed would be implemented.

It was amazing that the preliminary meeting for this effort was conducted on June 27th 1975. I previously stated this was the meeting I was denied by my management to attend. My supervisor attended in my place. He had no knowledge of these socio-economic programs at Electric Boat Division. He never participated in any reviews conducted by the Navy Department or the Small Business Administration. I gathered all the statistics on a quarterly basis for these reviews and submitted the appropriate reports. I was asked by my supervisor to write a job description. I had stated previously, it was not my job to write a job description about my position. I was listed on the Management Organization Chart as the Company's Small Business Administrator and the Minority Business Enterprise Administrator. I wondered what was the criteria for listing me in a management position?

The Corporate Manager of Material requested that my comments should not be limited to the activities currently taking place within Electric Boat Division, but should include any potentially rewarding activities which I felt should be considered for an overall Corporate Plan. The objective was to provide effective help to the small business, minority business and labor surplus communities, to improve our base of suppliers and to obtain recognition of our achievement when justified. It was necessary to avoid "lip service" to the program.

On July 8, 1975, Lillie and I traveled to Yonkers, NY to attend the wedding of our oldest daughter Ellen. She was married to Mr. Leroy Edwards, a radio broadcaster.

I was sure the Corporate Office was sincere in an effort to be a good corporate citizen. I observed many positive efforts coming from the Corporate Officers. The obstacles placed in my path by our Procurement Department management were destructive. There were management personnel in my department whose agenda was to sabotage my efforts.

On September 19th, 1975, I submitted my memorandum to the Corporate Office defining my plan for an effective socio-economic program. I basically explained the template that was used to implement our program, when it was put into effect on June 30th 1972. Some important aspects necessary for effective programs are senior management support and training.

With the New Year rapidly approaching, I decided to request that the Director of Procurement assign a new person to administer the Division's socio-economic programs. I had been attending night classes at a local college pursuing a degree. I was scheduled to graduate on May 22nd 1976.

I was completely frustrated with certain Managers in my Department who were fighting every effort I was making to do my job properly. From the start, they looked at a Minority Business Enterprise as a start up company or an inferior entity. It was not difficult to see the bias by these individuals. I had the misfortune of working for these individuals for a considerable period of time.

I had agreed to spend time working to get another individual on board administering these socio-economic programs. The Small Business sector was already established when I took over the program but the Minority Business Enterprise Subcontracting Program was new to the Division. The source list of suppliers and all procedures necessary for the suppliers to form a business relationship with Electric Boat Division were in place.

On June 28, 1976, our daughter Ellen and her husband Leroy were blessed with a daughter. This was my first grandchild. They named her Miesha Nadine Edwards.

I was finally assigned to the Trident Specialties Section for a period of four months and later transferred to the Casting/Forging Section. This action allowed me to assume the duties for which I was initially hired.

The Casting/Forging Section was familiar to me because of my military experience on submarines. This was a smooth transition back to the buying function. I had been assigned to a special government purchasing program in 1971 after completing a course in the Negotiation of Contracts and Cost/Price Analysis.

I was happy to be back as a Buyer after four years. The four year period was a detour in my career. I kept up to date on the buying function. Most of this time period, I was still buying on a part time basis and evaluated as a Buyer. This section also purchased raw material.

The month of May finally arrived. The commencement exercises were conducted on May 22nd 1976. I was inducted into the Mitchell College Society of Scholars and received the Nathan Hale Award. I was fortunate to have my family present when I received my degree.

A new Director of Procurement was assigned early in the New Year. On May 26th 1976 after my graduation, I received a personal memorandum from the new Director. The subject of the memorandum was graduation. "Congratulations both on receiving your degree from Mitchell College and receipt of the Nathan Hale Award. Your graduation while working full time speaks for your persistence. The Nathan Hale Award certainly speaks well for the quality of your scholastic efforts. I think you can be very proud of your achievements".

After being assigned to the Casting/Forging Section, my initial objective was to study every book I could find on the Casting and Forging Industries and how raw material is produced. I had purchased these items previously in 1971. I selected two books to study for the purpose of enhancing my technical knowledge of the Casting and Forging Industries. The Steel Casting Handbook by the Steel Founders Society of America and the Forging Industry Handbook by the Forging Industry Association were my favorite books.

I purchased castings and forgings made from various alloys. These alloys were steels, bronze, nickel aluminum bronze, different series of stainless steels, and nickel alloys. I made various trips to foundries, forge shops and steel mills to observe how metals are poured, cast and forged. I purchased different types of castings based on methods of manufacture, there were static, investment, continuous and centrifugal castings required for submarine construction. In the forging area, some are manufactured by the open frame method and others by closed die. The open frame method uses different forging hammers and dies uses presses.

A few of our major forging suppliers poured their own raw materials while others purchased their raw material from mills prior to the forging process. I was able to observe the manufacture of these parts. I also witnessed the destructive and non-destructive tests used during manufacture for chemical and mechanical properties in the finished product.

One of my first trips to a casting foundry was to observe the centrifugal casting of large rings at the Wisconsin Centrifugal Company in Waukesha, Wisconsin. This company was one of my major accounts. They produced the hatch ring (stainless steel) and the locking ring (nickel aluminum bronze) for the twenty four missile tubes on each Trident submarine. These rings are in excess of eighty inches in diameter. These rings are shipped to the company fabricating the missile tubes. These rings are finished machined and welded in the hull insert casting.

I observed how the centrifugal casting process is used to make castings. By spinning the mold in which the molten metal is being poured, centrifugal force acts to distribute the metal in the mold. Wisconsin Centrifugal Company was the only known company approved by the government to cast these large rings for the Trident Submarine.

While at Wisconsin Centrifugal Co. I asked the Sales Engineer about the refining of stainless steel by the Argon-Oxygen Decarburization process. He called one of the Metallurgists and we had a discussion about the process and when their company would be processing stainless steel by that method. I was informed their company was presently working to include this process in their manufacturing cycle.

My curiosity of this process was the result of my research into the history of refining stainless steel. I read everything I could find on melting and refining steel and other metals that were used for submarine construction.

I was purchasing the stainless steel hatch rings for the Trident submarine missile tubes. This process was of refining stainless steel and developed by the Linde Division of Union Carbide Corp. and proved out by Joslyn Mfg and Supply Co. of Ft. Wayne, IN. I made a concerted effort to learn as much as possible about the manufacture of the parts I had the responsibility to purchase.

This method of refining stainless steel by this process should decrease the price of this material because the steel producer could use a cheaper high carbon ferrochrome material and free the electric furnace from the dual role of melting and refining.

Melting could be done in an electric furnace and refining in an (AOD) vessel. The argon-oxygen mixture in the vessel reduced the level of unnecessary elements in the alloy and, improved machining and welding of the stainless steel.

I never took my job for granted. I wanted to be well informed in all areas of manufacture and purchasing on materials to build submarines. As a previous crewmember aboard submarines, I knew the importance of new technologies and quality control methods to ensure my knowledge of the items I purchased.

I had other accounts that centrifugally cast smaller diameter parts. One of these suppliers was US Pipe and Foundry Company. I purchased hydraulic accumulator cylinders for various hydraulic systems throughout the submarine. This company had patented a process whereby they could centrifugally cast two types of stainless steel (300 and 400 series). There is a fusion zone between the two series of stainless steel. I tried to obtain competition for this cylinder. Other foundries attempted to duplicate this process but failed. They were unable to produce a fusion zone between the two metals.

I was given major accounts to purchase structural equipment and raw material for the shipyard. My experience on submarines helped me to understand the impact of purchasing material that complied with strict quality assurance standards. I was the only member of the Procurement Department that had experience serving aboard nuclear powered submarines.

In addition to the large cast rings, each missile tube had a nickel copper forged ring. This ring was the upper section muzzle end ring. This ring must be forged for additional strength. Unlike the large cast rings, I received competitive bids for the forged rings. During my evaluation of the bid for the cast rings from one supplier, I had to do an in-depth cost analysis to justify the reasonableness of the pricing.

At the time I was purchasing the forged rings, the cost of each ring was approximately $70,000. Each submarine had twenty four tubes. The cost for one ship was $1,680,000. I negotiated this pricing because the supplier requested progress payments. This allowed the supplier to purchase raw materials. Occasionally, I requested a penalty clause be placed in the contract to ensure that the contract delivery date be met, in order that our shipyard schedule to the government is preserved. All materials purchased for the missile tubes were shipped to the missile tube fabricator.

Electric Boat Division had three suppliers who competed for the contract to fabricate the missile tubes: Westinghouse of Sunnyvale CA., Babcock & Wilcox of Barberton, Ohio and FMC Corporation of Minneapolis, MI.

Upon completion of the finished missile tube, the successful supplier would ship the tube to our plant to be welded into the hull of the submarine.

It was good to be back purchasing material for the construction of submarines. There were courses in non-destructive testing. I studied the liquid penetrant procedure along with ultrasonic and magna-flux examination of metals, in addition to x-ray examination of metals and read books on metallurgy. It was necessary to be the best I could be as a Buyer and knowledgeable on the technical side of submarine construction. My military experience was valuable in my technical knowledge. My experience as a negotiator and knowledge of purchasing procedures was synergistic to my technical expertise.

I asked my Supervisor and Manager when I would be considered for a promotion based upon the complex contracts I was given the responsibility to administer. My Manager stated there were no openings in our casting and forging group for another Buyer Specialist. I was a Senior Buyer at the time. I didn't understand why I was doing the work of a Buyer Specialist but couldn't be advanced to that position. The following week, there was an opening in our group for a Buyer Specialist. I asked my Manager if I could be considered for the position and he answered in the affirmative. I was interviewed and was subsequently advanced. There were a few other personnel in the Department that started off being a Buyer in the same group I was initially assigned to purchase material. At this time, they were supervisors and managers. I felt stuck in a Department whereby my advancement would be limited by factors beyond my control.

This was the Supervisor that informed me "Jim, as long as you are in this Department, you will have difficulty being advanced because you are on the s—list because you made a complaint about racial discrimination in nineteen seventy four".

I was determined to work at peak performance and let my accomplishments speak for my ability. I took my job very serious. I made the complaint because I was placed in a political position to administer a program that was very unpopular at the time. I was informed "you were placed in this position because you are the only minority in the Department". I was hired as a Buyer and then denied the opportunity to be a Buyer. I was stuck in a dead end job after three and one half years.

My son James Jr. was a student at a local community college, and was in his second year when he decided to enlist into the military. His rationale was to serve an enlistment and be eligible for the GI bill, and go back to school to obtain a degree in Broadcasting and Communications.

He enlisted in the Air Force on August 30th 1976. I asked him why he chose the Air Force. He replied that he was interested in aviation and remembered my story about being denied an opportunity to attend flight school years ago. I was hoping he would complete school prior to a military career. He knew the military history of his family. I was in the Navy for twenty years on active duty and served in the reserve for an additional ten years. James Jr. had two uncles who served in the Air Force, one uncle in the Navy and one uncle in the Army. I felt our family had provided enough military service. It was time for other families to make a commitment to serve this country in military service.

He departed for San Antonio, Texas for basic training at Lackland Air Force Base. Upon completion of basic training, he decided to go to school to become a jet engine mechanic. He had decided that in the future he would obtain a license as a pilot. I was happy that he had a vision for his future and was pursuing his dream for the future.

In the meantime, I was happy to be back buying material for submarine construction. I purchased material from many casting and forging suppliers in addition to raw material suppliers. My purchases ranged from a few pounds (investment castings) to forgings made from ingots weighing in excess of 200,000 pounds.

In 1977, my second son, Thomas left high school and wanted to work in a trade. He enrolled in the Apprentice Trade Program at Electric Boat Division and aspired to be a welder. He was an outstanding basketball and football player at the high school but was not interested in attending college. He always told me he enjoyed working with his hands and had a strong mechanical aptitude for repairing items. I informed him to follow his dreams and do the type of work he enjoyed because college is not for everyone.

During January of 1978, I was chosen by the management of the company to participate in a plant wide inventory. This task lasted one week working eight hours a day from January 22nd to January 29th 1978. I was given a certificate of appreciation in recognition of," invaluable service, personal interest and participation in the plant wide inventory". The certificate was signed by the Director of Material and the General Manager of Electric Boat Division.

In February of 1978, my son James Jr., was home prior to being transferred from Chanute Air Force Base in Illinois to Plattsburgh Air Force Base in New York (Strategic Air Command) and assigned to the 380th Field Maintenance Squadron. The urgency was to overhaul the engines of a squadron of planes to be deployed to Europe. He later informed me his group was working twelve hours per day to complete the task.

After the task was completed, he received orders to report to the 376th Field Maintenance Squadron at Kadena Air Force Base on the island of Okinawa. He was transferred in May of 1978.

I received the most devastating news of my life when my son called on July 7th, 1978. He informed me he had been diagnosed with acute lymphatic leukemia. It was as if I had been stabbed in the heart. I had worked in the past as a laboratory technician reading bone marrow slides of leukemia patients. During this period of time, this diagnosis was a death sentence. The only chance for a person to survive was a bone marrow transplant.

Our son Thomas was visiting his maternal grandmother in South Carolina when he was notified that Jim was in the hospital in Washington, D.C. He hitch hiked from Florence, S.C. to Washington D.C. to be with his brother at a critical time.

This was a complete shock to me. I thought he was still in Okinawa. The phone call came from the Walter Reed Army Medical Center in Washington, D.C. The doctor informed me that my son was air lifted to the Tripler Army Hospital in Hawaii and then to Washington, D.C. It was explained to me that aggressive treatment had to be started immediately. I explained to the doctor that I would be traveling to the hospital the next day which was a Saturday. He convinced me that aggressive treatment had to be initiated immediately. I gave permission to start treatment prior to my arrival at the hospital. The next day, my wife and I left for Washington, D.C. Our son was in good spirits despite a poor prognosis. I was very proud of his inner strength and his faith in God. My wife and I made a commitment to travel from Connecticut to Washington, D.C. every weekend to visit him and to give him hope for the future. An aggressive regimen of chemo-therapy was in progress. In July I requested a week of vacation to spend more time with our son and it was granted. We intended to spend from July 24th through July 28th. On July 26th, I received a phone call from Pittsburgh that my father had died of a massive heart attack. I called my employer and explained the circumstances I was facing. They informed me I could take as much time as was necessary.

My sister informed me the funeral would be on July 31st, 1978. We left for Pittsburgh on July 27th 1978 and informed our son we would be back as soon as possible. He loved his grandfather and stated "it's a shame". Jim informed me that some people are worse off than his disease.

We attended the funeral in Pittsburgh on July 31st, 1978 and returned to Washington, D. C. for a few days prior to returning to Connecticut.

During this period of time I was having automobile problems during my trip to Washington DC on weekends. I decided to purchase a used vehicle for my weekly trip. Approximately two days after purchasing this vehicle, I was leaving work and found the left front tire slashed. I had to purchase a new tire. I was told a sheet rock knife was used to destroy my tire. You can imagine how I felt because I needed this vehicle to visit my son who was sick hundreds of miles away.

I was informed on September, 18th that my son was in remission after his chemo-therapy and could return to Connecticut. The next day, I left for Washington D.C. with my son Thomas to bring Jim back home.

Upon his discharge from the Walter Reed Army Medical Center, his doctor's orders stated he must report to a Veteran's Administration Hospital on a weekly basis for blood work to be performed. The nearest hospital was in West Haven, Connecticut which was only about an hour away.

A few weeks after Jim came home, Thomas decided to join the military. He went to the recruiting office and joined the Marine Corp. The Recruiter informed Thomas he would receive his recruit training at the Marine Corp Base at Parris Island, SC. Thomas requested to be sent to the Marine Corp Recruit Depot in San Diego, CA. His request was approved and he left for CA.

We received notification from the Air Force stating that Jim was being medically retired from the service and would receive veteran benefits.

Jim asked me to help him find a car before he started back to school in the spring. We went to a few dealers before he decided upon a vehicle. We saw a new 1978 silver grey Audi Fox at a dealership in Groton, Connecticut. He decided to purchase this vehicle.

I asked him if he needed me to co-sign for him. He stated I can make the payments. I was unaware at the time he had purchased an insurance policy from the finance company and designated me as the beneficiary. The purpose of this action was if something happened to him, the car would be paid for in full. I was sorry to hear that his thoughts were not positive about his medical prognosis.

He asked me and his mother if we could help him get an apartment and furniture. We were able to help him get an apartment in New London and started to shop for furnishings.

I co-signed for his furnishings. He always wanted a water bed, so he purchased a king size water bed. He was all prepared to finish his education and make the weekly trip to the Veterans Hospital. He was very happy to have a dependable car.

He needed a vehicle for his weekly trips to the Veterans Administration Hospital in West Haven, Connecticut for his laboratory blood tests.

Jim's younger brother Merv who was twelve years old at the time loved horses and told us one day he was going to buy a horse. He had a newspaper route delivering papers in an area of approximately one half mile. Mr. Silva one of his customers informed Merv that a friend of his who owned the Little "B" Barn and Tack Shop had a horse for sale. On June 16, 1979, we went to North Franklin, Ct. to see the horse. My wife and I decided to purchase the horse and made arrangements with Mr. Silva to board the horse at his facility.

The price of the horse, saddle, bridle and pad was $801.75. The horse was a Bay Quarter type mare named "Torrie". When the horse arrived at the Silva Horse Farm, all immunizations were up to date and we agreed on a monthly fee for boarding. I located a nearby place to buy hay and feed. I informed Merv that taking care of a horse was a daunting task but he was determined.

Merv had an extended newspaper route. He delivered approximately one half of his newspapers and returned to the house to pick up the balance. During this cycle, he stopped by Mr. Silva's farm to feed the horse. I knew he was motivated to care for his horse because most of his money from his newspaper route went to buying hay and feed. Jim was happy that Merv finally realized his dream of owning a horse.

When there was inclement weather, we drove Merv to deliver his newspapers. On June 28, 1979, Merv's niece Miesha was celebrating her third birthday. We had a party for Miesha and she got a ride on the horse and had pictures taken. I knew Jim enjoyed the festivities of the day.

Jim had planned a trip to San Diego, California to visit his Aunt Yvonne and get brochures from San Diego State University. The trip was made on the one year anniversary when I was first notified about his illness. He had a nice visit with his Aunt and his cousins and returned to Connecticut after a week's vacation.

Prior to his trip to CA. he informed me he wanted to buy a new Audi 5000 which was a top of the line Audi. I thought about the reasoning behind his decision. I convinced him not to buy another car because his Audi Fox was practically a new vehicle.

During this period, one of my suppliers was having labor problems. The producer of the primary shield tank top forgings, The Ladish Co. went on strike on April 11, 1979. This supplier was single source for these forgings. This presented major problems for our company and its prime contracts with the US Government.

I sent a memorandum to our Engineering Department stating, it is requested that a review be conducted to determine if alternate methods of manufacture of this item is feasible. Historically, we had been unsuccessful in obtaining cost and pricing data from the Ladish Co. to support their priced proposals. It is anticipated that a waiver of cost and pricing data and cost accounting standards requirements of Public Laws 87-653 and 91-379 would be requested from the Secretary of the Navy. It has been noted that the Ladish Co. has continuously failed to state its position with regards to compliance with these public laws in a manner which is clear and unequivocal.

In order to protect the construction schedules, it was necessary to determine if alternate methods of manufacture can be employed. Historically, the lead time for these items to be manufactured has been approximately thirty weeks. If other manufacturing methods are acceptable, other suppliers may have the capability to quote our requirements. Please evaluate and advise.

On August 9, 1979, a meeting was scheduled in the Shipyard Office to discuss alternate method of manufacture for this requirement. Personnel from Nuclear Design, Trident Engineering, Materials Engineering and I represented the Purchasing Department. It was determined that three alternate methods of manufacture be explored, a plate weldment, whereby six inch plate could be purchased from US Steel or Lukens Steel. This plate would be to Electric Boat Division specification 24113 which is "fine line" for inclusion shape control. Another method would be a redesign by other forging suppliers, possibly a single extrusion by Curtiss-Wright Corp. or Cameron Iron Works. The final alternative would be a casting if other methods fail. It was agreed upon that inquiries would generate costs for plate and extrusions. Subsequent to our meeting, Ladish submitted a quote for the top and mid-ring forgings, however, no delivery could be quoted because of the work stoppage at their plant.

I requested a determination be made as to the commitment of funds by Electric Boat Division to The Ladish Co. for raw material purchases with an option date to cancel in the event that another manufacturing method is chosen for this requirement or in the event the strike at the Ladish Co. continues. I anticipated a very busy summer.

The summer went rapidly. Our family went to a company picnic on my fiftieth birthday. It turned out unseasonably cold. Most of the events for the small children were cancelled.

In the latter part of August, Lillie became ill and was diagnosed with bleeding in the lower alimentary canal. She was transferred from the Lawrence and Memorial Hospital in New London to the Yale-New Haven Hospital in New Haven. She underwent surgery and recovered rapidly. Lillie was also suffering from hypertension and taking medications prescribed by her primary care manager. She continuously worried about Jim and the battle he was waging against his disease. I tried to give as much support as possible to my family because we were experiencing difficult times.

Jim enrolled again at Mohegan Community College to complete his two year degree and planned to enroll at San Diego State University to complete his four year degree. He decided to play on the basketball team again. I was hoping he would not put more stress on his body but he insisted on playing.

He was voted to the College Senate and was very popular with the student body. He participated in a series of college plays and enjoyed acting.

While a student, he enrolled in the Barbizon School of Modeling and completed the course and received his certificate. He participated in shows wearing casual wear and business attire. I was very proud of his accomplishments.

He was very upbeat about his future. On some weekends, he participated in sky diving at the Chester Airport. Sometimes I wondered why he was participating in so many activities, but I was happy to see him having a good time and staying active.

We had a nice Christmas holiday season and looked forward to the New Year. Jim was still traveling to the Veterans Administration Hospital every Wednesday for his laboratory tests.

We tried to see all of Jim's home basketball games. In January, the family went to see one of his games. He played an outstanding game but his team lost by two points in the last six seconds of the game.

The first week of February, Lillie and I went to Hartford, Connecticut to see Jim perform in a fashion show. The following week we went to New York to see Jim's sister Ellen perform in a fashion show on her birthday. Jim was very proud to see his sister perform in a fashion show. At this point, I never knew that the next month I would get devastating news about the health of my son.

On March 26th, I received a call from Jim stating that the doctor from the Veterans Hospital wanted him to stay over night. I called the doctor and he informed me that the cancer had returned. This was a major concern for me based upon my knowledge of the progress of this disease.

I continued with my job as a Buyer while visiting my son at the Veteran Administration Hospital in West Haven, Connecticut. Jim received another regimen of chemo-therapy. I could easily see he was slowing losing his battle against this disease but remained positive. I was very proud of his determination to defeat this disease.

I often wondered why this disease came upon him so suddenly. He was always very healthy and active. It was strange to me why he would get gravely ill in a period of one month. Only God knows the answer to this question. There is no family history of this disease even though I know genetics may play a part in addition to exposure to certain chemicals and foreign substances.

I thought it would be good to make a trip to the hospital for his mother's birthday and our twenty sixth wedding anniversary. The date was April 3rd. This would be a nice two days prior to the weekend. This was a four day period to spend with our son.

In May of 1980, Jim had been on a new regimen of chemo-therapy and his resistance to infection was severely compromised. He requested permission to visit his mother on Mother's Day which was May 11th. Permission was granted by his doctor however, he had to be back to the hospital by noon. I picked him up at the hospital at seven in the morning and returned him back to the hospital prior to noon. He was able to spend two hours with his family. Jim had a small puppy, a Siberian Husky. He spent a considerable amount of time with his dog prior to coming back into the house. I could see the pain on his face when we had to return to the hospital.

Later in the month, his puppy left the yard and was hit by an automobile in front of the house. His hip was fractured and he had minor injuries. I notified Jim and told him what had happened. He asked me to take care of his dog because an animal has feelings and should be respected. I took the puppy to a veterinarian and his hip was repaired. I notified Jim about my actions and he was pleased.

We decided to spend the Memorial Day weekend at the hospital visiting Jim. Memorial Day was on Monday giving us a long weekend. We were able to take Jim outside in a wheelchair. He had to have a blanket and a facial mask because of his compromised immune system. We had a nice long weekend. I never thought this would be Jim's last day outside.

Early Saturday morning on May 31st, I received a call from the doctor informing me that Jim had developed an abscess in his groin area. I knew this was a major problem because of his immune system. When we arrived at the hospital, Jim was experiencing a considerable amount of pain and had to be sedated. This experience was taking a heavy toll on his mother who was also experiencing medical problems. We stayed over the weekend at a local motel and returned back home on Monday.

I returned to work and tried to put in as many hours as possible during the week to make sure my workload was up to date. During the month of June, I made the trip to the hospital after work sometimes during the week for a few hours. I was very concerned about the progress of my son's fight against the disease.

On June 17th, while at work, I received a phone call from the doctor at the Veterans Hospital informing me that Jim needed a donation of platlets. I immediately volunteered to be the donor. The doctor stated that the donation should be made by a person under the age of forty. My age at the time was fifty. I had to sign a form not to hold anyone responsible if I was adversely affected by the procedure. The platlets would be extracted from whole blood by the electrophoresis method. I did not hesitate to do anytime to benefit my son. My wife and I traveled to the Farmington Medical Center to undergo the procedure. After the procedure was completed, the Hematologist advised me to have a complete blood count at least twice a year to follow-up on the regeneration of my blood cells.

One week later on June 24th, Jim's doctor wanted to talk to me about his medical condition. She told me there was nothing else they could do for my son and was requesting my permission to stop all medications except for pain. My reply was, as long as you are living, you have a chance. Only God decides when the end of life comes.

I started to make the trip after work every day to visit my son and try to give him hope. Our last weekend with Jim was June 28th and 29th. We took our granddaughter, Miesha with us for the weekend because June 28th was her fourth birthday.

The year before after his classes, he occasionally took Miesha to the store with him to buy pizza. He enjoyed spending time with his niece. On one occasion, he took Miesha to the college with him. He had an assignment to complete and spent an hour or so in the library.

It was difficult for me to imagine that one year ago, he was active in sports at the college. He was a member of the basketball and baseball teams. I recall seeing him playing centerfield for his team at the US Coast Guard Academy the prior summer.

Jim's stepbrother, Ernest who lived in New York called and planned a trip to the hospital on July 4th. I informed him the family would be there for the weekend. It was nice having everyone there for the holiday. Ernest, Rose and their sons, my grandsons Renwick and Sean drove up from New York.

The morning of July 7th, I was called at work and was notified that Jim had taken a turn for the worst. I left work and picked up Lillie and we left for the hospital. Jim had been heavily sedated but still alert. He couldn't talk but he was staring at us. I felt he was trying to communicate with us. Four doctors came into the room and were discussing the rash he was developing. They couldn't explain the appearance of the rash. I heard one of the doctors say," I have seen many leukemia patients but never a case like this".

It was about eight thirty in the evening when one of the doctors informed us they would be examining Jim and we could leave and come back in the morning. I had a strong feeling not to leave the area at this time. Lillie and I decided to go home and come back early in the morning. I was very concerned about our son and his prognosis. We arrived back home prior to midnight and went to bed. The phone rang at five in the morning and we were informed that Jim died at four forty. We immediately left for the hospital which was about fifty miles away. When we arrived back at the hospital, the doctors explained to me again, they had never seen a case of leukemia such as the one that killed our son. Jim died two years and one day after he informed me of his diagnosis. His funeral was on July 11th, 1980 with full military honors. This was a sad day for our family but Jim was no longer in pain.

After Jim's death, Lillie and I talked about the strange circumstances of his initial diagnosis and the period of his treatment and comments made by the doctors during the last month of his life.

When Jim was transferred from Plattsburg Air Force Base to Kadena Air Force base in the latter part of May 1978, he became gravely ill in a period of one month. I often wondered what immunizations he received prior to leaving for the Far East.

We also wondered why a member of the military from Kadena Air Force Base on the Island of Okinawa made a visit to see our son while he was at the Walter Reed Army Medical Center in Washington, D.C.

Jim had been on Okinawa for approximately one month and probably knew just a few people. Years after his death, I received a tape from one of his friends on Okinawa during the period of his illness. The tape was made by independent researchers studying human retro-viruses. I believe that one day, some things will be revealed about our son's illness and death.

I always knew Jim was a special person because of his generosity and compassion for other people. During his illness, he frequently stated "some people are worst off than my condition". After his death, I found out he donated a portion of his meager veteran's pension to the United Nations International Children's Emergency Fund (UNICEF) on a monthly basis. This revelation did not surprise me because I knew he was a compassionate person.

He lived a blessed life doing things he thought made the world a better place. He died at the age of twenty three. I believe you measure the worth of a person's life on earth by their accomplishments, not by their chronological age. It was very difficult for my wife and me to accept the death of our oldest son. Our faith in God helped to ease our burden during the most difficult period of our life.

I went back to work with a heavy heart after the funeral. I reflected on a statement made by my father in nineteen seventy three when he stated, "you always assume your children will outlive you". My younger brother Harold Lloyd died of asphyxiation. Here in nineteen hundred eighty, I lost a son.

The first evaluation of my performance after the death of my son, the period was March 1980 to March 1981. I will never forget the statements made at the most difficult time of my life. The assessment started off positive. My supervisor stated "Mr. Mosley has assumed follow-up duties as well as buying and is very knowledgeable in regards to operating procedures. During 1980, he placed purchase orders with the value of $3,261,718. This was 26.5% of the group total. He achieved a cost reduction of $115,290. He is very well organized and keeps detailed records and his data base information is always up to date. Mr. Mosley also attended another seminar on negotiations". The negative part of the evaluation was about the late placement of some purchase orders. I recall my supervisor calling me at home right after the funeral of my son stating " Jim, you have to get back here right away because a special purchase order had to be placed". My son was buried on July 11, 1980 and I had to take my wife to the hospital on July 14, 1980. I informed the supervisor I had to take my wife to the hospital that Monday and I would be in as soon as possible. It appeared he held this against me for the entire evaluation.

I wrote a rebuttal to his evaluation. My comments were, I had an interview with my supervisor and I was informed that in certain areas I should make efforts to improve. I have been told this for thirteen years and I totally agree that improvement is possible and necessary in all areas of work as well as life.

I was informed that I should be more aggressive in conducting negotiations. My reply was I feel that I can be aggressive and perform a creditable task of negotiating in a manner other than being boisterous or visibly upset. Using a bold and energetic pursuit of one's ends is to me an important element of negotiating.

In another area which is a little painful for me, I was informed that last year I was late placing some purchase orders. In some specific instances, I missed certain days because I was at the hospital with my son who was dying of Leukemia. He was in the intensive care unit for about six weeks.

During this period, there was considerable stress on me to visit him as I am sure most people can understand. Many days I left work at 4:30pm and went to New Haven to see him and returned home at about 1:00am. If I am to be penalized for my actions during this trying period, I accept the penalty. My son died on July 8th 1980.

Notwithstanding the above, during frequent periods in the past, I performed and issued purchase orders for people who were either out sick or leaving the company. In one case, I worked on one individual's desk for eight weeks in addition to my own work. This was difficult for me to forget under the circumstances.

In other instances, I was penalized for the late placement of orders. I explained I had to wait for the Engineering Department to forward the drawings. This was necessary for the bidders to quote a price for the item. In some cases, I had to wait over six weeks for the necessary drawings. I am sure the supervisor writing the evaluation was aware of factors beyond my control.

Additionally, it took an average of three to four weeks for potential suppliers to quote on certain casting and forging requirements. At this time, I was directed to solicit a new potential supplier for HY-80 castings. This was an area beyond my control as my supervisor was continuously informed. It was easy to see the retaliation that was taken against me because of my past history of a complaint that was truly justified and continues.

I was so busy at this time that I only had time to concentrate on my duties as a Buyer and to stay informed on all activities relative to the accounts that I had the responsibility to administer. The supplier for our fairwater plane bearing and rudder assemblies was having problems with the machining of these parts. I had to make a trip to our supplier Janney Cylinder Co. in Philadelphia, Pa. to discuss our concern about the late schedule change. I met with the VP of Sales, Production Manager, Quality Assurance Manager, Plant Manager and the Production Control Manager. Our discussion focused on the machining problems and shipment to meet our construction schedule and commitment to the government.

I was aware of the difficulty machining stellite parts due to the nature of the material. Another important aspect of delivery schedules remains in some instances, the responsibility of our company. The Quality Assurance Manager informed me that in some instances, film reading approval, vendor information requests (VIR), and vendor Procedure approval requests (VPAR) and source inspection requests to our company should have shorter turn around times. When our company is delinquent on any of these issues, the contract delivery date may have to be adjusted.

Approximately eight week later, I had to make another trip to Janney Cylinder Co. with two engineers from our company to discuss an Engineering meeting relative to a proposed change to the fairwater plane bearing assemblies, as outlined on a change notice. The proposed changes to the sleeve (alloy 21) portion of the assembly were primarily dimensional in nature and the machined surface finish. An additional requirement proposed for the first time on this alloy was for two attached coupons for the tensile test which must be taken in the longitudinal direction and the elongation value should be provided for information only. This change would require another spinning die and the casting would be an additional three to four inches to facilitate test material.

The Engineering Notice also required a temperature dimensional adjustment which Janney Cylinder Co. must study further. The proposed changes to the bushing (Alloy16) and the spherical bearing (Alloy 20) were primarily dimensional and machined surface finish. Most of the proposed changes present no problems to Janney Cylinder Co., i.e. dimensions, feature control symbols, lubrication holes, hardness tests for the bushings etc.

Janney Cylinder Co. must wait authorization from our Engineering Department to machine test coupons from one sleeve casting from one of the two orders presently on hold for our company. The testing would be accomplished at a local test laboratory. If the ultimate tensile strength is 85,000 pounds per square inch, our Engineering Department can advise this company whether to machine a ship-set of sleeves for one submarine from the old design or incorporate the new design, the lead time for these items is approximately twenty six weeks I would have to negotiate new pricing for these items due to supplemental changes.

I had previously been contacted by a foundry in Orrvile, Ohio who was interested in supplying bronze valve bodies for our shipboard use. Electric Boat Division had a foundry that produced bronze valve bodies. We needed another source for these castings due to our production schedule to satisfy our prime contract requirements.

I was contacted by our Quality Assurance Department and was requested to attend a survey of this supplier, relative to their compliance to the government's quality and inspection systems. I considered this an honor that our Quality Assurance Department had this respect for me in this area.

I accompanied our company's Quality Assurance Engineer to Orville, Ohio to conduct the survey at the Orrville Bronze and Aluminum Co. We met with their President and Quality Assurance Manager. We spent two days at their facility and found their records and procedures were in compliance with the government and Electric Boat Division's specifications.

I loved my job and continued to improve my knowledge in the technical area of material specifications, and how metals are prepared for the manufacture of castings and forgings.

I received a requisition to purchase K-Monel bar stock to be used for the secondary propulsion machined parts. I received quotations from three potential suppliers. The low bidder had a price of $102,766.73. While analyzing the previous buy for an earlier ship, I noticed an extra ship-set of material was purchased and put into an excess material account. I notified the Engineering Department and had this requisition cancelled. This was a cost avoidance of $102,766.73 for the company. I decided to keep a record of any cost reduction or cost avoidance for my personal records. The manager signed the Cost Reduction Sheet. In the past I never kept personal records of my savings because I thought it was just doing your job. I was informed by a member of the Department that it is a part of your evaluation and he advised me to keep records. I started to keep personal records of all my cost savings for the company.

My supervisor assigned a very complex component for me to purchase for the Trident submarine program. This was something that I felt was a challenge for me to accomplish. This item was to be manufactured by the extrusion method. The only known supplier was Cameron Iron Works in Houston, Texas. In addition to the forging presses, this supplier uses, it also had extrusion dies whereby the metal is pushed through the die in order to manufacture long tubes with small wall thickness.

I studied this manufacturing method. The product which was assigned to be purchased was the Sonar Cable Trunk. This thin walled tube was approximately forty-five feet in length with a very critical wall thickness. I knew when the item was to be shipped to our facility after manufacture it required special transportation to limit the camber for this part. The camber was the complexity, arching or curvature of this long, thin tube. This was another single source item assigned to me where cost analysis was required to determine the reasonableness of the quoted pricing.

I was curious that most of the complex requirements were always assigned to me to purchase. I always looked at it as an opportunity to learn and progress. I was optimistic in accepting all challenging situations as an opportunity to grow.

I reflected back on my earlier years in the Procurement Department, when I was transferred rapidly through the various buying groups. I felt at the time, the objective was to frustrate me and hope I would voluntarily leave the company. The results of these actions were I was educated in all segments of the buying functions.

One of the most memorable events in my life occurred early in June of 1981. My wife Lillie went to the grocery store and when she was leaving the store, she observed a small elderly woman standing outside waiting for a taxi. Lillie decided to drive her home. She lived in an apartment complex in New London, CT.

When Lillie returned home, she informed me of her encounter with this elderly woman. This woman was Pearl F. Blanks who was born in Statesboro, GA. on July 8, 1901 and had no living relatives. She was seventy nine years old and would be turning eighty in July. She had one sister, Blanche Lipsey and parents Emma and Frank Lipsey. Her husband Fred Blanks had died a few years after moving to New London from Stamford in 1975. Lillie asked me whether we should "adopt" her and assist in taking care of this elderly single woman. We both agreed to assist Pearl in her day to day activities. Lillie took her grocery shopping and to her frequent visits to wash her clothing.

Pearl informed us about her past history relative to her parents and her work history. Most of her life she worked as a domestic to some famous families. She had worked for an Army General, the Honeywell family and for President Franklin Delano Roosevelt. She worked at the President's southern White House in Warm Springs, GA. Eleanor Roosevelt gave Pearl a dress but she had to do major alterations because the First Lady was close to six feet tall.

Pearl met Fred Blanks when they both worked at the Bureau of Engraving in Washington, D.C. They were married on July 10, 1936. This union lasted forty four years until Fred died in 1980. Pearl also told us of horrible events that happened to her family during the early years of the twentieth century in rural GA.

We took care of Pearl until my wife Lillie died in 1985. I continued my commitment to Pearl. She called me when she needed transportation etc. When I married again in 1988, my wife Gloria Mosley supported me in my commitment to Pearl.

It came a time when Pearl was having a difficult time taking care of her daily activities. She was placed in a Nursing Home at the age of ninety two. We visited her two or three times a week. We lived less than a mile away.

We were attending a relative's college graduation in December of 1998 in Florida when we were notified that Pearl had died at the age of ninety seven years of age of Alzheimers disease on December 10, 1998. The New London Day which is the local newspaper interviewed me about the life of Pearl F. Blanks.

I had another opportunity to concentrate on an issue other than my duty as a buyer. Our youngest daughter Patricia graduated from Waterford High School in June of 1981, and aspired to be a beautician. She was very interested in that field. She informed me and her mother that she was pregnant. This was a major surprise to both of us but we were determined to support our daughter.

We were invited to visit our eldest daughter Ellen for Thanksgiving dinner at her home in Yonkers, NY. Later in the evening, Patricia started to have labor pains. We went to St. John Riverside Hospital and Patricia delivered a healthy baby girl. She was named Felicia Anne. Patricia spent a few days at the hospital prior to being discharged. We returned back to Yonkers to bring Patricia and the baby back home. On our trip back, we visited my brother William, his wife Emiko and daughter Emmy who lived in Wilton, Ct. Lillie was very excited about buying baby clothes for a new granddaughter. We helped Patricia find an apartment and purchase furniture. This helped me to take my mind of the problems I was having with some individuals in the Purchasing Department. The name of the Department was changed from Procurement to Purchasing.

The order for the sonar cable trunk was placed on July 13, 1981. I was notified later that based on current lead times, January, 29, 1982 would be Cameron's contract delivery date. The material was scheduled and poured on November 2, 1981 to meet an extrusion date of November 23, 1981. This would have allowed Cameron to complete all work required by the end of January. However, the heat of material poured suffered ingot cracking and the heat was scrapped. I was notified and decided to take a trip to Cameron Iron Works to meet with the Production Manager and the Sales Engineer. I arrived at Cameron Iron Works on December 1, 1981 to discuss the status of this specific contract.

Mr. Harlan, the Sales Engineer accompanied me to meet with the Supervisor of ingot preparation to find out why the heat of metal was scrapped. The heat scrapped weighed 100,000 pounds. This heat would have been for my current purchase order. The scrapping of the heat of material was due to thermal shocking of the ingots during heat treatment. I found out the error resulted from the material being heat treated to 1250 degrees Fahrenheit instead of 1200 degrees as required. The scrapped ingots had to be re-melted. A new contract delivery date was December 2, 1982. I was given a new manufacturing schedule for our requirement.

While in the Houston, Texas area, I also had an account in the Beaumont, Texas area. I arrived at Beaumont Well Works' business office early in the morning of December 3, 1981. I met with Mr. Bert Wilms, a Sales Engineer with the company who was responsible for our accounts. I attended a meeting with the Sales Engineer and the Production Manager to discuss the schedule for our open contracts. Our contract delivery dates were discussed and found to be on schedule.

This trip was beneficial from the standpoint of following up on open purchase orders, personally meeting with the appropriate people, touring the facilities, and observing various manufacturing operations which enhances personal growth and knowledge of the products.

The following year, a new supervisor was assigned to our buying group. I had previously worked with this individual as a peer in an earlier time period. I was hoping this person would be fair in evaluating my performance.

The next evaluation for the year ending March 1983 was more indicative of my performance. The supervisor stated that "Mr. Mosley awarded 176 purchase requisitions/supplements totaling $2,161,600 during 1982. He achieved cost reduction/avoidance of $314,259, or 14.5% of his total dollar awards. Jim is thorough in performance of his job and maintains an excellent working knowledge of departmental policies and procedures.

He utilizes his time effectively. Mr. Mosley should continue to be assigned larger and generally more complex items to buy". I finally started to feel more positive about the evaluation of my performance.

The following year, I was assigned purchase requisitions to purchase more complex and new items in support of the Trident submarine program. During 1983, I awarded 253 purchase orders totaling $3,291,326 with a total savings of $699,057 or 21.2% for an increase of 6% in saving over 1982. I was also effective in coordination of new requirements for the Trident submarine fairwater dive plane bearings and was able to obtain delivery of these items in support of our shipyard schedule. I previously stated that I keep a personal record of my cost savings after being signed off by my management.

In 1984, I processed a considerably greater number of buying transactions than the previous year. The awards totaled $7,713,860 with cost reduction/avoidance of $986,951 or 12.7% of total dollars committed.

My three major objectives for the following year were to develop three alternate sources for stellite parts for the fairwater plane and rudder bearings. Very few centrifugal casting companies would even consider manufacturing these items because of machining problems. Stellite is a cobalt based alloy and is very difficult to finish machine. There is a considerable amount of scrapping during the machining operations.

While buying stellite parts for the fairwater planes and the rudder bearings from the Janney Cylinder Co., I noticed a major discrepancy in the way we were buying shipboard and logistical support items.

On one occasion, I received a requisition to purchase a shipboard item on March 22, 1984 and then received another requisition from the Industrial Sales Department to purchase the identical item for logistical support on March 31, 1984. I received one quotation for both inquiries with different pricing.

The shipboard requirement was for two pieces priced at $5209.00 each and the logistical support item was priced at $6250.00 each. I brought this to the attention of my Supervisor and Manager and informed them of the discrepancy and stated this pricing appeared inconsistent with what I considered to be reasonable. I informed my management I would call the supplier in order to understand the rationale behind the pricing.

I called the supplier and requested an explanation for the price difference for identical items. The Vice President of Sale informed me, our requirements were considered two separate purchase orders with the materials coming from two separate inventories of stock. I refused to accept the explanation but our management felt that nothing could be done.

The period from April 1984 to the time I submitted my suggestion on May 3, 1984, no changes were made to our purchasing methods. I submitted and was assigned Suggestion # 18731 (Logistical Support Orders) by the Chief of Employee Suggestions for Electric Boat Division.

I had to explain our present method of purchasing and the method I proposed that would be more cost effective. In the present method, purchase requisitions are received in the Purchasing Department on an inquiry basis from Industrial Sales. The assigned buyer prepares inquires for solicitation of potential suppliers. The bidders are requested to quote a firm price for a specific period of time, i.e., sixty, ninety, one hundred twenty or one hundred fifty days. Upon release for purchase, the buyer places the order. In as much as Industrial Sales requests that Purchasing solicit quotes on a vast number of commodities, it is surmised that some suppliers are conditioned to the fact that these are primarily spare parts and quote prices accordingly. A good example of this fact is that recently two inquiries were sent to a potential supplier for the same item within a time frame of nine days. I received different pricing.

The new method I proposed was upon receipt of a potential requirement from Industrial Sales, the assigned buyer should review the commodity relative to previous purchase orders for the same or similar items. Additionally, discuss the commodity with a buyer from the appropriate buying group who normally purchases this item for shipyard allocation, based on prime contract requirements. This review in turn would provide the buyer of logistical support parts greater leverage with potential suppliers despite the fact that it is not a current buy item and the quantity may be small. At times, with proper planning, concurrent buys can be made for maximum price advantage after negotiations.

The advantage of this approach is that savings of thousands of dollars can be realized along with a more effective method of purchasing these support commodities. Additionally, with all the current negative publicity about defense contractors' purchasing practices, it seems prudent at this time to effectively purchase spare parts at reasonable pricing after effective negotiations.

I was surprised that on June 25, 1984, I received a reply to my suggestion. It stated your idea is a very good one however, it is regretted that your suggestion must be considered ineligible because it was an idea which was under consideration prior to the submittal of your suggestion.

Purchasing Management recognized the need to strengthen the procedure for the procurement of logistical support material for the Industrial Sales Department. Accordingly, in February 1984 the Purchasing Department altered its approach and began assigning the logistic support purchasing requisitions to the commodity buying group. This worked successfully and eventually resulted in a total re-structuring the logistic function within Purchasing. He further stated that on June 4, 1984, the logistic support function was assigned to a different Buying Manager and a new Chief of Purchasing was named to coordinate the total buying and expediting effort. The buying will continue to be done by the responsible commodity buying group and the expediting by a separate section under the direction of the newly named Chief of Purchasing.

The work I put forth constructing this suggestion was stolen from me by my supervision. I brought this issue to the attention of my management in March of 1984. They informed the Chief of Employee Suggestions they had made changes in February 1984. My suggestion was reviewed by my supervisor and Manager prior to submission. I had also talked to other Buyers stating my submission of the suggestion.

It is sad that supervision took my suggested changes and back dated them to February. I am sure they over looked the fact that I first brought this issue to their attention the first week of April after I had received the quotations from Janney Cylinder Co. It was strange that the changes made by Purchasing Management did not occur until the first week of June and I did not receive the memorandum from the Chief of Employees Suggestions until June 25, 1984. The period from April 1984 to the time I submitted my suggestion on May 3, 1984, no changes were made to our purchasing methods. There is something wrong with this picture.

I was able to resolve one of my objectives early in the year. Electric Boat Division had one domestic supplier for NIALBR bar, plate and forgings in 1984 and previous years. This constituted a single source supplier. The specifications for this material included MIL-B-24059 and QQ-C-00465B. Competition was developed by my research in the marketplace and finding an off-shore potential supplier. The Navy (NAVSEA) was notified, the off-shore supplier submitted samples and they were approved. The material was shipped to one our current raw material suppliers and we would purchase the material.

This task resulted in considerable savings during the year and into the future. The unit price was reduced from $5.50 per pound to $2.80

per pound. We purchase thousands of pounds of this material each year. I considered this task a major accomplishment in my years as a Buyer.

My final objective was to find another source for the Primary Shield Tank Top Forgings. This tank surrounds the reactor vessel in the submarine. I knew it would be difficult and would take time to develop a competitive source. Ladish Co. in Wisconsin was the single source for this forging. I was given the responsibility to purchase this item for the Trident submarines. In the casting, forging and raw material area, most commodities were purchased on a competitive basis. Most of my major accounts were single source. I think the reason for this was most of the people in my group had no training in detail cost analysis.

The first Trident submarine had the Shield Tank Top made from fabricated alloy steel plate. The Navy decided to change the material specifications to forged parts for added strength and safety. I made a trip to the Ladish Co. in Wisconsin to observe the forging process for large complicated items. This supplier forged parts by the closed die and open frame method. During my visit I observed the forging of very large parts. The first day of my visit a large forged steam chest for General Electric Co. was completed. The following day I observed a set of wing flaps forged for a jet liner. The set weighed in excess of 29,000 pounds and consisted of eight forgings in lengths up to 18 feet. The material was 300M, an ultra—high strength 4340 modified steel.

This company had capabilities to manufacture closed impression die forgings up to 56,000 pounds which was the weight of the General Electric Co. steam chest. Additionally, seamless rolled rings to 350,000 pounds, diameter to 28 feet and heights of 10 feet. The forgings I observed being manufactured were closed die and open frame forgings. My next trip I would see the start of the manufacture of our Primary Shield Tank Top Forgings. These parts would be by the open frame forging method whereby, forging hammers would be used. During this period, I was assigned the responsibility of purchasing the rail section forgings for the primary shield tank.

I was fortunate to have an account where there was competition for the part. There were two qualified suppliers, the E. M. Jorgensen Co. of Seattle, Washington and the National Forge Co. of Burnham, Pennsylvania. Both of these suppliers were familiar to me because I had other accounts where I utilized these suppliers.

When the Ladish Co. was prepared to start the production of our part, I knew how much of an alloy steel they had to purchase from a mill to make these parts. A mill-run of this material was a 200,000 pound ingot billeted to 98,000 pounds prior to shipment from the mill to the forger.

Because of the weight of the material to be shipped from the mill, it was necessary to take a pre-planned route to the destination of the forger and ultimate machining of the parts.

It was unfortunate for me to have a new supervisor assigned at this period of time. The new supervisor had no buying experience and previously been an Expediter to follow-up on orders that had been placed.

During this period of time, I accomplished one of my objectives of finding competitive sources to manufacture stellite parts. Janney Cylinder who produced our rudder and fairwater plane bearings closed on 5/31/1985. I was able to get Wisconsin Centrifugal Co., Techni-Cast Co. and the Stoody Co. qualified and approved to manufacture stellite parts.

During my next evaluation, I knew at the time this supervisor would never evaluate my buying performance fairly. The reason for this was he had no buying, cost analysis or negotiation experience. In the absence of this, his focus was only on suppliers and on contract delivery dates.

I was determined to develop a competitive source for the tank top forgings. I talked to one of the metallurgists in our Material Engineering Department about my task of finding and developing a competitive source for the primary shield tank top forgings. We knew that the Ladish Co. purchased the raw material from a mill on a competitive basis.

The metallurgist informed me that there were four possible sources to investigate. He advised me to contact US Steel (Homestead Works) Bethlehem Steel, Earle M. Jorgenson Steel in Seattle, Washington, and A. Finkel and Sons of Chicago, Il. I found out that Bethlehem Steel and US Steel had the capability to mandrel forge a ring (rectangular cross section) from which the tank top pieces can be machined. However, usually the forging shops are not interested in or required to perform necessary machining to convert the rectangular ring into the finished pieces that we require. The machining costs were probably one if not the largest item in the total cost of the pieces.

In my discussions with the Material Engineering Department, if I could buy the rectangular ring to a special chemistry and ultrasonic requirements we need from the melt/forge shops, it may be possible to find someone else who could convert the ring into the required pieces. The machining supplier would also have to perform the heat treatment required and the necessary mechanical (tension and impact) testing required. For the size ring being forged, heat treatment must be performed after the shapes are partially machined from the ring due to the large section of the ring relative to the finished piece thickness.

I had meetings with representatives from US Steel and Bethlehem Steel. The latter informed me that in the future, they could be solicited for our requirement.

This is a long lead time item therefore I had to have a supplier who could perform all functions of the contract without subcontracting out part of the work because the contract delivery date was critical relative to our commitment to the US Government.

I considered finding a competitive source for the primary shield tank top forgings a major priority. On April 11, 1979, our one source, the Ladish Co. had a work stoppage by the union and a strike was called. Our Engineering Department had to discuss alternative manufacturing methods to produce these parts. Fortunately, the strike was of short duration. I thought if I could develop a competitive source, this would alleviate the problems we had in the past.

For the eighth Trident submarine, I solicited Bethlehem Steel Corp. in addition to the Ladish Co. Both organizations submitted bids for the forgings. I evaluated the bids and Ladish Co. was the low bidder. This was an important event for me because I now had adequate price competition for this requirement.

I was happy I had accomplished the major three objectives in finding competition for major single source suppliers. My next solicitations for stellite material, NIALBR material and the forgings for the primary shield tank top forgings would be competitive bids.

In the third quarter of 1984, I scheduled a visit to three of my forging suppliers in CA, E.M. Jorgensen Co. in Los Angeles, Shultz Steel Co. in South Gate and Carleton Forge Works in Paramount. My objective was to follow up on open purchase orders and tour their facilities. I had made arrangements to spend one day at each facility. I scheduled my visit for December third, fourth, fifth and sixth of 1984.

A preliminary meeting was arranged at E.M. Jorgensen Co. for 9:00 AM on December 4th in the General Manager's Office. Present at the meeting was the General Manager, Manager of Insides Sales, Manager of Quality Assurance and the Production Department Supervisor. One of our orders had a very tight delivery date and I asked for a sequence of events in the manufacturing cycle.

The Production Department Supervisor outlined the current order status and explained each event which included work to be accomplished by their subcontractor. I was given a copy of each event and the date of completion. The Manager of Quality Assurance explained the chemical check of the tensile specimens, the magnetic particle and ultrasonic testing. The finished forgings would be shipped on December 28, 1984. This date would satisfy our shipyard schedule.

After the meeting, I was given a tour of the facility by the General Manager. He informed me that E.M. Jorgensen Co. was presently installing a new ring expander which would give them the capability to supply 180 inch diameter seamless rolled rings.

The following day, December 5th, I arrived at the business office of Shultz Steel Co. at 9:00 AM. I met with the President, Assistant to the President, the Manager of Sales and the Customer Service Representative. We discussed our open purchase orders. During the tour of the manufacturing facility, I observed the forging of an upper section missile tube ring on one of our orders. Three rings were forged during the day's operation and one piece was rough machined. Additionally, six missile tube operating rods were completed and source inspection was requested. The open orders seemed to be processing smoothly.

Shultz Steel Co. had a very impressive facility with the latest state-of-the-art machinery, including a CAD/CAM system (Computer Assisted Design/Computer Assisted Manufacturing). A new 28,000 ton computer controlled press and a three dimensional coordinate measuring machine.

The following day, December 6th, I arrived at the business office of Carleton Forge Works. I had two open purchase orders with this supplier. One order was for the locking rings for the logistic escape trunk and the other order was for the Fairwater Diving Gear Connecting Rod.

I had a meeting with the Sales Manager, Production Manager and the Customer Service Representative. Both of these orders were delinquent to the contract delivery date but not to the material availability date. The latter date is when the material is required by the trades in our shipyard. One of the locking rings had been received by our Receiving Department however, the balance of two pieces were on hold pending a disposition by our Engineering Department on a Vendor Information Request (VIR). This request is for non-conforming material. There was a groove on the outside diameter of both forgings. I called our Engineering Department and they informed me that in all probability the (VIR) would be approved as the pieces will conform to the final machining dimensions.

The other order for the Fairwater Diving Gear Connecting Rod, the forging failed the ultrasonic inspection and had to be scrapped. It was subsequently re-forged and the shop dimensions were in error. The re-forging operation was scheduled for the week of December 10th. Based on the sequence of events, the material available date for our shipyard would be met.

After the meeting, I was given a complete tour of the facility by the Production and Sales Manager. Carlton Forge Works had a very modern and clean facility.

In summary, the trip was beneficial from the stand point of following up on open purchase orders, meeting with appropriate people who service our accounts, touring the facilities and observing various manufacturing operations, particularly those relating to work in process on our purchase orders.

When I returned to Electric Boat Division, I was assigned a few other major accounts. I was assigned to purchase the forged sixteen inch main sea water valves (MSW). There are four valves for each submarine, two hull valves and two backup valves. These valves are critical for the safety of the submarine. I was familiar with these valves because of my experience in the US Navy as a crewmember aboard submarines. These are very large valves, when completed with the actuators in place, each valve is approximately six feet high.

There are potentially a few suppliers with the capability to forge and machine these large valve bodies. In all probability, they would be forged and machined by the E.M. Jorgensen Co. at their facility in Seattle, WA. This facility had the capability to melt the steel, forge and machine these large valve bodies. I studied the sequence of events in the manufacture of these parts. National Forge Co., in Burnham, PA., also had the capability to manufacture these parts.

I was also assigned to purchase the eight inch auxiliary sea water valves and the lug and link forgings for the steam generators.

I knew the challenges that lay ahead for me but I knew I was up to the task and was eager to learn and build upon my experience. I felt this was an opportunity to learn more about the forging industry.

There was a United Kingdom office here at Electric Boat Division and I was informed I would be buying main sea water valve bodies for the British Navy as well as our submarines. I assumed there was an agreement between the two governments relative to buying parts for nuclear submarines. It was cost effective due to quantities to be quoted.

I had previously stated when I was on active duty in the US Navy aboard the USS Skipjack (SSN-585), members of the nucleus of the first British nuclear submarine was embarked on our ship for many months getting acquainted with the operation of our nuclear power plant. The

British Navy's first nuclear submarine had the same power plant we had on our ship. The power plant was the S5W reactor plant made by the Westinghouse Electric Corp.

While I was going through this difficult period of losing my wife and accepting many more complicated accounts, it appeared to me that my supervisor was still making a concerted effort to make my job more difficult. In some instances, I had to follow up on orders negotiated and awarded by other Buyers. My performance was partially based upon the contract delivery date being met in areas where I had no control, i.e. contingencies for time relative to adequate lead time and allowance for source inspection by Electric Boat Division (EBSI) or by the government (GSI).

I explained to my supervisor I had no control over other people's work especially from the Quality Assurance Department. They scheduled the source inspection prior to the supplier shipping the material. I could easily see this individual was making me responsible for other Buyer's work. This technique was for the purpose of discrediting me in the eyes of others as part of the conspiracy started on September 15, 1974 and had been passed down and rubber stamped.

I awarded my first order for these valve bodies, to the E.M. Jorgensen Co. of Seattle, WA. I requested a copy of their manufacturing sequence and informed the Sales Manger that I would be scheduling a trip to their facility in Seattle, WA. I had previously been to their facility in Los Angeles, CA. I was hoping I would be in Seattle, WA. for the forging operation. When the steel is melted, two ingots weighing 72,000 pounds each are required for the four valve bodies.

I was assigned a new supervisor the first quarter of 1985. I knew this would be a trying period. This supervisor was never a Buyer but he had to evaluate my professional performance as a Buyer. He had always been an expeditor in the past. His previous function was to follow up on open purchase orders. The most frustrating event that happened to me was when one of our forging supplier, Cann & Saul Forge Co. in Royersford, Pa. went on strike and was late delivering material and this supervisor blamed me because I was not aware of the company's work stoppage. This supplier's Sales Engineer called me the day the company went on strike and requested a new contract delivery date for the material. This information was forwarded to the appropriate people at Electric Boat Division. I advised the originator of the requirement to place an emergency order with Delaware Alloy Forge Co. who had the capability to forge these products.

The strike was terminated at Cann & Saul Forge Co. and a new contract delivery date was assigned.

The month of April 1985 was a devastating period of time for me and the rest of my family. I could not imagine how my life would be turned upside down dealing with the new supervisor and my challenges at home.

My wife Lillie and I decided to celebrate her fifty second birthday and our thirty first wedding anniversary at our daughter's residence in Yonkers, N.Y. on April 3, 1985. Our plan was to spend a few days with our daughter and granddaughter and return to CT. on April 6, 1985 prior to Easter Sunday the next day.

We had a nice visit with our daughter. Felicia, our granddaughter who was three years old at the time accompanied us on our trip. When we left N.Y. to return to CT. on April 6, 1985, our granddaughter Miesha, age ten years old wanted to spend a few days with us in CT. We arrived back home in the evening and planned to visit a few friends the next day.

On Easter Sunday, we visited some friends in Groton, then an elderly friend, Pearl who lived in an assisted living housing complex in New London. Lillie bought some Easter lillies and a rose to give to Pearl who loved flowers. We enjoyed a nice Easter Sunday.

The next morning I returned to work. At approximately two o'clock in the afternoon, I received a call from my granddaughter Miesha. She said "you have to come home, grandmother is sick". I left work and when I got home, Lillie was on the couch unresponsive. I called 911 immediately and the ambulance was at the house in less than ten minutes. It was apparent to me she had suffered a stroke because of her medical history of high blood pressure.

She was admitted to the Lawrence and Memorial Hospital in New London and placed in the intensive care unit. I notified her mother, son and siblings about her medical condition. Additionally, I notified our two sons who were living in CA. They immediately returned to CT. to be with the rest of the family.

I went to the hospital every day after work to be with my wife. Most of the time, she was unresponsive and unable to recognize any visitors. She died the following Sunday after being admitted. Most of her siblings were able to attend the funeral and pay their last respects to a loved sister. Lillie's mother was unable to attend the funeral because of health issues.

My youngest son who was a college student in CA. decided to remain in CT. and enroll in a state university. The fall semester he enrolled at Western Connecticut State University. He decided to attend this school because they were interested in his football ability. The fall semester was his first season on the football team.

Lillie's health started to fail after the death of our oldest son in 1980. She grieved for many years after James Jr. died. The doctor had informed me, her blood pressure was very difficult to control despite the medications prescribed. I guess she never got over the trauma of our son's death. Lillie stated to the end of her life that Jim's sickness and death was of a suspicious nature. She continuously asked me to find out what immunizations he was given prior to his transfer to Okinawa. I was never able to gain total access to his military medical records.

After Lillie's death, I fully immersed my time in my buying function and my activities after work. It was a difficult adjustment living alone after thirty one years of marriage. I spent my hours after work being a member of a bowling team and playing basketball. I attended church services on Sunday and spent time visiting my children. My youngest daughter Patricia lived about two miles away in New London, CT. My oldest daughter Ellen lived in Yonkers, NY. and my youngest son Mervin was a college student at Western Connecticut State University in Danbury, CT. My other son Thomas was in the US Marine Corp. I stayed active and was able to take my mind off some of the problems I faced at work.

The following year 1986, I was assigned another supervisor from our group who had been a Purchasing Agent and recently promoted to a supervisory position. The Purchasing Agent position was open and I requested to be considered for the opening. I was informed the position would not be filled. The accounts the new Supervisor had as the Purchasing Agent were assigned to me relative to accountability.

A few months later, the Purchasing Agent position in our Casting and Forging Section was assigned to an individual from another group with no experience purchasing castings and forgings. I still had the bulk of the accounts in our group. I guess my job was to train the new Purchasing Agent.

The next evaluation period was very interesting relative to the way my supervisor described my performance. "Mr. Mosley processed one hundred eighty two awards totaling $4,917,466. He obtained a cost reduction or $163,347. Mr. Mosley expedited approximately two hundred seventy five line items and has maintained a contract delivery delinquency under three percent. Mr. Mosley's work is fully satisfactory and he works with Engineering in the development and solicitation of new HY-130 steel suppliers and new design of inconel forgings for the new generation of submarines". The HY-130 is a high yield steel to be used for the hull plate on submarines. Previously, we used HY-80 and HY-100. The yield strength of these grades of steel, are 80,000, 100,000 and 130,000. The inconel 625 is a nickel-chromium-molybdenum alloy which provides high strength without a strengthening heat treatment. This alloy would be used primarily in the new piping systems that previously used copper nickel alloy. I was determined to learn and understand engineering and metallurgical principles that applied to materials I had the responsibility to purchase.

When I read my evaluation, I informed my supervisor, my cost reduction was $578,402.not $163,347.I learned earlier to keep records of my cost savings. It appears from year to year my performance was deemed satisfactory. Most prudent people would look at this as the individual is barely performing his job function. There was never a superior or excellent performance despite the positive things I had accomplished over the years that were well documented. I knew a promotion was impossible when year after year the same statement of satisfactory performance was rubber stamped on my evaluation.

Prior to signing my evaluation, I had my cost reduction savings corrected and attached a rebuttal sheet to my evaluation. I was tired of holding the frustration in and wanted to express my feelings. I knew this would further alienate my supervisor but I felt it was necessary to voice my opinion about an injustice being perpetrated on me as an employee.

I stated this performance review is one element of retaliatory measures systematically taken against me since I filed a complaint of discrimination in 1974. I initially refused to sign this review sheet because of a familiar pattern of statements made over the years, which are not true. The objective of these statements was to discredit me. One of the most familiar is the late placement of orders to material availability dates. I refused to sign the review sheet in 1973 because of the conspired distortion of my performance during the review period. This unfair act was explained and documented in a letter dated September 15, 1974.

The various subtle elements exercised against me over the past thirteen years were for the primary purpose of denying promotional opportunities. These activities are conducted by a small group of individuals. I was informed years ago that as long as I was a member of this Department, I would never advance.

During my performance review, the most positive accomplishments over the year are generally never mentioned, e.g., prior to 1985, the purchase of Nickel Aluminum Bronze Alloy bar and rod was assigned to me for purchase. We had one domestic source for certain diameter bars therefore, single source buying was necessary. A considerable quantity of this alloy is purchased for various applications. During that period of time, the average price per pound was approximately $5.50. I developed an off shore source and as a result, the price was stabilized at $2.80 per pound. Once competition was developed, most of this alloy was being purchased by other Buyers other than all being assigned to me for purchase when it was primarily a single source item. Activities such as this are never mentioned in the performance review. This is only one example of many over the years.

There is no doubt a conspiracy has been conducted against me in this Department for years by a small hard core group of individuals and they know who they are. I have been a Buyer in this Department for eighteen years however my salary is between $20,000 and $30,000 per year. Compensation and promotional opportunities are not commensurate with my years of service, experience and documented performance which nobody can deny.

This group leader was promoted to a supervisory position from our group a few months ago. This left the Purchasing Agent position open. I was informed the position would not be filled but abolished. I wonder why the position was abolished. I felt I earned an opportunity to fill the position particularly since a considerable amount of the work previously performed by the Purchasing Agent was assigned to me. I never received any feedback on my rebuttal relative to this evaluation.

It was interesting that during the year I was frequently complimented on aspects of my performance but conveniently overlooked during performance reviews.

During the following period, I had more available time to spend studying the technical aspects of submarine construction. I was the only employee in the Department who had military experience serving aboard a nuclear submarine. My previous military experience as a Senior Chief Petty Officer and years of submarine service made the task easy for me to assimilate.

While in the military assigned to pre-commissioning crews at Electric Boat Division, I was able to observe how the systems were assembled and tested. Many of these parts I was purchasing at this time.

I was frustrated by some of my evaluations when it was stated, a few of my orders were placed late and the material available dates were not met. I had verbally asked my supervisor to talk to the Material Ordering Department to release requisitions designated as long lead time items so the orders can be placed in time to support shipyard schedules. It appeared my request fell on deaf ears.

I decided to make an official request to my Supervisor, Manager and the Director of Purchasing relative to the late receipt of requisitions I had the responsibility to process. The subject was Forgings Purchased for the construction of the Package which included the Reactor Compartment. This request was made by memorandum for documentation purposes.

I stated the following forgings are affected by late generation of purchase requisitions from the Material Ordering Department and subsequent late order placement. The six items adversely affected are Steam Generator Foundation Lugs, Steam Generator Foundation Links, Primary Shield Tank Top, Primary Shield Tank Top (Rails), Pressurizer Ring and the Main Coolant Pump Foundation Rings.

These forgings are classified with long lead time (LLTM) numbers with the exception of the Pressurizer Ring and the Main Coolant Pump Foundation Rings. I asked my management to evaluate and advise what actions can be taken in order that materials can be ordered and received to support schedules. The Buyer's hands are tied until he receives the purchase requisition. It was unfair to penalize the Buyer for late receipt of purchase requisitions from another Department.

One of my major accounts, the Ladish Co. who manufactures the primary shield tank top forgings which is a single source item took exceptions to various articles in our terms and conditions. I received an official letter from their Senior Sales Engineer.

I contacted our Legal Department relative to this problem. General Dynamics' Electric Boat Division EB-2 Rev.7/83 Conditions of Purchase under US Government Prime Contracts would be a contract requirement for this supplier. It was proposed by our Legal Department to have an "Overriding Agreement with the Ladish Co. The articles to be modified were Article 4 (Changes), Article 8 (Title& Risk of Loss), Article 10 (Warranty), Article 25 (Assignments and Subcontract Approval) and Article 57 (Rights in Technical Data and Computer Software).

On May 19, 1986, I sent an official letter to the Senior Sales Engineer at the Ladish Co. detailing the "Overriding Agreement" proposed by our Legal Department. Article 57 applies only to the data specified to be delivered on the face of the order.

I stated if the foregoing clearly sets forth our understanding, please sign and return a duplicate copy of this letter which shall thereupon constitute an agreement between us, which however shall be terminable by either party upon at least thirty days notice to the other. I signed the letter as the Buyer Specialist who would be placing the order. The "Overriding Agreement" was approved by the Ladish Co. This exercise was another learning experience for me that helped me grow as a Buyer in our Purchasing Department.

I was also assigned to purchase the missile tube access doors and torpedo tube doors. The missile tube access doors were manufactured from bronze castings and I had a few potential sources to solicit on these items based on past history. The torpedo tube doors were forged for extra strength. Each tube required a breech and muzzle door. My military career on submarines helped me to understand the significance of these parts. During my qualification aboard submarines, I had to learn how to load a torpedo into the tube and the sequence of events to fire and reload another torpedo into the tube. This made me aware of the significance of the torpedo tube doors.

The specifications for the torpedo tubes required them to be purchased from the Wyman-Gordon Co. in MA. I decided to research the history of these forged doors for the torpedo tubes. In the past, the US Navy negotiated a contract with the Wyman-Gordon Co, to manufacture forging dies to produce these parts. Wyman-Gordon Co. retained title for these dies for the exclusive use by the US Navy. The title holder had the responsibility for the upkeep and repair of these forging dies.

On August 19, 1986, I received a letter from the Professor of Radiological Science at the University of Lowell in MA. I was invited to join a delegation of thirty people to travel to the People's Republic of China in the summer of 1987. The delegation members would examine the various aspects of nuclear radiation protection with their Chinese counterparts. In addition, delegates would learn about China's approach to this important subject as the country attempts to achieve its modernization goals. The Professor stated your background and interests would contribute to the delegation. Our delegation would be meeting with Chinese officials from the National Nuclear Safety Administration, the Ministry of Nuclear Industries and a variety or other ministries, institutes and relevant organizations to discuss areas of radiation protection, education and training. Our team would be composed of educators, commercial and government training specialists, representatives of regulatory agencies, nuclear instrumentation companies and radiation emergency planning specialists.

I had previously stated I was a member of the National Health Physics Society. In the military, I had taught nuclear accident training and was the USN Submarine Base Director of the Disaster Control Branch.

I also received a letter from the Director of Energy and Resource Development from the Citizen's Ambassador Program out of the US State Department. He stated, in your role as a Citizen Ambassador, you will help further the ideals of People to People International, a non-political private sector organization dedicated to promoting international understanding. Since its founding by President Eisenhower in 1956, People to People had developed many different activities that enable citizens to establish friendships with their counterparts in other nations. The Citizen's Ambassador Program supports the People to People goal by focusing on the desire of specialist professionals to share ideas and experiences with their colleagues in other cultures. Technical exchanges in many disciplines of medicine, science, engineering, agriculture, law, architecture, and industrial technology provide opportunities for delegates and their counterparts to develop lasting professional and personal friendships.

The success of any People to People project is due in large part to the delegates themselves. The make-up of the delegation would have a direct impact on the professional benefits derived by each team member. Although the major criteria for acceptance of delegates would be their professional backgrounds and experience, the ability and willingness to contribute on a people-to-people level are also of considerable importance. The Honorary Chairman of this program was President Ronald Reagan.

It was an honor for me to be chosen as a delegate for this team. I had to decline because I had promised my son we would take a vacation trip to CA. during the summer of 1987. This would be our first vacation together since his mother died.

Prior to the trip to California with my son, I attended my fortieth high school reunion in Pittsburgh, Pa. The Chair Person of the Reunion Committee had taken the year book and had each student's picture duplicated and we were given badges with our yearbook pictures to wear. This was a good idea because it allowed us to recognize each other after a forty year period.

The reunion was very well planned and everyone had a nice time and vowed to keep in touch with each other and meet again in ten years for our fiftieth reunion.

I was also able to visit with my brothers and sisters that still resided in Pittsburgh. I knew I would be back in the area soon because I was administering a contract with a supplier in this area who was manufacturing powdered metal valve bodies for our Seawolf class of submarine. Later in the summer I took my son to California to visit my sister and his cousins in San Diego.

When I returned from our trip, I continued to work on a unique order that was assigned to me earlier in the year in addition to my other accounts. The US Navy decided to purchase three and five inch flow control valve bodies for the Seawolf Program. These valves were to be manufactured by the hot isostatic pressed method commonly referred as (HIP'd). Powdered metallurgy was common with the aerospace industry and oil drilling industry, but not with submarine construction.

I knew I had a complicated challenge ahead. This subcontract was to be a lower tier to a prime contract with the Westinghouse Bettis Atomic Power Laboratory. I had to obtain consent from Westinghouse Electric Corporation prior to placing the order with Crucible Compaction Metals a Division of Crucible Materials Corp. Westinghouse Electric Corp. was familiar with Crucible Compaction Metals because both companies are located in the Pittsburgh, Pa. area.

I received a response from Westinghouse Electric Corp. after I solicited Crucible Compaction Metals asking me why Electric Boat Division recommends using a General Dynamics audit in lieu of Bettis requesting a Defense Contract Auditing Agency (DCAA) audit. Westinghouse Electric Corp. also asked if unlimited rights to technical data were obtained from Crucible Compaction Metals.

I talked to the Sales Engineer at Crucible Compaction Metals about "unlimited rights to technical data". I received a letter from the Sales Engineer on October 20, 1987 expressing their proprietary rights.

The container evacuation parameters and procedures, container design and manufacture and technical standards are proprietary. He further stated that Crucible Compaction Metals had expended considerable time and money developing these items and it is for that reason that his company considers them proprietary and do not consider them to be subject to the "unlimited rights" clause in our terms and condition of performance under government prime contracts.

I forwarded this information to the Westinghouse Electric Corp. In my reply I explained at the time of the original request for quotation on January 15, 1987, the contract was under the cognizance of the Naval Sea Systems Command (NAVSEA). The programmatic need date was October 2, 1988. The date was predicated on the award date to Crucible Compaction Metals. The period of performance was quoted as one year after receipt of an order.

I explained that Electric Boat Division generally requests a General Dynamic audit based on an agreement with the Supervisor of Shipbuilding

(SUPSHIPS) which represents the US Navy at our shipyard. If a potential supplier refuses an audit by General Dynamics, they have the option of requesting a DCAA audit. The potential supplier would accept an audit from a government agency or the customer. A General Dynamics audit was requested on September 15, 1987.

Crucible Compaction Metals took no exceptions to Electric Boat Division's terms and conditions (Form 2 Rev. 7/83) based on their interpretation of Article 57 relative to Rights in Technical Data and computer software. This potential supplier would not grant "unlimited rights" to General Dynamics or the government.

The Electric Boat Division's estimated price or rough order of magnitude was $195,944. Crucible Compaction Metals' proposed profit relative to its acceptability would be evaluated upon receipt of the final audit report.

I decided to research the past history with this technology being used for other applications. The material to be used was inconel 625 alloy. In the past, Crucible Compaction Metals worked closely with wellhead equipment manufacturers to produce a wide range of HIP clad components. This included valve bodies, bonnets, closures, tees, crosses, flanges etc. The weight of the components ranged from two hundred pounds to six thousand five hundred pounds. This company is well known in the oil drilling industry. The inconel 625 mechanical properties were impressive. The tensile strength was 143,500 psi, yield strength, 83,000 psi, 35.5% elongation and 40.5% reduction in area. I had to understand these statistics because I would be required to accompany one of our engineers to their facility to observe the work in process. This was an educational experience for me in purchasing an item for submarine application for the first time.

I was familiar with the Westinghouse Bettis Atomic Power Laboratory because it is located in the suburb of West Mifflin where I attended middle school and my older brother worked at Bettis as an Electrical Engineer previously. My brother Donald resides in that township today.

My son Merv was a student at Western Connecticut State University in Danbury, CT. and a member of the football team. Prior to his mother's death, he was attending a college in CA. I was planning on attending his home games and a few of his away games.

One of his away games was at Norwich University in Vermont. I talked to my other son Thomas who was living in Plainfield, NH. We decided to meet at the school and watch the football game.

We had a group leaving from Danbury via a chartered bus. The people in the group would be staying over the weekend at a hotel in Montpelier, the state capital. I had made arrangements to have Monday off from work.

After the game which was on Saturday night, my son Thomas returned home to NH. Our group returned to the hotel. We went sight seeing on Sunday and had a very good time prior to our return trip on September 14, 1987.

When I got back home, I was notified my daughter Patricia gave birth to her second child on September 13, 1987. It was a boy and she named him Corey James Mosley. I lived approximately one mile from my daughter's apartment. Her daughter Felicia Anne Mosley was five years old and loved having a baby brother.

During this period of time, I met Gloria who worked at the JC Penney store in Waterford, CT. We were both single and started to date and spend time together. Gloria had three children from a previous marriage, Joseph, John (twins) and Linda. The boys had graduated from high school and were enrolled at Tuskegee University in Alabama to study Physics and Mechanical Engineering. Linda was in middle school.

We had been dating for about six months when we decided to get married. We informed our children about our future plans and set a date of January 30, 1988 to be married.

While I was heavily involved with these complex accounts, I was informed the US Navy was contemplating using titanium metal in the ball valves aboard submarines. My assignment was to locate the major titanium sponge producers in the country and be prepared to solicit those suppliers via inquires about titanium prices. The titanium would be used for the balls in the valve bodies.

The sponge is a porous form of titanium that must be processed, which I was informed was very labor intensive. I located three potential suppliers. Titanium Metals Company (TIMET) located in Henderson, Nevada, Oregon Metallurgical Corporation (OREMET) located in Albany, Oregon, and Reactive Metal Inc. (RMI) of Ashtabula, Ohio.

I scheduled meetings with representatives from these companies and forwarded a report to my management. After a few months, I was informed by my management, the US Navy decided not to put titanium balls in the valves because of the exorbitant pricing of these balls that were to be placed in various valves. I looked at my efforts as another opportunity for learning and experience another potential way of manufacturing parts for the construction of submarines.

The date of January 30, 1988 arrived and I married my fiancée Gloria. We were married by a local Justice of the Peace and decided to postpone our honeymoon. I was very busy at work during this period of time. Members from both of our families attended the ceremony.

The months of January and February were extremely busy for me particularly with the subcontract with Crucible Compaction Metals. This was the most complex order I had the responsibility to administer. The classes I had in the past from the American Graduate University on Cost/Price analysis and Negotiation of Contracts were very helpful in determining reasonableness of quoted prices since this order was a first for our Department in the field of powdered metallurgy. This would be the first time this technology would be used in submarine construction. I was proud to know the confidence placed in me to administer this contract which was the first of its kind.

On May 5, 1988, I asked the Director of Purchasing when will I be considered for a promotion. His reply, "you are a specialist Buyer, if you were promoted, you would have people working for you". My response was I was a Supervisor in the military for sixteen of my twenty years on active duty as a senior non-commissioned officer. Having people working for me is not a new concept. I also was the Supervisor of a Clinical Laboratory at a Naval Hospital among other tasks. I took this as an insult.

On May 10, 1988, I received an inter-office memorandum from the Director of Purchasing. He stated congratulations on your achievement of greater that 17% cost savings for the first quarter of 1988. It is my pleasure to recognize your outstanding effort in support of the Division's commitment to improve our competitive position within the shipbuilding industry.

There were rumors about the possibility of a strike in our shipyard. The General Manager in a memorandum to salaried employees stated actions were being taken to improve Electric Boat's competitive position to hold the line on payroll costs.

The salaried personnel accomplishment and development review was conducted in March. My supervisor stated "Mr. Mosley had 141 transactions for $2,700,000 and had cost reduction/cost avoidance of $340,073 for a 12.5% total which exceeds the goal of 8% minimum. Mr. Mosley is responsible for follow up on approximately one hundred shop order line items and has met or bettered the 3% contract delivery date delinquency rate consistently. Mr. Mosley negotiated and placed this group's first order for powered metal (HIP) castings for the SSN-21. Mr. Mosley interfaces with engineering in the development and solicitation on new suppliers and new design Inconel forgings for the SSN-21 program". During these evaluations, the problem of late receipt of purchase requisitions is never addressed as I stated before about long lead time items.

In July, the Metal Trade Council Union for Electric Boat Division voted for a strike. This action practically crippled the shipyard. The supervisors had to do the work normally done by their subordinates. The salaried personnel in many departments were transferred to the shipyard to work in the various trades.

My workload was very heavy at this time, particularly orders with long lead times and potential delinquencies. I was hoping major items to support schedules would be shipped to support our schedule if the strike was of a short duration.

I was notified I had to be transferred to the Paint Department in the shipyard, painting the inside of the main ballast tanks on submarines being constructed. I asked who would be doing my work while I was working in the shipyard. I was told it would be put on hold. I knew that once I got back to the Purchasing Department, I would be penalized because my work would not have been accomplished. This was the game being played. A few of the Buyers terminated their employment because of the hazard of painting inside of tanks. I am sure my assignment was made hoping I would voluntarily leave the company. I was one of the most senior people in the Casting/Forging Section.

Prior to my notification to work in the shipyard during the strike, our Engineering Department requested that I accompany one of their employees to attend a meeting at Crucible Compaction Metals. The purpose of the meeting was to discuss and evaluate the progress on the three and five inch flow control valves for the Seawolf Program and to discuss and evaluate the Standard Form 1411 pricing proposal. This form broke expenses down into three major categories: 1. Cost of manufacture of the valves, 2. engineering, and 3. tooling. Engineering rates were based on average salary rates. I had to basically do another audit on their overhead, direct labor and indirect labor rates, general and administrative expenses and proposed profit.

The meeting would be attended by three representatives from Crucible Compaction Metals: The Vice President of Finance, Sales Engineer and the Engineer. Electric Boat Division would be represented by our Engineer and me the Buyer.

When the engineering meeting started, the vendor's Engineer gave the current status of the valve bodies. The dimensions were taken on the valve bodies and they were off slightly from the specification. It appeared that the area of the flange was tilted slightly from the vertical and the bridge wall had an area that was slightly bulged. The dimensions were taken by a Cordax computer. Our Engineer discussed with their Engineer and Sales Engineer methods whereby the design drawing can be fine tuned to where tooling will provide bodies which meet all design dimensions by utilizing gussets to strengthen internal areas of the valve body. One of the three inch valve bodies would be used for the qualification test which includes shock and vibration testing.

The tooling for the five inch valve body was received the same day we arrived. The second iteration of the five inch valve body would be hip'd on September 21, 1988. It was explained that if gussets were used, the assembled container is secured to a vibrating mechanism for compaction and loaded with powdered metal. The loaded container is then hot out-gassed while pulling a vacuum on the fill stems. Fill stems are crimped and then seal welded. The sealed container is loaded into the autoclave and hip'd at a specified pressure and temperature to 100% density. The fixturing would strengthen the bridge wall and the neck below the flange at a time when the internal pressures and temperatures are making the powder metal more dense or compact.

The next day, I had a meeting with the Vice President-Finance to discuss in detail the Standard Form 1411 (Contract Pricing Proposal) prior to a General Dynamics audit. I requested the following information be provided:

1. A letter from DCAA approving Crucible Compaction Metals' Cost Accounting Standard (CAS) disclosure statement.
2. If available a letter from DCAA approving specific rates e.g., direct labor, overhead and General and Administrative (G&A).
3. Submit actuals, for engineering hours committed as of this date.
4. Rationale for 10% rejection hazard and back up historical data of actuals.
5. Rationale for 18% G&A which is applied to all orders.
6. Defining of cost centers and department rates.
7. Formula explaining standard labor rates which are computed from current rates.
8. Design, Process and Project Engineers (800 hrs estimate).

9. Despite the fact that container technology is proprietary, invoices from your suppliers are requested.

The Vice President-Finance addressed each request with an explanation of the pricing structure for our purchase order. Additionally, a written package was made a part of my report to assist the General Dynamics auditor in making an evaluation.

On September 8, 1988, I received a letter from the Vice President-Finance of Crucible Compaction Metals with attachments addressing my comments I made at their plant on my visit last month. The letter read this packet should address most of the questions you raised in your recent visit. I attempted to give you the actual data that was available. I only hope it answers more questions than it opens. Any details that may be missing could hopefully be cleared up with a phone call. I would gladly entertain any questions from your auditing people.

The strike lasted for one hundred and three days at Electric Boat Division. When the work started again at our plant, it was necessary for material to be delivered immediately to meet the construction schedule for the applicable submarine.

My next evaluation period was in March of 1989. My supervisor finally started to detail some of the positive events I accomplished during the past year, my supervisor stated, "Mr. Mosley had 148 transactions for $3,636,624, and had cost reduction/cost avoidance of $143,382. Due to rapidly escalating raw material pricing and current market conditions, no buyers in the Raw Material Group could meet goals for cost reduction/cost avoidance. Mr. Mosley was awarded a certificate for $1,000,000 cost saving via form 2960 reporting and was the only raw material recipient. Mr. Mosley's shop order line items averaged 100 and contract delivery delinquency averaged 3% or less". I felt I was finally getting recognition for my accomplishments in the administration of major complex contracts.

On August 21, 1989, I was transferred from the Raw Material Section which included the Casting/Forging Group to the Valve Group. Purchasing valves was familiar to me because in the early 1970s I was in a special group purchasing valves and other components for submarine overhaul, and later some new construction contracts.

I received a surprise when I was given the task of negotiating and subsequent closing of many delinquent orders placed by other buyers. I felt this was a set up for me to either get fired or placed in an untenable position. The amazing thing about this issue was many of the Buyers with these delinquent purchase orders were still working in the Valve Group. I had inherited their problems.

I asked the Manager of this group why I was given this batch of delinquent orders. His response was "I know you can accomplish this task". The problem orders included many single source and maximum priced purchase orders. Upon completion of the manufacturing cycle, the purchase orders had to be negotiated and a final firm fixed price determined by a supplement to the orders prior to the submission to the US Navy for approval.

On many of these orders, some of the material was never delivered to Electric Boat Division. I never understood why someone should not have known many of these parts were never shipped. I think the reason for this lapse was poor expediting of the material. The most challenging of the delinquent orders were Valve and Primer Co. of Schaumberg, Il., Drilling Engineering and Mining Co. (DEMCO) of Oklahoma City, OK. and Crosby Valve Co. of Wrentham, MA. The latter two companies manufacture special butterfly and swing check valves used in the submarine ventilation systems.

During the decade of the 1980s, parts were purchased for many submarines under contract with the US Government. Sometimes parts were purchased for four or five submarines. During the construction period, some parts are lost or ruined. To keep up with the ship's construction schedule, parts were "stolen" from future ships to satisfy the current construction schedule. Replacement parts should have been ordered at the time but apparently this was an oversight by the Material Ordering Department. The Buyer would ultimately be blamed when there is a shortage of material for future requirements.

When the buyers placed orders for replace material, the lead time could not support the ship's construction schedule in many instances when purchase requisitions were late arriving in the Purchasing Department. Situations such as this would be a major headache for me because when the trades in the shipyard needed material, they contacted the Buyer administering these contracts. My name continuously came up because of the quantities of delinquent orders I was given to oversee.

I was amazed that three of these delinquent orders were four to five years old and still open. I could not understand why the Supervisor and Manager were not aware of these potential problems.

I put forth my best efforts to close these orders properly in addition to the other orders I had the responsibility to place and expedite. I spent a considerable period of time working on these delinquent orders and contacting the suppliers.

One of the most crucial orders I was attempting to close was open for four years. The Supervisor of Shipbuilding (SUPSHIPS), the US Navy's representative at the shipyard requested an expedited closing of this order which had been open for four years and three months.

When the original Buyer placed the order, it was a maximum priced order to be negotiated prior to closing of the order. The subcontract audit was to be part of the negotiations. The original Buyer was to supplement the order after a fixed price was agreed upon. It was strange that the Supervisor did not assign this order to the original Buyer for negotiations. I think the reason for this was because of the length of time this order sat dormant. I felt this order was going to be a major problem and someone had to take the heat for the delinquency.

I documented each step of my negotiations. I wrote a memorandum to file for my Manager and my records. The subject was Final price negotiations with Crosby Valve and Gage Co. for swing check valves. The purchase order was for swing check valves and was identical to material previously awarded to this supplier. Due to schedule considerations, the award was made to Crosby Valve and Gage Co. on a single source basis on May 7, 1985. The award was made on a maximum price basis of $282,769 subject to downward revision only following a General Dynamics audit and final price negotiations.

The Subcontract audit memorandum dated July 28, 1989 advised the Purchasing Department that no documentation existed relative to final price negotiations for the subject purchase order. A subsequent review revealed that all purchase order items had been delivered and paid for at the purchase order maximum price. Further evidence revealed that through an inadvertent error, the original Buyer did not proceed with final price negotiations. As the result of the audit, I proceeded to negotiate with Crosby Valve and Gage Co. after I was assigned to the Valve Group on August 21, 1989. My negotiation objective was based on the findings of the General Dynamics Audit Report #PP-1288 dated September 26, 1985. The recommended baseline for negotiations was $50,392.85 of costs for non-acceptance and $34,713 for consideration.

Negotiations with this supplier were conducted during the period of August of 1989 through November of 1989 in an attempt to reach agreement on a firm fixed price. The supplier remained adamant in their position stating that the valves had been delivered and accepted by

Electric Boat Division and no price adjustment could be made at this late date. My continued attempts did not result in a price reduction. Finally a meeting was held at Electric Boat Division on November 1, 1989. I presented my position in detail by cost elements however the supplier refused to consider any price reduction. Their rationale was their methods of cost allocation comply with Federal Regulations. The supplier agreed to execute a Certificate of Current Cost or Pricing Data. After consideration, an agreement was reached at the maximum price as stated in the original purchase order.

The $50,392.85 as recommended by the auditor for non-acceptance was partially based on projected labor and burden rates, however the supplier remained firm on their maximum price as costs that were actually incurred.

My Manager had to report to the Director of Purchasing the results of the negotiations prior to forwarding the results to the Supervisor of Shipbuilding (SUPSHIPS).

The Manager's note to the Director of Purchasing stated "I have reviewed in detail the purchase order. The supplement submitted for your approval definitize the purchase order that was issued on May 7, 1985. All material had long been delivered however the original Buyer had never properly closed out the order.

The negotiation team included a representative from Subcontract Audit, a Cost/Price Analyst, and Jim Mosley, the negotiation team leader. The Chief of Purchasing reviewed the negotiating process. The vendor's representative (Sales Manager) stated he had lost money in producing the valves and he was not prepared to offer any price reductions to Electric Boat Division.

Based on the fact the purchase order is under-budget, and the negotiated number is the best achievable, it is recommended the supplement be approved. The Crosby Valve account is now current and the valves would be bought and expedited by Mr. Jim Mosley in the future".

I was happy to see this nightmare disappear and was hopeful I would not be assigned any more delinquent orders from other Buyers.

I was informed by my Supervisor that my responsibilities would be the procurement/administration of specialty valves and associated parts for all programs, logistic support orders and to clear up old delinquent orders from other Buyers. I was very busy for the next six to eight months primarily clearing up many of these delinquent orders that presented major challenges.

In January of 1990, I received a purchase requisition to purchase swing check valves from Crosby Valve and Gage Co. This supplier was single source for these valves. The valves were identical to those previously purchased with the exception of Item #2 which was purchased for the first time.

My negotiation objectives were to lower the unit pricing of each item to conform to the results of the price analysis I had conducted. Additionally to improve the delivery date of each item particularly Item# 2. This item was urgently required. My final price analysis was developed to make a comparison to previous pricing after quantity and escalation adjustments. There were five types of valves for various applications. Item #1 showed an analysis 21.4% higher than the previous price after quantity and escalation adjustment. The previous quantities were for three valves and the present quantity was for two valves. The two price quantities were allocated for one ship therefore, no increase in quantity is applicable to follow on ships. The alloy for these valve bodies is copper nickel (70/30).

This supplier must purchase copper nickel castings in a quantity of two in lieu of three relative to the purchase order. The raw material at the time was $1.03 per pound for copper and $3.44 per pound for nickel.

The set up charges were allocated over two valves in lieu of three, this supplier's direct labor rate had been audited and accepted. Item# 2 was purchased for the first time. I conducted price analysis by parametric relationships and comparison to similar items, i.e., sizes and alloys. Item #3 was purchased in a quantity of nine in lieu of five. By increasing the quantity, the unit price was decreased by 18%, this resulted in a savings of $2016 for this item.

The quoted price for Item #4 was 0.2% higher than the previous price. The previous quantity was for ten valves and the current quantity was for fourteen valves. The applicable indices used for pricing projections did not contain provisions for metal price increases that are passed from the casting supplier to the valve manufacturer. The quantity for Item #5 was increased from three to seven valves since the previous order. After adjustment for quantity and escalation, the final negotiated price was 3.4% lower than the previous price. After my final price analysis and negotiations, I deemed the award price for this purchase order was in line with what it should cost to manufacture these valves. The negotiated price was under the budget for this order.

The supplier's contract delivery date was in line with our shipyard schedule and would advise later on improving the delivery date after determining the lead time for obtaining the castings and a schedule for machining operations. The supplier was aware of the fact that Item #2 was urgently required.

Based upon my price analysis, negotiations and purchasing target data, the award price of $35,000 was judged fair and reasonable.

My next evaluation was conducted in March 1990. I felt for the first time in my twenty two years in the Purchasing Department I was being evaluated objectively and the Supervisor was not one of the co-conspirators. He personally congratulated me for my performance since I had been in the Valve group. He stated on my review,"Mr. Mosley transferred to the Valve Group from the Raw Material Group on August 21, 1989. His performance in both groups during the evaluation period was both competent and professional. In the Valve Group, he quickly assimilated his responsibilities and became an immediate contributor to the group's overall objectives, His dedication to the learning and performance of his job has been excellent. He has already grasped many of the technical aspects of the valves under his cognizance established a firm sense of urgency, and responds positively to critical shipyard developments.

Additionally, he has earned the respect of his co-workers and has established sound working relationships both within the Division and with his vendors. Highlights of his Valve Group performance included 1) the negotiation and subsequent closing of numerous "old dogs" maximum priced purchase orders with Crosby Valve and Gage Co., 2) active involvement in the subsequent resolution of the DEMCO valve operator problem in support of urgent shipyard schedules. During the latter part of 1989, in the Valve Group, he committed a total of $149,239 on forty four transactions with a combined cost avoidance/reduction savings of $16,964 or 11.35% of the award dollars. Jim has demonstrated the capacity and desire to conduct business conducive to shipyard support at minimum expense. He has become a valued member of the Valve Group. On planning next year's objectives, aid in the development and placement of purchase orders with additional small disadvantaged business concerns which is a major objective of our Department".

This was an objective that was very close to my heart. Small Disadvantaged Businesses were the combination of Minority Business Enterprises, Native American Businesses and Women Owned Businesses. I administered these programs from 1972 to 1976 when they were resisted by many Buyers and some members of Management when I was appointed to implement these programs for Electric Boat Division.

I knew this would be a major challenge because most of the purchase orders I was to administer were specialty valves that were primarily purchased from single source suppliers.

Another one of my major objectives was to attempt to negotiate a Master Price Agreement (MPA) with Crosby Valve and Gage Co. for swing check valves and to administer the Automatic Switch Co. account to ensure timely support of contract commitments. Both of these suppliers are single source suppliers for important submarine systems.

In March 1990, there was an opening for a Purchasing Agent position in the Valve Group. I applied for the position along with a few other Buyers. I submitted my resume which included my education, experience in Purchasing and special accomplishments over the years. The promotion was given to an individual who had less experience and a lot less time in the Purchasing Department. This individual was one of the six individuals who never completed the purchase order that I had the responsibility to resolve when I was transferred into the Valve Group. I thought I had an impressive resume.

In May of 1990, our son Merv was drafted into the Arena Football League. We traveled to Pittsburgh for a family reunion at this time and made plans to return to Pittsburgh because his team, The Albany Firebirds was scheduled to play the Pittsburgh Gladiators in July. Our son had an outstanding game. I was very proud of him. He signed many autographs and was interviewed by the local news media.

During my next evaluation period, the Valve Group was split into two segments. I had the unfortunate luck to be assigned to a new Supervisor. I was familiar with this individual because we worked as peers in the early 1970s. I always considered this individual as a closet racist and this would be his opportunity to come out of the closet. I was going from a Supervisor whom I felt evaluated me fairly to one that had an "ax to grind". I recall when I worked in the same Buying Group with this individual earlier in my career, I never recall him ever speaking to me as a peer and co-worker. He appeared to resent me because I was in the Purchasing Department. It appeared this individual felt I was in this Department because of affirmative action.

I was still working on delinquent orders inherited when I came into this Buying Group in addition to the new accounts I had the responsibility to administer.

I was informed on March 21, 1990 my suggestion of processing the primary shield tank top forgings and the main coolant pump ring forgings would be made from a modified chemistry from the steel mill. It had been approved by our Engineering Department. The Material Ordering Department created new part numbers for these items and directed the Engineering Bills of Material to utilize the new part numbers. The suggestion number for this project was #28502 which is on file with Electric Boat Division.

This adopted suggestion could have saved millions of dollars in the past if adopted earlier. Unfortunately despite my efforts to put it in the pipeline earlier for the last ten ships, the savings of $110,140 only applied to the eighteenth and last ship of the class. My resistance came from Supervisors in the Purchasing Department. The date this change took effect was December 21, 1990. I submitted this suggestion when I was a member of the Casting/Forging Section of the Raw Material Group.

I was in this group for a short period of time when I realized just how easily my new Supervisor could make my job more difficult. I was penalized for problems originating in the Engineering and Quality Assurance Departments. I alerted the Vice President of Material, Director of Purchasing, Inventory Control Department, my Manager and Supervisor about a major problem with a purchase order for swing check valves with the Crosby Valve and Gage Co. I documented the entire sequence of events from the time I received the purchase requisition until I awarded the order. My Supervisor stated I did not award the order on a timely basis after receiving the requisition.

I received the purchase requisition on April 20, 1990 as an emergency requirement. The request for quotation was typed on April 23, 1990 and mailed on April 24, 1990. It was received by Crosby Valve and Gage Co. on April 27, 1990 with a bid due date of May 11, 1990. When I didn't receive the bid by the due date, I decided to call the Sales Manager at the bidder's plant. He informed me he was having a problem with our requirement. I informed him this order was an emergency requirement and I needed to know the extent of the problem. He assured me he would call me back after the weekend.

He called me on May 14, 1990 and stated he would not be able to quote our requirement until he resolved an issue with the supplier of the material for the bushing and bumpers of the valve assembly.

Crosby's quotation was dated July 6, 1990 and was received on July 9, 1990. I read the quotation and many exceptions were taken relative to our request for quotation. These exceptions were major items that had to be resolved by our Engineering and Quality Assurance Departments. I alerted the appropriate Departments via Internal Reply Memoranda. I assigned a number to each, and informed them of the problems and dated the messages. I sent out six Internal Reply Memoranda and waited for a reply. This is a listing of those sent out to the appropriate Departments: A1464068 dtd 7/20/1990, A1464070 dtd 7/23/1990, A1540180 dtd 8/6/1990, A1513937 dtd 8/30/1990, A1469113 dtd 9/30/1990 and A1484252 dtd 10/2/1990.

I explained to my management the steps I was taking to resolve the issues that prevented me from placing the order. Crosby Valve informed me of the multitude of problems relative to the request for quotation. Their first exception was to the material to be used for the bushing and bumpers in the clapper assemblies in addition to exceptions taken to the raw material for PC-18 of the two inch valve and EB Specification 2678G. On February, 2, 1990, The Dixon Division of the Furon Corp. notified Crosby Valve that Rulon A would no longer be manufactured however Rulon AR which is an improved material will now be utilized as an alternate.

The drawings invoked on the request for quotation were Charles Wheatley Drawing #6861 Rev. C and EB Drawing 2621-927-01 Rev. A, 2621-927-02 Rev— and 2621-927-10 Rev. C These drawings referenced Rulon A bearing material to be used in the clapper assemblies which was obsolete material. The Dixon Division of the Furon Corp. was sole source for this material. With the multitude of problems related to the descriptive definition of these valves, I requested permission to return the requisition to the originator to update the nomenclature and revise the EB drawings. My request was denied. As long as I was charged with holding this incorrect document, I would be penalized by my Supervisor.

On July 20, 1990 I requested Department 952 to review Crosby's exceptions relative to the drawings, material specifications and the deletion of Standard Clause 12-17 which applies to Electric Boat Division supplied material. On July 23, 1990, I requested Department 457 to initiate the applicable drawing revisions, as the seller refuses to accept an order until the drawings are revised. On August 6, 1990, I requested Departments 457 and 459 to revise our drawings to reflect the change of the bearing material. Department 459 stated that no budget was available for this task. The request was subsequently forwarded to Department 952 to have the material file updated.

On August 30, 1990, I advised Department 312 that all orders or quotations affected by Rulon material would be placed on hold by Crosby Valve until a resolution is made relative to material changes. On September 20, 1990 the Supervisor of Shipbuilding (SUPSHIPS), the US Navy

Representative approved the D Revision of Charles Wheatley Drawing. #6861. The Electric Boat Division drawings had not been revised as of that date to reflect the new Rulon AR bearing material. On September 24, 1990 Department 323 (Quality Assurance) disapproved the placement of the order due to non-compliance with Electric Boat Division Specification 2678 Revision G. On September 30, 1990, Department 312 was directed to supplement twenty three part numbers to update the nomenclature in lieu of our drawing revisions. On October 2, 1990, Department 323 granted permission to place the purchase order.

To summarize, the purchase order was finally placed on November 5, 1990 and supplemented on November 13, 1990 to incorporate the revised parts nomenclature. On November 14, 1990, I received a message from Crosby Valve requesting the deletion of certain standard clauses that do not apply to the purchase order in addition to Item # 12 which only applies to Electric Boat Division supplied material.

I forwarded another Internal Reply Memorandum A1577337 dated November 15, 1990 to Department 952 for evaluation of the Crosby Valve message of November 14, 1990. I requested from Crosby Valve an assurance that a concerted effort would be made to improve deliveries on this purchase order.

I informed my management that in the future, it would be prudent to think that upon receipt of an incorrect document that cannot be processed in a reasonable period of time, should be returned to the originator for correction or completion. It is not feasible to think that six months is a reasonable period of time for me to be charged with an incorrect document and ultimately be penalized for things beyond my control. I had been charged with the delinquent purchase requisition for a period of six months. This is one of many instances of discrediting me because of a built in bias exhibited by this Supervisor.

One of my new accounts was the Automatic Switch Co. I had awarded a purchase order for a solenoid trip valve and a three way bypass valve for the Seawolf Program. These valves were familiar to me because of my submarine service in the US Navy. The solenoid trip valve is part of the 12,000 gallon per day Distilling Plant located in the Engine room. The valve trips when the unit is over pressurized from its safe setting.

I had no idea the solenoid trip valve would be modified after the order was placed by Engineering upon a request from the US Navy (NAVSEA).

I awarded the purchase order on June 28, 1990 with the delivery date for the solenoid trip valve January 10, 1992 and June 29, 1991 for the three way bypass valve.

After the order was placed, the US Navy (NAVSEA) contacted our Engineering Department about the modification of the solenoid trip valve and assigned a research and development task number to the modification. I was contacted by the Engineer from Automatic Switch Co. who informed me he would be coming to Electric Boat to attend an engineering meeting to discuss the valve modification and changes to be made on the delivery of the valve after the order is supplemented with the new requirements.

The engineering meeting was conducted on August 20, 1990 in the Fourth Floor Conference Room in the Engineering Building. In attendance at the meeting were three Engineers from Electric Boat (Department 457), one Designer from (Department 459), two Engineers from Automatic Switch Co. and myself representing Purchasing (Department 630).

The meeting was held to discuss a Modification Kit Design that would reduce the noise levels associated with the tripping action of the Distilling Plant overpressure trip valve. The modification design by our Engineering Department was presented to the representatives of Automatic Switch Co. who stated they would prepare a proposal that would incorporate the new design modification and assured us this proposal would be at Electric Boat on September 4, 1990.

When the proposal was not received on the agreed date, our Engineering Department notified the lead Engineer at Automatic Switch Co. on September 6, 1990. The lead Engineer informed our Engineering Department that the drawing of the modification kit that was provided to them by Electric Boat was not dimensionally correct in some areas. They would have to re-dimension and re-draw some of the items shown on our drawings and indicated because of the additional changes the projected proposal delivery date is now September 12, 1990.

On September 25, 1990, I received a facsimile from the Engineer at Automatic Switch Co. He asked me to please confirm that the valves on this order are the ones to be converted to quiet operations. If yes, this order is on hold until it is supplemented with the quiet operation information. I passed this information on to my Supervisor and our Engineering Department who had the responsibility of writing the supplement to the purchase order.

On October 1, 1990 I sent a facsimile to the Engineer at Automatic Switch Co. stating the valves on the referenced purchase order are to be manufactured in accordance with the drawing and specification invoked. Any changes to the order will be by a supplement to the order. The supplement will be dictated by our Engineering Department. My Manager and Supervisor were well aware of the problems with this order due to potential changes with the design.

My Supervisor did not respond to these problems until he sent a letter to Automatic Switch Co. on March 8, 1991. It appeared he had held conversations with their representatives but had no authority to supplement the order. The change must come from Engineering.

He stated in his letter the valve was to be manufactured to Revision P of the drawing but the purchase order which is a legal document references Revision L. He should have known a supplement to the order is required to change the drawing revision to incorporate the new design.

Automatic Switch Co. agreed to proceed on a best efforts basis while awaiting our supplement. They had issued a purchase order to their foundry to obtain the body castings for the valve. I also requested their Sales Manager quote the three way bypass valves for two Trident submarines. I referenced the two requests for quotations I had mailed to their facility.

My Supervisor also advised the supplier that the purchase order will be supplemented on or before March 22, 1991. Additional costs and delivery delays associated with this modification would be the subject of a future negotiation.

The date of March 22, 1991 had come and gone and our Engineering Department was still reviewing the proposal submitted by our supplier. On April 4, 1991, I received an internal Memorandum # A1812380 from our Engineering Department. The subject was engineering review of Automatic Switch Co. proposal for the quiet operation trip valves. After review of the proposal, we find it technically acceptable pending the incorporation of true clevis mounted dashpots brackets into their design. Engineering is concerned that their present design shown on their drawing does not allow for free pivoting of the dashpots at both ends as specified in the request for quotation which will be incorporated into supplement #1 to the order. This pivoting is vital in order to avoid side loading of the dashpots which inhibits their sound dampening efficiency. This was discussed with the Engineering people at our supplier. They are aware of this discrepancy and had expressed a willingness to comply with our Engineering request. Engineering recommends that Purchasing place supplement # 1 with the supplier with the supplier noting the reservation and agreement stated during their conversation. It was important for my Manager and Supervisor to remember that the purchase order was placed on June 28, 1990 and due to changes requested by the US Navy (NAVSEA), Automatic Switch Co. received the go ahead to manufacture the valve in April 5, 1991. It took approximately eight months for this supplier to get the official go ahead to manufacture the valves on this purchase order. This is one purchase order that will be etched in my mind forever. My Supervisor had stated that I held up the manufacture of these valves for eight months. This was a lie and he knew the history of this purchase order. This was eventually placed on my evaluation. My Supervisor and Manager knew the truth about this order.

On May 17, 1991 I received a memorandum from the Director of Purchasing stating I was to receive a monetary award for my suggestion # 28502 that was adopted and implemented on December 21, 1990. The old method was to process two purchase orders for the primary shield tank top forgings around the reactor vessel and the main coolant pump ring forgings in the reactor compartment from two different steel chemistries. The new method was to process one purchase order from a single steel chemistry. The savings result from the amount of steel to be purchased from the mill.

The ceremony took place in the office of the Vice President of Material. The award read: Presented to James M. Mosley for an adopted suggestion that directly contributes to the effectiveness and improvements of operations.

I had previously stated that it took years for me to get this suggestion out of the Purchasing Department. I finally had to get a Nuclear Engineering Supervisor to study my proposal before I was able to get it reviewed by a committee of Engineers and Metallurgists. Millions of dollars could have been saved if this suggestion had been adopted earlier.

I had another order in April of 1991 that was being held up because of problems our Engineering Department was having with the US Navy (NAVSEA). This requirement was for eight Trident submarines. This was another instance of my Supervisor discrediting me for problems created by our Engineering Department and our customer. In situations such as this, I always document my work and write a sequence of events. I received two purchase requisitions, one for seven submarines and one for the last submarine of the class. The requirements were for ¼ inch 3-Way Selector Valves for the Ship's Gas Management System. Crosby Valve and Gage Co. had produced the prototype valve and obtained shock test and drawing approval. These two orders were ready to be issued on April 26, 1991 however, they were placed on hold by our Engineering Department due to budget problems.

The rough order of magnitude that was reported for the last ship of the class was $50,000 for ten valves as reported to the customer. The prototype valve had a total price of $16,207. The total price quoted for the last ship of the class was $149,453 which exceeded the rough order of magnitude value. Under the task that was assigned by the customer, Electric Boat Division was not authorized to exceed the budgeted estimate without (NAVSEA) approval. The financial variance placed the price over the Gas Management task authorization. Crosby Valve and Gage Co.'s pricing was predicated on placing both orders simultaneously and manufacturing was to be accomplished concurrently. Our Planning and Engineering Department requested that I solicit additional sources in addition to Crosby Valve and Gage Co. I received a third purchase requisition to solicit additional suppliers to quote pricing for seventeen valves.

There were six suppliers solicited with four responses. On July 18, 1991, I returned the third purchasing requisition to the originator with the suppliers' responses in order that a technical evaluation could be conducted to determine an acceptable offer. The result of Engineering's evaluation was that Marrotta Valve Co. and Flodyne's design were not technically acceptable due to potential acoustic problems. Sargent Industries' design had no real detail to evaluate, the cost was prohibitive and delivery would not support the shipyard construction schedule. Engineering anticipated that the Crosby Valve and Gage Co.'s design would be the final solution.

As the result of the re-solicitation and evaluation prior to purchase order placement, approximately three to four months were lost, Crosby Valve and Gage Co.'s delivery schedule was forty three weeks after receipt of the order.

With a lead time of forty three weeks after the receipt of an order, if I was still in the Purchasing Department in 1992, my Supervisor would blame me for holding up the purchase order because the shipyard schedule would not be met. This is the reason I document the sequence of events in potential problem purchase orders beyond my control.

I was informed by my Supervisor that I had to make a trip to a supplier in Oklahoma City, Ok. to follow up on open purchase orders which were critical to our shipyard schedule. The supplier was Cooper Industries (DEMCO). This supplier manufactures "Butterfly Valves" that are used in the ventilation systems aboard submarines. In the past, problems had occurred during the installation of these valves. We had major problems on one of the Trident submarines during construction which impacted our schedule. I was hoping this would not happen again.

I arrived at their plant on June 17, 1991 and met with the Plant Manager. I stated that my purpose for the visit was to obtain the current status of open purchase orders particularly key event items, review their quoting procedures based upon early shipment control, review drawing approvals and submittals, receive a plant tour and to obtain a review of the manufacturing process at various work stations. My trip duration was for three days.

The Plant Manager arranged a meeting in the afternoon with representatives of their Sales and Quality Assurance Departments. Those in attendance were the Plant Manger, Sales Manger, Sales Engineer, Quality Assurance Manger and the Quality Assurance Engineer.

I asked for the status of our open purchase orders. The Sales Manager explained that purchase orders are grouped in accordance with our contract delivery dates. Some of the orders are processed and placed in storage. Approximately one month prior to the contract delivery date, the material is removed from storage and is sent to the Quality Assurance Department for final certifications. After this operation is completed, the material is shipped in order that it arrives at our plant within the time frame whereby early shipment control is not violated.

Early shipment control was instituted by Electric Boat for the purpose of having the supplier store the material at their facility until it was required by our shipyard. This policy applied to a majority of our suppliers.

I reviewed all open purchase orders to determine the current status. Based on the contract delivery date, some orders were processed for delivery within the appropriate lead times for immediate shipment, others were processed and placed in storage and some were released to the shop at the appropriate time. The raw materials had been purchased for the open orders.

The next area for discussion was the quoting procedure for our orders. The Sales Manager stated that two Buyers were responsible for quoting all Electric Boat requests. Cooper Industries (DEMCO) quoted to our part number description and their drawings plus all standard clauses on the request for quotations. Based on our required dates and early shipment control, our Buyers quoted a price for delivery after manufacture and an escalated price for dates in the future where early shipment control is invoked. The Buyer in turn conducts an economic analysis to determine the most cost effective method to utilize for the award price.

I talked to the Quality Assurance Engineer about the procedure for drawing submittals, non-destructive test procedure approvals and requests for non-conforming materials. I was very impressed with this supplier's Quality Assurance Department and Purchasing Department. I left their plant on June 19, 1991 and returned to Electric Boat Division.

The Sales Engineer gave me a tour of the plant. During the tour, many work stations were observed. The entire operation was discussed from the receipt of the casting material until the final assembly and quality assurance certification. This supplier appeared to have a very coordinated and efficient operation.

I returned from trip to this supplier's plant and assumed my regular duties. This same day, my Supervisor called me into his office and gave me my evaluation sheet. I was shocked at the negative comments he made about my performance. This evaluation without a doubt was the worst I had received in my twenty three years as a Buyer. His objective was still to drive me out of this Department. I was livid about the blatant lies he had on my evaluation sheet. I tore the sheet up, threw it on his desk and walked out of his office.

The Manager of our Valve Group called me into his office and asked me to sign a new evaluation sheet with my objections. I would not sign a bunch of lies and he was aware of my performance and the delinquent orders I was given when I was transferred into the Group.

The Supervisor stated in his evaluation, I had delayed the manufacture of solenoid trip valves awarded to the Automatic Switch Co. for eight months. This order was well documented and the Supervisor and Manager knew the entire history of this purchase order.

The purchase order was awarded on June 28, 1990 and the US Navy (NAVSEA) decided to modify the valves to a new design. For eight months the Electric Boat Engineers and Engineers from Automatic Switch Co. worked on a new design. On April 5, 1991, Automatic Switch Co. was given authority to manufacture the valves by our Engineering Department. I could not believe I was blamed for the delay. My Manager and Supervisor were well aware of this contract and knew our Engineering Department had to write a supplement to the order prior to manufacture.

I suggested to my Manager that we discuss this issue with the Director of Purchasing. We went to the Director's office and discussed this issue. I gave the Director the names and phone numbers of the two Electric Boat Engineers and the name and phone number of the Engineer at Automatic

Switch Co. These three individuals could set the record straight about this purchase order. The Director of Purchasing never looked into the issue.

In addition to the Automatic Switch Co. purchase order, I was penalized for orders placed by other Buyers. One of these orders was awarded five years before I came into the Valve Group and I inherited all the problems associated with this order. The original Buyer was still in the Valve Group. This Supervisor stated I was missing critical data in closing this delinquent purchase order. In the meantime, the previous Buyer was given an outstanding evaluation by this Supervisor.

We left the Director's office and I was awaiting a reply after our discussion. It would only take a telephone call to learn the truth about the manufacture of the solenoid valves. If the five year old order had been reviewed, the issue would have been laid to rest and I would have received a fair evaluation. I was sure the Director was well aware of my capabilities as a Buyer based upon my prior evaluation and the awards I had received.

On my performance assessment, my Supervisor stated:" Mr. Mosley performance during the appraisal period was satisfactory". This statement has been rubber stamped for twenty three years with the exception of the last evaluation period. "Mr. Mosley is a tireless worker and puts forth a maximum effort on all work assignments however, the quality of his work and the timing of problem resolution require improvement". It was difficult for me to correct problems created by other Buyers years ago. It was frustrating me to be set up this way to be discredited because of a complaint I made in 1974.

It was amazing that this Supervisor stated in his evaluation I should attend a company sponsored seminar on Cost/Price Analysis and Contract Negotiations. I had completed these courses in February and November 1971 from Sterling Institute, a company based in the Watergate Office Building in Washington, DC. and in October of 1980 and 1981 from the American Graduate University (Procurement Associates Inc.) based in Covina, CA. I have the certificates for my successful completion of these courses and still have the textbooks. I guess he forgot we were peers and classmates years ago.

The last purchase orders I placed with the Crosby Valve and Gage Co. was one month before my retirement. In my negotiations, I combined valve quantities for a Trident and Seawolf Submarine for negotiated savings of $51,719.

I was still awaiting a reply from the Director of Purchasing about my evaluation. After a period of one month had passed with no response, I informed my Manager I was retiring effective September 30, 1991. I was planning to work until I was sixty five years of age however they were finally successful in forcing me out of the Department after twenty three years and five months.

The month prior to my worst evaluation, the Vice President of Material and the Director of Purchasing awarded me a certificate and check for saving the company a substantial amount of money. I was complimented for my contribution to improve operations.

My previous evaluation by the Supervisor I was assigned to when I was transferred into the Valve Group evaluated me fairly and considered my work excellent. How could I go from being a highly productive worker to a non-productive worker in a short period of time?

The individual that considered my work excellent was the only Supervisor I had in twenty three years that was not in the Department when I was hired on April 3, 1968. I knew a conspiracy was constructed against me when I was hired and it became recalcitrant after I made an official complaint on September 15, 1974.

I was informed at one time that I was the "Jackie Robinson" of Purchasing. This individual probably thought this was a compliment but I knew from history the struggles and heart ache this baseball player endured.

I continued my duties hoping I would receive some feedback from the Director of Purchasing about my evaluation. Apparently, he never called the Engineers who would have told him the truth about the redesigning of the valves on the Automatic Switch Co. order and why it took eight months to give the go ahead by way of a supplement to the order from the Engineering Department after the applicable drawings were completed.

I became completely frustrated and on August 5, 1991, I decided to send a copy of my unsigned evaluation sheet to the Electric Boat Division's Equal Employment Compliance Officer with my rebuttal attached. I only wanted a fair hearing and an investigation of the negative comments placed in my personnel file from my initial date of hire. I stated this evaluation is a deliberate attempt to distort my performance over the past year. It contains false statements that can easily be refuted. A significant number of the accounts that I administered contains purchase orders that were never followed closely or properly by Buyers who are ranked higher and compensated accordingly. I had the responsibility to resolve the problems of their orders. The evaluator failed to compare last year's performance with the current period of evaluation. In my opinion, this is an important element in the supervision of personnel. It appears that a concoction of false statements had to be formulated to justify the negative comments.

It appears that my personnel file have been distorted for a considerable period of time, i.e., from the initial date of employment in the Purchasing Department on April 3, 1968 until the present time. I have always been ranked at the bottom relative to my peers "with no potential for advancement", and this stigma has been rubber stamped for twenty three years. Any positive accomplishments during the evaluation periods were conveniently overlooked. A few individuals in this Department have conducted a conspiracy against me since the date of employment as evidenced by my personnel file. As the result of this mentality, my family also was denied economic opportunity as the result of covert racism. I received no reply from the Electric Boat Division Compliance Office. It appears that the Compliance Officer only spoke to my Supervisor and ignored me as the person who made the complaint.

An official complaint was lodged with the Connecticut Commission of Human Rights and the Equal Employment Opportunity Commission in 1974 however there is nothing in my personnel file to indicate this action. The case number was FEP190-4/TB05-0635. There are also laws in the State of Connecticut commonly known as "retaliation" statues that prohibit an employer or their agents to discipline an employee for filing a discrimination suit. There were some individuals in the Purchasing Department who were violating these statues in the name of Electric Boat Division.

My treatment in this Department for twenty three years was a clear case of institutionalized racism by a small select number of individuals who vent their bigotry in the name of Electric Boat Division. In the history of this company, I was the first African-American hired as a Buyer and I was scorned from the date of hire. This was all documented in the case records of the suit in 1974. It was my intention to make certain individuals answer for the treatment and economic hardships that were forced on me as an employee and my family.

I never received a reply from the Equal Employment Compliance Office. They knew I would be retiring in the following month therefore the issue would be over.

I was determined to expose the individuals who made it difficult for me in a hostile environment to be treated fairly as an employee of the company. My record speaks for itself and is well documented relative to my accomplishments over the years.

Another amazing thing about my years in the Purchasing Department, during the period from 1972 to 1976, I had three job descriptions at the same time: Buyer, Minority Business Administrator and Small Business Administrator. The latter two job descriptions, I was representing Electric Boat Division in a management position as evidenced by the Management Manual. I was never evaluated by my Supervisors or Managers for administering these two government programs. They could not evaluate me because they were ignorant of the job descriptions. I was asked by one of my Managers to write the job description for these two programs. My reply was it is not my responsibility to write job descriptions.

I worked in more diverse positions than anyone in the Purchasing Department. I worked in every Buying Group in the Department with the exception of the Subcontract Farm-Out Program. This Group sends out material to be manufactured by a Subcontractor. Additionally, I implemented the Minority Business Program and administered the Company's Small Business Program.

My plan was after retirement, I would request another investigation into how a few rogue agents of the company could destroy the career of an employee and continue their personal animosity against future employees who they felt did not belong in the Purchasing Department.

The first week of September 1991, I was informed I would be honored by a retirement party sponsored by "my friends in Purchasing". A member of the Valve Group would be the coordinator. He asked me with a smile if I wanted any of our supervision to attend. My reply was if they wanted to attend, they would be welcome. I knew he was aware of the hardships placed on me when I was transferred into the Valve Group.

On September 11, 1991, I filed a complaint with the State of Connecticut Commission on Human Rights and Opportunities and had a case number assigned. The Case No. 9240133 was to be used on future correspondence. My purpose for this claim was to expose corrupt individuals and hope individuals in the future would be treated fairly. There are some individuals that have outlived their kind and outlived their time. The bottom line for this complaint is that I faced retaliation after I filled a discrimination complaints in September of 1974. Apparently this was taken out of my personnel file. Re: FEP190-4/TB05-0635.

In the past, I had filled internal complaints with Electric Boat Division's Equal Employment Compliance Office. The only people interviewed were the individuals I complained about. I was never interviewed or asked a question. What types of investigations were conducted over the years? My only request was for a fair investigation of the facts.

The retirement party was on September 26, 1991. The only Supervisor to attend the party was the only one who evaluated me fairly when I was first transferred to the Valve Group. I was not surprised that my previous Supervisors for the past twenty three years failed to attend because they knew how I felt about the injustices over the years. I personally felt sorry for them because of the weight on their consciences. Everyone must eventually pay for their actions whether good or bad. I put this behind me and moved forward to my retirement years.

A large group of my fellow employees attended the party and gave me many presents I revere to this day. The pocket watch I received is engraved: Best wishes from your friends in Purchasing, September 26, 1991. The Director's secretary baked a carrot cake for me and stated I make these cakes for highly respected people. It was nice seeing the number of people who had a genuine respect for me and my work history.

The date finally arrived for my retirement, September 30, 1991. I was ambivalent about leaving. I would miss most of the people in the Department however I wanted to forget the individuals that made my life miserable during my working years in the Purchasing Department.

I stayed in contact with many of my co-workers after retirement. I was given a Life Membership in the Electric Boat Management Association.

To reflect back on the past, I remember the hardships along the way. I enjoyed my job and the responsibilities that came with the day to day challenges.

I had many offers to work for other companies, including many of our suppliers. I declined because I did not want to relocate my family after a long military career. There were many things I remembered about my years with this company. In a Department the size of Purchasing, it was difficult for me to understand how a few individuals in middle management positions could carry out blatant discrimination without their supervision being aware of their actions.

I enjoyed my military career despite bumps in the road. I understood that when I joined the military, it was still segregated according to race. When I was in basic training, I was treated fairly and did not notice any discrimination. I appreciated the opportunities to enhance my education and views of the world. After I retired from the military, I was prepared to gain employment in a post military career and attend college.

Despite the fact I experienced discrimination during my military career I understood this as a dark period in the nation's history and accepted the reality of the time. I saw major changes coming to extract the full potential from all members of the military in order to make units more cohesive.

When I retired from the military and gained civilian employment, I thought most people would have gotten over the turbulent civil rights movement in the 1960s. I started my civilian employment on April 3, 1968. Many of my co-workers were still living in the repressive era of the early 1960s. I started to feel the sting of covert racism from the start of my employment from a few individuals. This activity was evident by the way I was being treated by a few of the Managers and Supervisors. I heard rumors that some individuals felt I was placed in the Purchasing Department because of affirmative action. Their assumptions were not accurate. I was hired because of my interview and knowledge.

Most of the people treated me fairly but a small group of employees resented the fact that an African-American was a Buyer in the Purchasing Department. A few years later, an African-American female was hired as a typist. I heard one individual make the statement, "we are being invaded".

I was administering the Minority Business and Small Business programs in addition to being a part time Buyer in the early 1970s when an African-American female was hired. I felt she was hired to take my place as a Buyer. She had a post graduate degree and they treated her as a Secretary or Clerk. After being frustrated for a few months she wrote a letter of resignation and left the company. I have a copy of the letter in my possession.

The Purchasing Department then hired an African-American male who graduated from Mississippi State University with a degree in Economics. He left the company after a short period of time because of the negative atmosphere. When young people see no future with a company, they leave and look for opportunities in other places.

The Management of our Department made a clever move. They had an African-American female transferred from the Inventory Control Department to the Purchasing Department and changed her job description to Buyer and then promoted her to the Purchasing Agent position. Her only buying experience was purchasing nuts, bolts and pipe fittings. The plan behind this move was if I brought up the issue of promotion again, the management could say we have an African-American female in a Purchasing Agent position. This was truly a device to generate tokenism and have people believe that the Department was committed to equal opportunity.

A few of these individuals I call rogue agents made comments about some of the female Buyers. In one instance when I was in the Valve Group, merit raises were being discussed by some Group Leaders and who would receive them. When one of the female Buyer's name was mentioned, I over heard the statement "she make enough money for a woman". If this was the mentality about women, I could imagine their thoughts about minorities.

When I retired on September 30, 1991, my pension was $843.00 per month or less than $10,000 per year. When I received my W-2 for the 1991 tax return, the number was $32,400. This was my largest compensation in my twenty three years and five months in the Purchasing Department. I had made very significant contributions over the years and it is documented. My compensation was $1700.00 per year over the minimum for my pay grade which was barely over an entry level salary. I received a life insurance policy of $1000.

On October 3, 1991 after I had been retired for a few days, I received a copy of a one sided investigator's report from the Human Resource Specialist at Electric Boat Division who worked for the Division's Compliance Office. The report was notarized and sent to the Regional Manager of the Commission on Human Rights and Opportunities. The report was based on information my last Supervisor and Manager gave to the Investigator. I was never asked a single question despite the fact the Investigator had a few weeks to get my side of the story before I retired.

If I had the opportunity to present my information, I could have showed documentation to refute the lies presented. The Investigator had no idea of the job descriptions I held in the Purchasing Department for twenty three years and five months. This is all documented information that people want to hide. The information in my personnel file was distorted however, I have records of my accomplishments, awards and accolades I have received from Electric Boat Division, the Corporate Office, US Navy, Small Business Administration and various organizations when I was the Small Business Administrator for the Company. I had represented the Electric Boat Division at a meeting in Washington, D.C. along with other representatives from General Dynamics Corp.

It was important for my Supervisor and Manger to remember and know, "if you are a liar, you must have a good memory". The sham investigation was analogous to a Prosecutor presenting his case and the Defendant was denied a defense and was judged guilty.

The Purchasing Department was a very large "elite" section of the company. I am sure over ninety percent of the people in this department know the truth about my performance. What is very amazing is the fact I will never believe that the top management in the Department were unaware of my performance in light of the fact that they presented me awards for outstanding performance. In 1989, I was awarded a certificate by the General Manager and Vice President of General Dynamics Corp. for $1,000,000 cost savings and was the only member of the raw material group to be honored, but according to my Supervisor, I ranked in the fourth percentile for performance. I was ranked relative to my performance at the bottom of the ladder from the date I made a complaint in 1974. If I had it done over again, I would not waver in my determination to voice my complaint. Some people define your reputation based upon ethnic bias. I define my character based upon innate qualities and work performance which is documented despite distortion of my personnel file.

A few individuals in the Purchasing Department were successful in driving a few professional minority personnel out of the Company in the 1970s. I was determined this would not happen to me because I had the resolve not to be intimidated by some biased people. It did not take me long to understand that some small people are placed in positions of responsibility to make large decisions relative to a person's work history.

The report submitted by the Electric Boat Division's Compliance Office was a cover up for what was going on in the Purchasing Department. I had to address each issue because of the distortions and lies. The Commission based their decision on the false statements given by the Human Resource Specialist.

CHAPTER 12

On August 30, 1992 I requested a reconsideration of the disposition of their finding. This request was based on the fabrications and distorting of facts given to the Commission by the respondent. Apparently this was the only defense that the respondent possessed. Appropriate documentation would detail the true facts of the case. The past history of events would validate this request.

I think it is important to address each issue given to the Commission by a representative of Electric Boat Division. Most of the information was incorrect and never challenged. The Human Resource Specialist stated, I was hired in 1968 as a Buyer and was promoted to the Administrator of the Minority Business and Small Business Programs in November 1974 and he voluntarily retired after not being given a raise in 1991. This was a complete fabrication. I was not promoted to administer these programs. It was a lateral transfer to a new job title I did not request. A program had to be put in place to comply with government contract regulations. I was the only African-American Buyer in the Purchasing Department therefore this job was shoved down my throat. I am sure my Manager remembers this incident on June 30, 1972. The respondent had the incorrect date that I was drafted into this job. I have a copy of the appointing letter with copies to the US Small Business Administration, the Naval Ships System Command, Supervisor of Shipbuilding, the General Dynamics Corporate Office and the Department of Defense (Pentagon). Despite this appointment, my title remained a Buyer. I asked how I was being evaluated at the time I was putting in place a new program for Electric Boat Division. I never received an answer. I received numerous accolades from the US Navy, General Dynamics Corporate office, the US Small Business Administration and private companies. I have the documented data. After numerous requests to the Director of Procurement by the US Navy Representative, my title was changed to Minority and Small Business Administrator on November 24, 1974 with no change in compensation despite my name being on the Department's Management Organization Chart. I held the job titles of Buyer, Minority Business Enterprise Administrator and Small Business Administrator at the same time and was only evaluated as a part time Buyer. On June 6, 1976, I was not promoted but I received another lateral transfer to Senior Buyer with no change in compensation. On June 29, 1980, I was promoted to Buyer Specialist after years requesting consideration despite the fact that I had been doing Buyer Specialist work for years. Despite all the responsible positions I held over the years, this $2900 per year raise in 1980 was the only promotional increase in 23 years and five months as a valued employee of the Purchasing Department. The biggest lie of all was I voluntarily retired after not being given a raise. The problem was my performance was distorted by my Supervisors over the years.

The Human Resource Specialist stated that assignments vary in complexity based on the technical difficulty and the overall volume of the work effort. "He was given less technical work". This is a joke. I am the only person in the Purchasing Department who had ever served on a nuclear submarine in the US Navy. Additionally I am the only person in the Valve Group including the Supervisor and Manager who had experience purchasing all major components used in the construction of submarines. Some of the Buyer Specialists in the Valve Group had one account while I had nineteen accounts. This disparity was never mentioned.

I was the only person in the Valve Group who had completed company sponsored courses in the Negotiation of Contracts, Contract Pricing Techniques, Cost/Price Analysis and the Truth in Negotiation Laws as set by the federal Government, with the exception of my Supervisor. This Supervisor was in my classes in the early 1970s and 1980s.

When I was transferred to the Valve Group on August 21, 1989, I was informed by my Supervisor at the time that I would be assigned accounts that had major problems for my resolution.

I was the only Buyer in the Purchasing Department that had experience in all buying groups in addition to my technical knowledge gained as the result of years of hands on experience serving on submarines during my military career. I would like to have explained to me how individuals who never spent one day on an operating submarine is more technically qualified on valves than my years as a Chief Petty Officer on submarines. Why was I given other Buyer's problems to resolve? I inherited one order that had six previous buyers, a Purchasing Agent, Buyer Specialist, and four Buyers.

The Crosby Valve and Gage account was previously administered by a Buyer Specialist and was in a terrible condition. This was a Buyer Specialist whose performance was ranked superior. This account was transferred to me for the resolution of problems that had lingered for four years. I was given low volume new work because my major assignment was to clear up problems on many accounts that had lingered for considerable periods of time due to the lack of contract administration by other Buyers. I should have known at the time that this maneuver was a set up to discredit me.

When technical complexity was assigned, why was I given nineteen accounts of which five had major problems that had been swept under the rug and ignored due to the lack of contract administration. I cannot understand why the Supervisor and Manager were not aware of these problems over the years. I had resolved the problems with two of the accounts and was in the process of resolving the others when I was penalized for work that should have been resolved years ago. The reason the Supervisor re-assigned these accounts was because of major problems. He knew I had the experience and technical capability to resolve the problems. However subversive acts against me were also an objective. The problems with these accounts took years to evolve and it is unrealistic to expect them to be resolved overnight.

Not one individual in the Purchasing Department can deny my experience, knowledge and capability in performing my assignments and assisting in the training of other Buyers. Why did the Supervisor re-assign problem accounts and orders from five or six Buyers to one individual? I would like to hear the Supervisor answer that question.

I previously documented the problem with the Automatic Switch Co. order. This was really an insult to me that I always will remember.

In the Human Resource Specialist's report to the Commission, the Supervisor stated my performance was deficient on a Crosby Valve and Gage Co. purchase order due to an engineering problem that had to be resolved by Electric Boat Division and Crosby's Engineering Departments. Why was this engineering problem mine to resolve? I was hired to purchase valves not to design them. The Supervisor informed the Investigator that I should have been able to resolve these engineering issues. I am sure the Investigator must have known this was a fabrication. I had detailed this particular purchase order earlier when the supplier of the bearing material to the valve manufacturer upgraded the material and drawings had to be changed and upgraded by the Engineering Departments at Electric Boat Division and Crosby Valve and Gage Co. Why did my Supervisor make these Engineering changes my responsibility? This was another way to discredit me in my job performance which had nothing to do with my duties as a Buyer.

The next issue in the report was my evaluation. It was revised due to lies and fabrications. I refused to sign the second evaluation because many of the lies were still a part of the evaluation particularly the Automatic Switch Co. and Crosby Valve and Gage Co. purchase orders which were detailed earlier.

In 1990, I was ranked thirty-one out of thirty-seven Buyer Specialists in the Purchasing Department. I was the third senior Buyer Specialist and had more overall experience than any Buyer Specialist in the Department and many of the Supervisors and Managers.

The report stated that in 1974, I filed a complaint of discrimination on the same issue that he was ranked near the bottom of his group and denied income because of his race and color. It is ridiculous that reports are written with no true facts to back up the information. In 1974 when I filed the complaint, I had three job titles, The Small Business Administrator and Minority Business Administrator for Electric Boat Division and a part time Buyer. How could I be evaluated against others for the first two job titles when no one else in the Company had these job titles? I stated earlier that I was never evaluated by anyone in our Department relative to my performance administering these government programs. My only evaluation was as a part time Buyer between 1972 and 1976. The only positive feedback during that period was from the US Small Business Administration, US Navy, Corporate Office, principles from Business and Industry and many of our suppliers. I was resented by some members of the Department management and some Buyers for doing my job in implementing the Minority Business Program. I did not ask for this job but was drafted to start the Program. The retaliation against me started after I filed the complaint in 1974 and lasted until I retired in 1991.

The next issue was concerning my suggestion relative to a change in the chemical composition for major components in the submarine reactor compartment. I tried to have the suggestion evaluated for years however I received resistance from my Supervisor at the time and some of our Department management. I had it thoroughly evaluated by Material Engineering and Nuclear Engineering Departments in order to move it forward. It was stated in the report that an Engineer was a co-author. That was a complete fabrication. This was my suggestion and my suggestion alone. This was another method to discredit me in my performance. I was given a monetary award for this suggestion which was shared by an Engineer who agreed with my reasoning. I received this award one month prior to the worst evaluation of my career at Electric Boat Division.

The next statement in the report, I was the only person who worked in the commodity group and administered to the Minority and Small Business Programs. I don't understand what this statement means, it is irrational and incoherent.

The company Investigator compared me to two Buyer Specialists in the Valve Group. Both of these Buyers were rated Superior in performance. One of them had one account, while I had nineteen accounts. The other Buyer who was rated Superior was the one from whom I inherited many problems. These problems had lingered for four years prior to my transfer into the Valve Group. The particular account was Crosby Valve and Gage Co.

In another statement, the Investigator stated that prior to 1988 in ongoing quarterly awards I along with other Buyer Specialists received an award from the Company recognizing "Outstanding Minority Business Enterprises". This event never happened. I don't know where this fabrication came from. In 1991, I was ranked thirty four out of thirty four. The year of 1974 was a critical year in my career at Electric Boat Division. The Investigator found no evidence of discrimination despite the evidence." The investigation did not reveal any statistical evidence that is reliable or relevant to the material issues raised in the complaint". I have documented evidence of my work history from my date of hire until the date of my retirement. I am happy today that I made that complaint in 1974 because I was justified in taking that action. I still wonder how investigations are conducted when the Complainant is not asked questions only the Respondent who automatically denies all allegations and only one side of the dispute is heard. I will always say that my record of accomplishments speaks for itself, no one can erase it.

Approximately two weeks after the disposition of my complaint, I requested a re-consideration of the disposition of the finding. The request was based upon the fabrications and distortions of facts given by the respondent. Apparently, this was the only defense the Company investigator possessed. Appropriate documentation would detail the truth of the case. The past history of events would validate the request.

My letter addressed each issue and finding made by the Commission's Investigator dated August 18, 1992. Many of the events detailed by the

Investigator were incorrect including dates, in fact, some of the events never happened and it can easily be proven. In one instance, it was stated that some work is distributed among Buyers. It was not mentioned that purchase orders from six different Buyers with critical problems were transferred to me for resolution. I kept very good records including the name of each Buyer whose problems I inherited. I am sure these records cannot be destroyed.

My request for re-consideration was to have the opportunity to present my information which is well documented and cannot be refuted.

It would not be possible for members of the Purchasing Department to destroy all evidence relative to records in other Departments at Electric Boat Division. Apparently the Investigator never questioned the statements given by the biased few members of our Department.

In my request for re-consideration, I gave the names of people in other Departments who could clear up many of the false statements made by my Supervisor. I didn't think this was too much to ask for in order that many issues could be clarified.

One of the worst fabrications was I received a promotion when I was appointed to the positions of Small Business Administrator and the Minority Business Administrator for Electric Boat Division. There was one Administrator for these two programs at each Division of General Dynamics Corp. on a national level.

I received copies of the Department Organization Chart on a regular basis from the Division's Manager of Management Services. It stated "attached for your information, is a copy of Organization Chart No. 15.0. You will be provided with a copy of each future organization chart on which your name appears. A file of these can serve as a personal record of the management positions you have held at Electric Boat Division". These are records in place at the Company in addition to my personal records. I held these positions for four years prior to going back to buying materials for submarine construction.

On June 29, 1980, I was promoted to Buyer Specialist after years requesting consideration despite the fact that I had been doing Buyer Specialist work for years.

Despite all the responsible positions I held over the years, this $2900.00 per year raise in 1980 was the only promotional increase in twenty three years and five months as a valued employee of the Purchasing Department.

CHAPTER 13

I received notification in September of 1992 that my request for re-consideration was rejected. The letter stated that my case #9240133 was dismissed for the following reason. "You filed a timely request for re-consideration. Your request has been carefully reviewed by the staff who recommended it be rejected. I have accepted the recommendation and denied your request. This denial of re-consideration is the Commission's final decision on your complaint. Denial may be appealed by filing a petition in the Connecticut Superior Court for the judicial district where the discriminatory practice is alleged to have occurred or in the judicial district where you reside or transact business within forty five days after mailing of this letter". After retiring with a pension of $10,116.00 per year, I could not afford to retain an Attorney to pursue justice. In the scriptures, God stated that I will supply all your needs. I always will believe this and I have seen this come to past for the entire period of my life.

I decided to close the book on a dark era of my life. The truth was never brought to light however wicked acts perpetrated by wicked people will be answered by a higher Being.

We are not yet a color blind society. This is not only unfair but unnecessary. Many people overlook continued documented discrimination in employment and economic opportunities which are vital areas of our lives.

I have always believed that racism is not an individual act but an institution in our society. Individuals that practice racism are aware of the fabric of our society as it relates to different institutions.

I am a firm believer in the Scriptures. Luke 6:38 states, the measure you give will be the measure you get back.

If I had been assigned to any Department other than Purchasing, my career would have probably ended on a positive note. Most people are good, decent and value your work ethic and performance, not the color of your skin.

In the 1960s and 1970s, some people were still denying equal opportunity for some citizens including military veterans. When I started working in the Purchasing Department, I had spent one half of my life as a member of the United States Armed Forces. Most of the people in this Department had never served in the military.

On June,14,1992, my son Thomas Robert Mosley after his service in the US Marine Corp married Miss Starlit Stoher and resided in Lincoln, Ne.

In the latter part of 1992, our friend Mrs. Pearl Blanks was a resident in an assisted living facility and wanted to purchase a small trailer and live with my family. She stayed at the facility for another year until February 1, 1993. I helped her purchase a small trailer and she had it moved to the rear of our house.

This arrangement lasted approximately ten months until she was starting to suffer from dementia. Her doctor informed us she needed to be in a skilled nursing facility. She was transferred to a local convalescent home in the fall of 1993. We visited Pearl approximately twice a week. I didn't want her to feel that she was abandoned. We had basically taken care of her since June of 1981.

I had made plans to spend more time with my family including grandchildren after retirement. In January of 1993, my wife and I started to plan to attend some of the upcoming college commencements exercises. We had eight relatives graduating from college. Six of the eight were three sets of twins. One set of the twins (nephew and niece,(Stacey and Tracy) attended different Universities, one at Iowa State University in Ames Ia., and the other one at Georgetown University in Washington, D.C., One set of twins (our sons, Joseph and John) attended Tuskegee University in Alabama. One set of twins (our nieces, Kyra and Kirsten) attended Prairie View University in Texas. Our niece Emmy attended Georgetown University in Washington, D.C. and our nephew, Karl attended Harvard University in Cambridge, Ma. We were unable to attend all of the graduations however we were fortunate to attend the commencements at Tuskegee, Georgetown and Harvard Universities. It was rewarding to see these young people furthering their education. By completing their degree requirements, they invested in their future for further growth.

The latter part of 1993 and early 1994, we started traveling to different areas of the country to visit relatives. These trips took us too many parts of the country. Some of these trips were for the purpose of attending football games in the Arena Football League which we had been attending since 1990. Our son Merv played for the Albany Firebirds and the Connecticut Coyotes.

On March 9, 1995 we were notified of the tragic death of my stepson John. This was a very difficult time. We were comforted by the scripture John 3:16-"For God so loved the world that he gave his only begotten Son that whosoever believeth in him should not perish but have everlasting life". John was buried March 16, 1995.

Our daughter Patricia was married May 20, 1995 in Waterford, Ct. to Mr. Joseph Bove and resided in Uncasville, Ct. Her new residence was approximately five miles from our residence. One month later on June 22, 1995 my first grandchild Miesha Edwards graduated from high school in Yonkers, NY. She decided to further her education at a University in Virginia. In August we traveled to Richmond, Va. to help her get enrolled at Virginia Union University.

While we were in Virginia, I had the opportunity to visit with some of my relatives that lived in the state. My Aunt Ruth Taylor Pearson was in a Nursing Home. She was turning eighty two years old in November and was doing well. She was born on November 14, 1912 in North Carolina. One of her daughters Merdice Pearson Parham who lived in Richmond was the Financial Aid Officer at Virginia Commonwealth University. Aunt Ruth talked about her early years in North Carolina and when the family moved to Virginia in 1922. She was ten years old at the time and my mother was fourteen.

She talked about the difficult time adjusting after Uncle Luther died the prior year on October 4, 1994. The last time I saw Luther Pearson was in June of 1973. He developed Diabetes and suffered from the complications including leg amputations prior to his death. He lived to be eighty two years old. He was born May 12, 1912 in Virginia.

During the summer, I worked around the house doing handyman projects. I love landscaping and maintenance projects which keeps me busy most of the time. I generally have a small vegetable garden in the back of the house that produces items such as tomatoes, squash, cucumbers, collard greens and peppers. In the fall, I am very busy raking and removing leaves that fall from the large oak trees surrounding our property.

The prior year, 1994, I enrolled in a tax preparation class at H&R Block. After completing the course, I decided to do seasonal tax preparation for H&R Block in order to stay busy during a certain segment of the winter months.

I prepared various tax returns for clients of H&R Block. Some returns were simple and straight forward while others were more complex. It was necessary to conduct an interview with each client prior to starting the return. The purpose of the interview was to ascertain that the client had all necessary documentations to insure that the tax return would be done properly. In case of an audit by the Internal Revenue Service, I would be available to accompany the client to answer any questions.

I learned to complete most individual tax returns and performed various studies to find answers to tax questions primarily through the Internal Revenue Code. When you complete a tax return for a client who owns a business with many assets to depreciate, you must be aware of the proper method of depreciation. The tax code made a very important change in 1986 relative to depreciation. From 1981-1986, the method used was an accelerated cost recovery system (ACRS). Prior to 1981, a class life asset depreciation range system (CLADR) was used. The word depreciation is used in two ways in the tax system. First it means the general process of deducting the basis of an asset over a number of years and thereby use the (CLADR) system. After 1981, (ACRS) was used. In 1986 the Congress passed a tax reform act which modified the (ACRS) method of depreciation. This act affected most businesses including home businesses.

With these changes, it was necessary to remember that when Congress makes a change to the tax code concerning depreciation, the defining factor is when the asset was first placed into service in the business. If a building was placed in service in 1978, and was being depreciated by the straight line method of declining balance, it will still use the (CLADR) system.

Starting in 1987, the modified accelerated cost recovery system was used (MACRS). The major difference between (ACRS) and (MACRS) is the number of recovery years in depreciating an asset.

I learned to calculate short and long term capital gains for individuals who sold stock, bonds, mutual funds during the tax year. The tax laws change frequently on taxes relative to capital gains and deductions for capital losses, the key point is the basis of the asset.

I frequently advised clients on methods to decrease their tax liability by being prudent in their tax planning. I advised many people to pay estimated taxes if their income is such that their tax liability to the government exceeds $1000. If they receive a refund in excess of $1000, they gave the US Treasury an interest free loan. I am sure the Government would not give the average citizen an interest free loan.

I worked part time preparing taxes for a period of time and then decided to do only selective returns for my children and grandchildren.

My wife Gloria Mosley and I started to make plans for our trip next year. Gloria's family in Tuskegee, Alabama scheduled a reunion every two years in order to keep the family in touch with each other. The reunion was scheduled from July 1, 1996 to July 5, 1996. We also planned to visit my relatives in Virginia to continue a project I was working on. I had been working on a genealogy project for many years and decided this trip would give me the opportunity to talk to some of my relatives. We would stay a few days prior to our return home to Connecticut.

I had contacted my cousin, Sallie Louise Taylor-Person in Lawrenceville, Va. in February about our trip to the South this summer and would be staying a few days in Virginia gathering information for my project.

Our son Merv was married to Miss Joyce Marie Speliades in March of 1996. He lived in Connecticut therefore we did not have to travel far to attend his wedding. We were going to have a busy itinerary for the remainder of the summer so we started to plan our trips to Alabama and Virginia.

On April 21, 1996 my cousin Sallie Louise sent pictures of her family including children and grandchildren. Additionally names of some people who knew some of my father's relatives. I knew this would be a difficult task because my father was an orphan. His father died when he was two years old and his mother died when he was six years old. His uncle Benjamin raised him and took care of Miss Emoline the mother and grandmother.

Gloria and I attended the family reunion during the first week of July and had a good time visiting with the Chisholm family. Family members had traveled from as far away as California to attend the reunion.

We left Alabama on July 8, 1996 and headed north toward Virginia. We had anticipated staying a few days while I was gathering information for my genealogy project. We visited with the Taylor, Pearson and Ingram families on my maternal side and the Palmer family on my paternal side. I was able to obtain some valuable information to add to my thirty years of research.

My father had two living relatives in the area at the time, Mary Mosley and Clarence Leonard Palmer, a cousin on his maternal and paternal side. I had an in-depth discussion with Mr. Palmer that lasted a few hours. I was unable to contact Mary Mosley. I was told that she never married. My cousin Linwood Travis Taylor Jr. informed me she was about eighty six years old at this time.

When we left Virginia, we planned to return the next year to further my research. This was important because of the medical history of family members. I have always been interested in molecular biology and genetics. I had been researching and trying to obtain as much history as possible about my lineage. This task had been occupying some of my time for over thirty years.

Through various means such as microfilm and other information from the Bureau of Census etc., I have traced my ancestors back to Northampton County, North Carolina and Brunswick County, Virginia. My great-great grandfather on my maternal side was born on a farm in Northampton County, North Carolina in 1810. My great-great grandmother Emoline Mosley on my paternal side was born in Brunswick County, Virginia in 1830. What makes this research significant is the probability of its impact on our medical history.

Very few people my age can say they met their father's grandmother. I was ten years old at the time and she died about two months later at the age of one hundred and ten years in 1940. One of the most amazing things about Miss Emoline as she was called was the fact that she had been blind for seventy years, probably from glaucoma, macular degeneration or other ocular diseases that were not fully understood at that particular time in our history. My father died in 1978 from complications of diabetes. He also had glaucoma. My father and mother had thirteen children and many of us are afflicted with diabetes. I am curious if genetics plays a part in our family's medical history. This fact re-kindled my interest in molecular biology and genetics and future study of my lineage.

Some of my relatives were found in the 1870 census, which was five years after the Civil War. My great-great grandfather Nick Taylor was sixty years of age at the time and my great-grandfather James Nicholas Taylor Sr. was twenty seven years of age. My maternal grandfather James Nicholas Taylor Jr. was born August 5, 1870 and died September 27, 1958. My maternal grandmother Fannie Jackson Taylor was born January 6, 1884 and died July 3, 1958.

My maternal grandparents had thirteen children and my mother had thirteen children. On my paternal side, I was able to go back to 1830. My maternal uncle Eugene Taylor told us stories of his great grandmother Sally Jackson who was a slave and was forced to wash the master's feet every night.

My mother died in 1948 at a young age. I had been in the military for about six months at the time. My father was left with ten children at home. The oldest was a son who was seventeen, two other sons fifteen and thirteen and seven daughters, the oldest one was twelve. My father with the help of my oldest sister and a housekeeper took care of his family until he re-married in 1957. I have continued over the years looking for information about my family tree. In some cases, it becomes very difficult because of the history of slavery. In many cases, there were only slave schedules whereby a slave holder counted only the number of males and females that he owned. It was intriguing to find out the state of North Carolina had less slave holders than any other of the southern states. In that state in the early 1800s, many of the African-Americans were allowed to raise families and they appeared in the US Census by name, sex and occupation in addition to their monetary value.

Most were listed as farm laborers or housekeepers. There was little separation of slave families during this period in North Carolina. The initial tracing started with word of mouth of the elders, obituaries and then the US Census that dated back to the first census in 1790.

I will continue to research my family roots. It is very interesting relative to medical history and genetic markers that identify many chronic diseases. These advances have been made possible due to the mapping of the human genome. My interest in family medical history will eventually lead me to the study of genetics and African-American history.

My oldest sister Alma Mosley Kitchings died on August 2, 1996 of congestive heart failure. Her daughter Bernita Kitchings and grandson Anthony Kitchings were there from Phoenix, Az. at her side when she passed away.

The latter part of the year was pretty uneventful with the exception of my daughter Patricia giving birth to a son on September 28, 1996. Patricia and Joseph named their son Jared Taylor Bove. Another event that happened after we returned from Alabama and Virginia, our friend Pearl Blanks who was in a Nursing Home received a birthday card from President Bill Clinton and the First Lady Hillary Rodham Clinton on her ninety—fifth birthday.

Gloria Mosley and I were planning to take a Carnival cruise in the near future. We had never taken an ocean cruise and this would be a nice vacation to get away and relax. On June 12, 1997, our son Merv and his wife Joyce were blessed with their first child, a son and named him Austin

Lane Mosley. It is always a happy experience when your first child is born. I can reflect on my becoming a father for the first time in 1955.

During this period of time, our friend Mrs. Pearl Blanks was in a Nursing Home and we visited her a few times each week. We had made plans to visit her next month on July 8, 1997 on her ninety sixth's birthday. She always looked forward to our visits. I told her in a joking manner that when she reached one hundred years of age, I would bring her a cake with one candle. The nursing staff at the facility informed us Pearl's dementia was increasing. We continued to visit her on a regular basis. It was convenient because the facility was approximately one mile away.

In October 1997, I was asked to join an organization committed to protecting military and veteran benefits. A chapter of the National Association for Uniformed Services was established in Groton, Connecticut. I was appointed as a Chapter Officer (Vice President for Legislation).

The purpose of the Association: To protect and enhance the earned benefits of uniformed service-members, retirees, veterans and their families and survivors, while maintaining a strong national defense, and to foster esprit de corps among uniformed services personnel and veterans of the United States, through nonpartisan advocacy on Capitol Hill and with other government officials. This organization is the service-member's voice in government and includes all members of the Armed Forces, active and retired.

We have Registered Federal Lobbyists in Washington, D.C. who meet regularly with Congressional leaders and occasionally with members of the Administration on bills before Congress that affect service-members, retirees and veterans.

It is also important to note which House member and Senator sponsor a bill and the co-sponsors for any potential legislation affecting the military or veterans.

The following year 1998, we started to make serious plans for a Carnival Cruise in the fall of 1999. In the meantime, Gloria's sister Helen who lived in Alabama invited us to attend the graduation of her son Todd from Florida A&M University in Tallahassee, Fl. in December. We accepted the invitation and made plans to attend the commencement exercises. The graduation was in the first week of December. We had planned to stay a few extra days before we returned to Connecticut. We received a telephone call on December 10, 1998 informing us that Pearl had died at 6:40 AM December 9, 1998. The Medical Examiner listed the cause of death as

Alzheimer's disease due to age. We left the next day for our return trip to Connecticut to make arrangements for her funeral.

My wife Gloria purchased clothing and flowers for the burial and we arranged with the Funeral Director to have a local Minister conduct a brief service and eulogy in the funeral home prior to internment.

The Minister had never met Mrs. Pearl Blanks and therefore asked me for any information I had about her in the seventeen years we were friends. Over the years, I had long in-depth conversations with her about her history. At the time of her death, she had no living relatives. Her parents Frank and Emma Lipsey and her sister Blanche were deceased. Pearl never had children of her own.

Pearl's first marriage ended with the death of her spouse Henry Brown. She later married Mr. Frederick Blanks on July 10, 1936 in Washington, D.C. They both worked most of their adult lives as domestics, except for a brief stint in the 1930s working at the Bureau of Engraving in Washington, D.C. Her work history as a domestic was very extensive, after leaving her parents as a young woman she worked for the Honeywell family and later worked for President Franklin D. Roosevelt at the summer White House in Warm Springs, Ga. Pearl and Frederick's final work as domestics was in Stamford, Ct. before they moved to New London, Ct. for reasons unknown in 1975. I spent about twenty minutes informing the Minister about the history of this amazing woman. Pearl was buried in Cedar Grove Cemetery in New London, Ct. on December 16, 1998. Each spring I place flowers on Pearl's grave along with my deceased late wife and son who are also buried in this cemetery.

The following day, I was contacted by the local newspaper who wanted the story of this woman's life born at the dawn of the twentieth century in the Deep South. Pearl was born in Statesboro, Ga. and talked to me about some of the horrors experienced by her parents when she was a little girl. Pearl didn't have much to say about politics or history, but what she witnessed and recounted told the story. When she was six years old and her sister Blanche was four, her mother took them to a carnival in Statesboro, Ga. A small group of young men approached them and knocked her mother to the ground for "standing in their spot". She never forgot that incident despite over a half century had elapsed.

After the story of Pearl's life was published in the local newspaper along with a picture of her, me and two of my granddaughters, I was contacted by a company in Tampa, Fl. who was interested in placing our local newspaper article and picture on a large plaque in memory of Pearl. I accepted the offer. I have the plaque on the wall in my home. Pearl was a part of my family for seventeen years. We unofficially adopted her in 1981 after her husband Frederick died.

We were hoping the following year of 1999 would be a better time period. Our grand-daughter Felicia would be graduating from high school and was looking forward to attending college.

Felicia graduated from high school and chose to attend Temple University in Philadelphia, Pa. In the latter part of August, we loaded our Van with her supplies and equipment and drove to Pennsylvania in order to register and enroll her in school.

When we returned to Connecticut, Gloria and I started to make plans for our Carnival cruise to the Eastern Caribbean. The cruise would start on November 21, 1999 and end on November 28, 1999. We would visit Nassau, Bahamas and our next ports of call would be San Juan, Puerto Rico, St. Thomas (US Virgin Islands) and then back to Miami, Fl. Our initial itinerary also called for a visit to St. Croix however, Hurricane "Lenny" hit the island on November 18th and caused extensive damage to the docking facilities and as a result of this event we were not able to visit the island.

We enjoyed our cruise and were able to relax and enjoy our vacation. This was our first cruise and I was sure we would take another one in the future. When we returned to Connecticut, the weather was very cold and we had to adjust from a week of mild and balmy weather to the weather of the Northeastern part of the country. We started to make arrangements for the Christmas holidays and the New Year, which was rapidly approaching.

Our daughter Patricia who was living nearby informed us their family was moving to Kansas in the near future. Her husband Joseph accepted a job in a suburb of Kansas City, Kansas. Patricia's brother Thomas and his wife Starlit lived in Lincoln, Ne. therefore, she could visit Thomas and his wife on occasions. Gloria Mosley and I decided we would visit our children in the Midwest when we had the opportunity.

We made a few trips to Philadelphia to visit with our granddaughter who was in school at Temple University. We visited many historic sites in the area. I was familiar with the city because one of my first duty stations in the US Navy was at the Naval Hospital in the southern part of the city.

In October of 1999 my stepdaughter Linda announced her engagement to Foster L. Ware III, a classmate from Tuskegee University. They planned the wedding for August of the following year.

Prior to the approach of the new century, there were concerns about potential computer problems e.g., the year 2000 could be interpreted as the year 1900. The New Year was ushered in with no problems. We were looking forward to Linda's wedding. August finally arrived and we went to Tuskegee, Al. for the wedding. The ceremony was a beautiful occasion held at the Tuskegee University Chapel.

On August 17, 2000, our son Merv and his wife Joyce became the proud parents of a daughter. They named her Alana Kalan Mosley.

The year 2001 would be a period in American History that few people would ever forget. In the early morning when people were commuting to work in New York, the World Trade Center in lower Manhattan was attacked by high-jacked planes from a Northeastern Airport. I was very concerned because my daughter worked in the financial district of lower Manhattan. By the grace of God, she was not in the area.

The very next day, Dorothy Irene Mosley (Stepmother) died from Acute Myelogenous Leukemia. One of my stepbrothers, Kevin Mosley who was a Pennsylvania State Policeman who lived in the Pittsburgh area was alerted the day before his mother died about the attack on the World Trade Center and United Airlines Flight 93 crashing in a field in Stonycreek Township near Shanksville, Pennsylvania in Somerset County. This area was about eighty miles southeast of Pittsburgh, and one hundred fifty miles northwest of Washington, D.C.

Of the four aircraft hijacked on September 11, 2001, the plane that went down in Pennsylvania was the only one that failed to reach its intended target. My Stepmother was buried in the Homestead Cemetery on September 17, 2001 and a group of Pennsylvania State Policemen attended her funeral out of respect for her son. My other step-brother Carl Mosley lived in the area.

In June of 2002, Gloria Mosley retired from the JC Penney Co. after seventeen years with the Company. We decided this would be a good time to make the trip to Kansas and Nebraska. The following month of July we decided to make our trip to the Midwest. We were both retired at this point and could enjoy our stay with our children and their families.

We arrived in Shawnee, Kansas and stayed a few days with our daughter and her family before driving to Lincoln, Nebraska to visit our son and his family. We had a very nice visit with our children and decided to stop in Gary, Indiana to visit with my brother-in law and his family on our return back to Connecticut.

This turned out to be a year we accomplished goals of visiting family members. We returned to Connecticut in late July and were happy to be home.

In August, my brother William Roger who lived in New York decided to visit us with his daughter Emmy, her husband and their two children. My brother was very proud of his two grandchildren. I know how he felt because at this time, I had six grandchildren.

On September 19, 2002 I was contacted by Mr. Glenn Knoblock who was writing a book about African-Americans serving aboard submarines. I was interviewed because I was a pioneer, so to speak in the "new" Navy after World War II. The military was de-segregated after I had been in the US Navy for two months. Later, I signed a release for the author to use my personal information. I was informed the book would be publishes in a couple of years.

In October of 2002, Linda and Foster became the proud parents of their first child. They named him Foster L. Ware IV.

After Christmas, we were invited to a party at my brother's home in New York. While at my brother's house, we were notified on December 29, 2002 that my older brother Mervin McKinley Mosley Jr. had just died in Pittsburgh of Adult Non-Hodgkin's Lymphoma. I always admired my older brother for his accomplishments. From an early age, his superior mental abilities were recognized. He excelled in school and athletics and showed a special talent and interest in the sciences. We were both stationed together in the US Navy. After leaving the military he attended Duquesne University. He excelled and graduated with honors in physics and electrical engineering. He did further studies at Columbia University and the Massachusetts Institute of Technology.

Mervin Jr. was a very spiritual individual blessed with profound wisdom, a deep understanding of the Scriptures and love for God. He positively influenced the lives of his brothers and sisters. As a role model, he taught us to strive for the best, work hard, stick together, think, show compassion for others, share, look out for one another and be truthful. I will always remember his leadership and example he set for his siblings. He was buried on January 3, 2003 in Jefferson Memorial Park next to his father Mervin McKinley Mosley Sr.

I will never forget what Mervin Jr. told me when I retired from the US Navy in 1968. He asked if I still wanted to attend medical school. I felt in this period of my life, I owed my time to my family and I would be over fifty years old when I complete a residency program and start to practice medicine. His response to me was, "how old would you be if you did not pursue your dream".

In December 2003, my sister Dr. Yvonne Johnson completed a Mosley Family Photo Journal (Three Generations-Volume I). This journal was distributed to her siblings as a memorial to our parents. My love of history helped me in the research over the years that assisted her in the compilation of this project. It was regrettable that Mervin Jr., our oldest living sibling died before the project was completed.

Yvonne stated in her introduction, "It is anticipated that this journal may serve to introduce our children to their many cousins and relatives and perhaps set the stage for them to organize a family reunion. Currently, we live in different parts of the country although our roots are in and around Pittsburgh, Pa." I felt this undertaking would make our family more cohesive and we could continue the Mosley family tradition.

In 2004, I decided to enroll in college again for personal enrichment. My plan was to take a few courses and gradually progress into a degree program. I wanted to major in Biology with a minor in Sociology. I decided to take my first course in Microbiology because I had taken the subject years ago when I attended Clinical Laboratory and Blood Bank School when I was in the military. I was an instructor in Microbiology later in my military career as the Supervisor of the Clinical Laboratory at a US Naval Hospital.

My first day of class was January 27, 2004. I was not shocked being the oldest person in the class. This was the first time in a college classroom since I graduated from Mitchell College in 1976. I finished the spring semester and decided to take a course in Ecology during the summer.

One of the Professors asked me if I was interested in the Fast Track Program. The School of Continuing Education allows certain students to earn a Bachelor of General Studies degree. This program offered by the school helps adult students earn credits for college level learning gained through work, volunteerism and other experiences. The Professor noted she was impressed with my military and civilian careers.

I decided to enroll in the Fast Track Program to gain credit for my lifelong experiences. The applicants met on a regular basis with the Seminar Instructor along with the regular courses of instruction you were pursuing in your degree program. The Instructor stated the students had to put together a portfolio. It is one of several "nontraditional programs" through which adults can earn college credit toward a degree. You must be able to describe your experience and identify the college level knowledge, skills and understanding you have acquired, and provide documentation of your learning from the experiences.

I understood learning comes from experiences of life. There is a theoretical and practical part of this equation. Prior to entering the class, I did extensive research on Bloom's Taxonomy of Educational Objectives. I studied the six categories in the cognitive domain. These included knowledge, comprehension, application, analysis, synthesis and evaluation. This taxonomy was a way for students, such as me to construct a mental model of college level learning against which to measure and evaluate their knowledge.

Research indicates that successful performance in many fields is based on knowing facts and procedures (factual or domain knowledge) and also on knowing strategies and skills (procedural knowledge) for applying that knowledge in real-life situations (Chi, Glaser& Farr, 1988). These research results also indicate that a significant portion of procedural knowledge may be implicit, that is, embedded in the context or routine in which it is learned, and not always available for conscious examination.

Factual subject matter knowledge alone often fails to provide adequate information about how actually to go about solving problems or putting knowledge of the domain to work. Even students who are academically successful may grasp factual knowledge but find that application eludes them (Sternberg, Okagaki, & Jackson, 1990): their knowledge doesn't go beyond the level of comprehension.

Research in the field of tacit knowledge indicates that the dissociation of task performance and verbal knowledge in the early and intermediate stages of expertise development may make verbalization of domain knowledge difficult for even relatively experienced students (Squire & Frambach, 1987). In addition, for some experienced adults, knowledge that was initially explicit has become automatized through years of routine use. The problem is therefore twofold: students have to recognize and describe what it is that they know that is college-level knowledge, and also be able to separate the factual from the theoretical parts in order to demonstrate satisfactorily both the range and depth of their knowledge.

Too often, Bloom's Taxonomy is seen as little more than a handy reference list of verbs that can be used to infuse action, color and life into an otherwise dull biographical narrative. I used the Taxonomy to produce a map or structure to organize my knowledge. One technique that I have found successful is to produce a written description of an experience from which I had gained significant knowledge. One experience I had in the US Navy aboard a nuclear submarine was when we had a leak in the Primary

System. I had the responsibility to advise the Commanding Officer about the potential future problems in the Reactor Compartment of the ship.

I had numerous experiences in my military and civilian careers that contributed to my college level learning. An experience can be a single event or an ongoing activity which may be dictated by your job. The task of working through several learning experiences makes an important impact on your life. The level of knowledge is grounded in my own experiences. When I look at the Taxonomy, I reflect on knowledge at Levels 1 through 3 which help to establish my factual knowledge of the domain, reflections at Level 4 through 6 enables me to put into words the theoretical principles contained in my knowledge.

By studying the six levels of educational objectives, I answered the questions to myself, why I qualify for college level credits based upon my portfolio. This Taxonomy helped me to organize what I know and have a tool to reflect an analysis that would have effects far beyond the construction of my portfolio. At this point, I started drafting my learning outcome statements and my focused essay. I was aware that verbs commonly used to express an individual's depth of understanding appear for each level of the Taxonomy. When I describe my learning, I would be certain to consider the full range of areas represented in the Taxonomy.

We attended workshops which include group sessions. These sessions are followed up by ongoing opportunities for individual consultations with the Instructor and informal small group meetings. A final follow-up group session with the Instructor is then scheduled. The workshop is designed to help students prepare a written Learning Portfolio that specifically details college level learning. The basic components of the Portfolio includes a resume, historical narrative and subject areas in which credit is being requested and presentation of learning you have acquired.

After I completed my portfolio, I had an interview with the Credit for Lifelong Evaluation Committee. The Committee members were full time faculty at the University. After the interview, they determined the number and types of credits to be awarded. I was awarded credits for History, Health/Physical Education, Chemistry, Physics, Biology, Business, Communications and Mathematics. I received a total of fifty one credits. With this project behind me, I started to concentrate more on the remaining subjects I needed to complete my degree program.

After my portfolio interview by the faculty members, one of the Professors who was my instructor for the Credit for Lifelong (CLL) seminar, advised me to write a book and use my portfolio as the cornerstone because my story must be told.

On October 7, 2004, I had another setback in my family life. My brother, William Roger Mosley died in New York from cancer. He was seventy three at the time. I recall that my mother always baked a cake for him because July 4th was his birthday.

Roger as we called him had served in the US Air Force as a radio operator during the Korean War. He was survived by a wife, daughter and step-daughter. With his death, I had lost three brothers who were military veterans. I still have one brother who is also a US Air Force veteran.

It was during this time period that Linda and Foster became the proud parents of twins, Lauren Ware and Logan Ware in March 2005.

On July 18, 2005, I received a letter from Mr. Glenn Knoblock who had interviewed me for a book he was writing about African-American Submarine Veterans. He was advising me the book had been published and was available for sale. In closing, he stated "thank you for your help in letting me tell your story, and for those who read the book, I hope you find my effort to tell the story of American's Black Submariners as worthy as the men whose stories are documented within its pages. This is a story that all Americans, young and old, Black and White, should be made aware of, so please pass the word on and let all your family, friends, acquaintances, and co-workers know about this book and the story it tells".

My granddaughter Miesha Edwards was married to Mr. Dario M. Lake in Yonkers, New York on 7/30/2005. I felt it was a milestone in my life to see a grandchild being united in holy matrimony. Miesha's husband Dario was from St. Marteen in the Caribbean. A second ceremony was performed on the island where many of his relatives met his new wife. Gloria and I were able to attend the second ceremony and had a nice vacation. Additionally, Miesha's mother Ellen Edwards and our granddaughter Felicia made the trip.

After returning to the states, *I started to prepare for the fall semester at the University. I enjoyed classes and the interaction with other students as I pursued my objective of graduation.*

In November, I was notified my sister Madge Mosley Maydwell was sick. She lived in San Antonio Tx. with her daughter Annette Fear and her family—husband Richard Fears and son Christopher Fears. We decided to make the trip to San Antonio.

My wife Gloria and I booked a flight and decided to stay for one week. We departed on December 2, 2005 and our return flight was on December 9,

2005. When we arrived in San Antonio, we met Annette's family for the first time. We had a nice visit for the week and toured some of the historical sites in the city. My sister Madge was in good spirits and enjoyed our visit. I anticipated a return to San Antonio in the next few years. I was impressed with the city and our stay at the Hill Country Resort in Canyon Lake, Tx.

I have a soft spot in my heart for San Antonio because of Lackland Air Force Base. My deceased son and my two brothers completed their basic training in this city.

The following year started with expectations of taking weekend vacations to local areas with my wife. I didn't want to spend all of my time either in the classroom or doing homework when I left the school.

I was notified I would be inducted into the Holland Club on June 10, 2006 based upon my career in the Submarine Service. The ceremony would be at the USN Submarine Base New London/Groton, Ct. There were forty four Submarine Veterans to be inducted after fifty or more years being qualified in Submarine Operations.

I was qualified on a diesel powered submarine, USS Volador (SS-490), a unit of the Submarine Force, US Pacific Fleet stationed in San Diego, Ca. in 1956. In later years, I became qualified aboard nuclear powered attack and missile submarines.

The Holland Club was established in May 1964. It was originally established to recognize those members who had been qualified in Submarines for fifty or more years and were the pioneers of the USN Submarine Service.

It was an honor to be inducted into this prestigious Club as a member of the US Submarine Veterans Inc. After the ceremony, all inducted members recited the USSVI Creed, "To perpetuate the memory of our shipmates who gave their lives in the pursuit of their duties while serving their country. That their dedication, deeds and supreme sacrifice be a constant source of motivation toward greater accomplishments. Pledge loyalty to the United States Government".

I was fortunate to have my loved ones attend the ceremony. My wife, children and grandchildren as well as two sisters from California were there.

On October 20, 2006, my granddaughter Miesha Edwards Lake gave birth to a girl and named her Dariana McKayla Lake. This event was a historical period in my life because I became a great grandfather at the age of seventy seven. I recall on July 7, 1977, I took Miesha to Pittsburgh, Pa. when she was one year old in order for my father to meet another great grandchild. The following year on July 26, 1978, my father died. I am proud that my father got to see my granddaughter.

Two months after the birth of my first great-grandchild, I was notified my sister in San Antonio, Tx. had died on December 6, 2006 at the age of sixty three. Madge had been sick with a chronic respiratory condition for a considerable period of time. Gloria and I were visiting with Madge and her family one year earlier to the day.

We contacted Annette and she asked us to send memorial tributes to the Porter Loring Mortuaries. Tributes were sent from many family members and friends. A memorial celebration of her life was to be conducted the following year in San Antonio. The scheduled date would be April 13, 2007 which would be the one hundredth anniversary of the birth of our father.

I was notified in the last week of January 2007 that a special African-American History Month event would take place at the Submarine Museum at the USN Submarine Base on February 9, 2007. This event would be a presentation by Mr. Glenn Knoblock to discuss his book "Black Submariners in the United States Navy, 1940-1975". Members profiled in the book were requested to be present.

"Despite the fact that Black men served valiantly in the Submarine force during World War II, and beyond into the age of nuclear submarines and continue to do so to this day, their accomplishments have gone largely un-noticed. It is now time to get them back onto the radar screen of history," declares Mr. Knoblock. Anticipated participants at the event would include many African-American veterans featured in the book. Mr. Knoblock would discuss his book during a lecture in the museum's theater. After the lecture, there was a book signing. The lecture was open to the public in order for people to gain an understanding of history. I was requested to sign many of the books that were sold.

After the book signing, I was talking to Rear Admiral Cecil D. Haney, an African-American who was the Commander of Submarine Group Two, who directs all of the Navy's fast attack submarines on the East Coast, when a representative from a local newspaper approached and wanted to interview me later for a newspaper article.

Rear Admiral Haney was the senior officer at the USN Submarine Base at the time. Significant progress had been made in the military over the years, relative to race relations. There have been seven African-Americans who had commanded nuclear submarines. Rear Admiral Haney was one of the seven. Before the age of nuclear power, there were no African-Americans who were submarine Commanding Officers.

During the month of March of 2007, I was interviewed by the local newspaper, pictures taken and the article was published on March 29, 2007.

Gloria and I started to make arrangements for our trip to San Antonio, Tx. for the memorial service for my sister Madge. We attended the memorial celebration with a few family members. I felt blessed that I was able to visit my sister a year before her death. During her life as a military dependent, she spent many years in Germany and Japan. This was the reason we didn't see each other often because I was in the military away from home for significant periods of time. I was in the US Navy and her husband was in the US Army.

This period happened to be a significant time in my life because the celebration was during the one hundredth anniversary of our father's birth. My father was held in high esteem by his children and everyone who knew him as a father and husband. He was always my hero and I thank him for all the sacrifices he made for his family.

This year was very important to me relative to memorials and accomplishments by family members. My grand-daughter Felicia completed graduate school at the University of Connecticut at the same time I was attending school at Eastern Connecticut State University. She was awarded a Master's Degree in Social Work.

She received an Academic Achievement Award from M. Jodi Rell, Governor of the State of Connecticut as a Graduating Senior Woman. The Governor stated on the official statement, "This is a tremendous distinction that I am certain you will carry with pride and honor. I commend your perseverance and dedication to education. Your commitment and drive is an inspiration to all of Connecticut's residents and is a testament to your strength and determination. You are truly an exceptional student and this testimonial is a tribute to your outstanding character. You have set a fine example for all Connecticut's students to follow. Therefore, I M. Jodi Rell, Governor of the State of Connecticut, do hereby convey honor and recognition to Felicia Mosley in the State of Connecticut. I urge all citizens to join me in recognizing your outstanding educational achievement and in wishing you the very best for continued success in all of your future endeavors". I was very proud of my grand-daughter's achievements and determination to complete her education.

I had to make a trip to Pittsburgh, Pa. for a memorial service for my mother who died fifty nine years ago and my sister who died fifty six years ago. The Braddock Cemetery had lost the records relative to the burial plots for my mother and sister. Through extensive research and determination, my sister Phyllis Mosley Colquitt was able to locate the burial plots for our mother and sister. We had new headstones made for both grave sites. We knew both graves sites were near our brother Harold Lloyd who was buried in 1973.

Bishop Nathan McAllister performed the memorial service at the grave sites. In attendance were six of my mother's surviving children. Lorraine Mosley Hayes who lived in Florida was unable to attend but she was there in spirit. This was a proud moment in our lives to see permanent grave markers, on our mother and sister's graves. I again thank my sister Phyllis, for her strength, perseverance and determination to find the final resting place of our loved ones. Phyllis was seven years old when her mother died. I also thank my sisters Norma Lampley Mosley and Yvonne Mosley Johnson for making this memorial service possible and producing Volume II of the Mosley Photo Album. This was a testament to the respect and love we all had for our departed family members.

I was still a college student at the age of seventy eight and was on course to graduate on May 18, 2008. This would be another significant event in my life because I would be graduating on my youngest daughter Patricia's birthday.

In October 2007, Linda and Foster became the proud parents of another son. They named him John Parker Joseph.

In January, l was notified the Administration wanted to interview me for an article to be placed in the Eastern Magazine which is published by the Division of Institutional Advancement for the benefit of alumni, students, faculty, staff and friends of Eastern Connecticut State University. The person conducting the interview titled the article, "Learning is Fun at Any Age". I was the oldest student to complete the Lifelong Learning Program at Eastern Connecticut State University. I was asked if I would be attending the graduate school. I replied if I decided, I would study Molecular Biology and Genetics. I had many years of experience in medicine and sciences allied to medicine. If not in this field, I would study African-American History. These are two areas I spend a considerable amount of time studying and researching for my own personal enrichment.

On April 21, 2008, my granddaughter Miesha gave birth to her second child. The baby was named Nya McKenzie Lake, my second great granddaughter.

The date for the commencement exercises finally arrived. Many members of my family were present including some from Bloomington, Il. My wife Gloria had a nicely decorated cake to commemorate an important day in my life. My children and grand-children were proud of me for graduating with honors as a senior citizen.

On May 21, 2008, three days after graduation, I received an e-mail from University Relations who interviewed me for the Eastern Magazine. She stated the magazine (next issue) is not scheduled to be sent out until September. They are adding more stories and doing the graphic design so that it can be sent to the printer. Copies of the articles were also sent to the local newspapers. When the *magazines are received at University Relations, she would like me to autograph her personal copy. She wanted to write a lot more about my life experiences but was limited to a certain length of the article.*

A few days later, I received a letter from the School of Continuing Education. I had been selected to be highlighted on the "Alumni Stars" web page for July 2008, beginning the first week of July. An enclosed gift card was presented for being highlighted on the top spot. "Your achievements are a testament to your dedication and perseverance. We are proud to have you as an alumnus".

I was relieved to be out of school and able to continue my hobbies and work around the house. I thank my wife for encouraging me to finish school and to write my autobiography.

The title of my book was based upon the history of the microscope. When you look at history, you must see the fabric of a life in detail. When I was attending Clinical Laboratory School in 1950, I was taught to understand the power of the microscope. When Anton van Leeuwenhook invented the microscope in the seventieth century, it revolutionized the medical field. It allowed the observation of the simple forms of animal and plant life. During the time I was in school involved in my practical work using the microscope, there was a low power, high power and oil emersion objectives to view various cells. Later we learned how to use the dark field condenser in order to observe the spirochetes that produces syphilis and yaws.

I used this analogy of the microscope to compare it to my life experiences in this society. Ironically, the microscope was invented to enhance the method used at the time to count the number of threads in cloth.

The following year was a historical period in American History because an African-American became the forty fourth President of the United States. I was proud to see this event taking place in my lifetime.

On January 20, 2009, Barack Hussein Obama was sworn in and vowed to renew the country in face of many challenges climaxing a once inconceivable journey. It was important for everyone including myself to remember the President was elected by all the people. I was proud to see many young people exercise their right to vote, l believe the future of our country is based on our youth and how they will create a society that will be respected all over the world.

A few weeks after the inauguration, I attended a meeting to discuss veteran benefits and whether the new Administration would be committed to protecting the benefits earned by members of our Armed Forces. I was personally asked if being an African-American helped or hurt Barack

Obama or has it played no role in the election to the highest office in the land.

My response to the question was, in the Presidential Campaign and ultimate national election, it was a minor issue. I am sure most people expected it because we are not a color blind society. The major issues were the economy and the future direction of our nation. We will see lesser emphasis on race as the voters become younger. The older generation of voters who lived to see changes made by first time voters, will ultimately change their attitude about race. It appeared that most voters looked beyond race and evaluated Barack Obama on his potential to lead and be a great President and help regain American respect around the world.

In 2010, I was asked for my opinion on some political science questions by some students at Eastern Connecticut State University. My degree is not in political science but they knew I love history.

> **What are the strengths and weaknesses of our Constitution? If you were creating the Constitution today, what things would you change and what would you keep the same?**
>
> I have read the Federalist Papers and determined that in my opinion, the Bill of Rights was the *major strength* of our Constitution. Based on the Federalist form of government without a statement explaining individual rights would have been a catastrophe and tyranny would reign. The ninth amendment basically clarifies the rights of the citizens but not for Native Americans and African slaves who were not considered citizens.
>
> In my opinion, the major weakness as a living document was that the founding fathers failed to understand that a nation founded on Christian principles would eventually abolish human bondage. Slaves were not considered citizens until the Fourteenth amendment was ratified in 1868. We all know that here in the twenty first century some states still deny equal protection under the law for all of its citizens. Some members of the judiciary still interpret the Constitution as the "law of original intent". We must never forget that judges of district, appellate and supreme courts have varied judicial philosophies. When the Constitution was ratified on June 25th 1788, it was considered a weak document because

it passed by a narrow margin of 89-79. A shift of five votes would have defeated the ratification process. The leading opponents to the ratification were Patrick Henry, George Mason and James Monroe.

If I were creating the Constitution today, I would change the basic foundation of federalism detailed in this document and use a different template for the document base. I believe that federalism infringes upon human rights. James Madison writes in Federalist #10 of the dangers of a democracy. His comment in itself explains the philosophy of a man who would become our fourth president. Much of the input for this document should come from the common man. We never had a common man as president until Andrew Jackson who was our seventh president.

The most important part of this document that must be saved is the *Bill of Rights* and what is stated in Article five about amendments. This is a living document and must be modified from time to time. The twenty third amendment should be repealed in order to allow the District of Columbia (seat of the federal government) to become a state with the appropriate representation.

Is the Constitution based on Christian Values?

We must first understand and define Christian values. After the colonists received their independence from England, they continued to enslave other humans. The Constitution did not apply to the Native Americans or the African slaves who were to be the burden bearers to build the new nation. In Article 1 section 9 of the Constitution it allowed the states to import slaves prior to the year 1808.

Can you find any evidence of religion contained in the Constitution text?

In the text of the Constitution, the first amendment specifically states that Congress shall make no law respecting an establishment of religion or prohibiting the free exercise thereof.

What role should religion play in American Government today?

I feel that religion should not play a role in American government. In the last decade we are seeing more religious leaders influencing politicians in many secular areas. One religious figure or leader should not try to influence the beliefs of other citizens. The citizens of the United States comprise many religious orders with various belief systems. I think it is a mistake to use religion to influence the legislation of laws that affect all citizens. First amendment rights apply to all citizens.

Evaluate the state of race relations in the United States today?

There has been some progress in race relations however we have a long way to go. The legacy of slavery is deeply embedded in the fabric of our society. Race relations will improve significantly when incomes, occupations and opportunities become fair to all citizens. The playing field must be level for all races. Every one should have the opportunity to succeed or fail based upon their ability and not based on their ethnicity. African-Americans have never been assimilated into this society unlike other immigrants. I think the reason for this is because the African slaves were brought to the colonies in chains as personal property. The major society of today is the beneficiary of slave labor. I feel confident that race relations will continue to improve and this will make America a much stronger nation. The strength of a nation is enhanced by utilizing the full potential of all its citizens.

Is Affirmative Action needed?

Affirmative action is needed because it is aimed at reducing inequality between groups. Those who view affirmative action as a quota system need to educate themselves about the true meaning of this program. Many people view affirmative action as a race issue which is not true. It is a conscious effort to increase the representation of women and other designated groups in particular organizations, occupations, programs and a wide range of activities. This program was primarily rooted in the unique historical experience of African-Americans in this country. African-Americans came as the property of others rather than as free individuals, while others were free to engage in the pursuit of property. This nation was built on slave labor. When all citizens are afforded equal opportunity, affirmative action would no longer be necessary. When I think of the genesis of this nation, the European immigrants were given affirmative action, and continues to receive it to this day.

Does race still impact what type of job you may receive?

In many instances, this is a reality of life in this nation. It has improved over the years however the institution of racism is alive and well. In most cases it is a covert action by individuals in positions of responsibility. A good example of how an applicant's race is a factor, we only have to look at the hiring of Division I and NFL head coaches. In 2002, the owner of the Pittsburgh Steelers brought up the issue and the NCAA discussed the issue of major college coaches. This is a very interesting discussion because of the number of African-Americans athletes in sports. Many organizations have a code to indicate the race of the applicant for employment.

Has being black helped or hurt Barack Obama or has it played no role?

In the Presidential Campaign and ultimate national election, it was a minor issue. I am sure most people expected it because we are not a color blind society. The major issues were the economy and the future direction of our nation. We will see lesser emphasis on race as the voters become younger. The older generation of voters, who lived to see changes made by first time voters, will ultimately change their attitude about race. It appears that most voters looked beyond race and evaluated Barack Obama on his potential to lead and be a great President and to help regain American respect around the world.

Should Federal Judges serve for Life?

I think that judges should serve for life because justice is to be blind and not influenced by political issues. Judges can be removed from the bench by articles of impeachment brought forth by the House Judiciary Committee and convicted in a trial by the United States Senate. If you recall, the United States Supreme Court was involved in the 2000 national election in Florida. In my opinion, this was a clear violation of the separation of powers.

In 1981, an African-American Federal judge (Alcee L. Hastings) was impeached by the House Judiciary Committee and convicted by the United States Senate (although not by the full Senate) and was removed from the bench. Mr. Hastings ran for Congress for a seat representing the twenty third congressional district of Florida in 1992 and was re-elected to the seat seven times. Theoretically if the separation of powers is actually the law of the land, judges should be impartial referees in the interpretation of judicial philosophy.

There are advantages and disadvantages to life service by judges. Judges should be non-political and procedures are in place for the removal of judges from the bench for the violation of the public trust. This violation could be in the sphere of high crimes and misdemeanors.

The role of courts in American would change in a negative way if we had a frequent change of judges. All judges have different judicial philosophies and as such politics will enter the administration of justice and the rule of law.

Can our Representatives in Congress serve the public good?

Our elected officials representing the people must design legislation for the benefit of their constituents. Congressmen and Congresswomen must always remember that their allegiance is to the people of their districts as well as the nation in general. Legislation should never violate the public trust. They are aware that the ballot box can remove them from office.

Should politicians be bound by public opinion when voting for legislation?

Public opinion may vary depending therefore on the issues. The legislators must make an informed decision relative to what is best for the general public. In any society, special interest groups make it very difficult for many legislators to be transparent in their job as social agents. Public opinion must be scrutinized carefully.

Should politicians vote their own independent conscience or what their constituents want based on opinion polls?

This question must be dissected in order to evaluate the pros and cons. A politician must not vote their own conscience because they were elected by many people with independent ideas of their own. It is a delicate balancing act for any legislator. Opinion polls should never be used to influence any legislation because polls in general are unreliable.

What should be more important to a member of Congress, local or national issues?

It is important to remember that the Congress of the United States as the legislative branch of government is obligated to serve the American public. Laws passed by the Congress affects all citizens in the nation. Local issues are important however, national issues should have priority.

CHAPTER 14

Breaking Barriers: African-American Firsts Reflections and Summary

1948: Top Recruit, Honor Man of an Integrated Company.

1948: First Group of African-American Hospital Corpsmen (Class A School). I finished second academically in class standing.

1953: First Group of African-American football players to compete against the University of Maryland (Byrd Stadium) in College Park, Maryland.

1956: First Group of African-Americans, (three) to attend the Submarine Medical Technician School. I finished first academically in class standing.

1956: First African-Americans Medical Corpsman to be designated "Qualified in Submarines". USS Volador (SS0490), Submarine Squadron Five, US Pacific Fleet, San Diego, California.

1958: First African-Americans Medical Corpsman to attend and graduate from the Nuclear Power Engineering School, profiled in Jet Magazine in November 1958.

1958: First African-Americans Nuclear trained Medical Corpsman to serve aboard a Fast Attack Nuclear Submarine.

1961: First African-Americans Nuclear trained Medical Corpsmen to serve aboard a Nuclear Powered Missile Submarine.

1963: First African-American Medical Corpsman to supervise the Clinical Laboratory at the Naval Submarine Base Hospital.

1964: First African-American instructor of the Atomic, Biological and Chemical Warfare School at the Naval Submarine Base and assigned to the EOD unit (Explosive Ordinance Disposal) at

Indian Head, Maryland. This unit was east of the Mississippi River. The unit west of the Mississippi was at the Sandia Base in New Mexico.

1965: First African-American : Director of the Naval Submarine Base Disaster Control Program and ancillary duties as the Brig counselor and acting Chief Master of Arms.

1967: USS Samuel Gompers (AD-37). The highest rated African-American on board this destroyer tender with a crew of 1200 personnel. My assignment was the H—Division Officer (administrator of the Medical Department) and the assistant Radiological Control Officer as a senior enlisted non-commissioned officer.

1968: First African-American Buyer hired by the Electric Boat Division of General Dynamics Corporation.

1972: First Minority Business Enterprise Administrator of Government Programs for the Procurement Department.

1972: First African-American appointed as the Small Business Administrator for the Electric Boat Division of General Dynamics Corporation.

1976: First African-American to receive the Nathan Hale Award at Mitchell College. The College is located in New London, Connecticut.

1986: First African-American selected to be part of a thirty person delegation to the Peoples Republic of China to discuss nuclear accident training with our counterparts. This endeavor was sponsored by the Citizens Ambassador Program out of the US State Department.

1997: First African-American appointed as the Connecticut Chapter-CT1 Vice President for Legislation for he National Association for Uniform Services. This organization is the service-member's voice in government.

2005: Only African-American Nuclear Trained Medical Corpsman profiled in the book, "Black Submarines in the United States, 1940-1975. The author of this book is Glenn A. Knoblock.

2006: First African-American Nuclear Trained Medical Corpsman to be inducted into the Holland Club. A prerequisite for this award is to be "Qualified in Submarines for 50 years and be a Life Member of the United States Submarine Veterans Association".

2008: The oldest person (78) to earn a degree through the School of Continuing Education at Eastern Connecticut State University in Willimantic, Connecticut.

This year of 2011, will be an important year in politics as politicians gear up for the next national election which is looming on the horizon. With all the problems facing our nation at this time, I wonder what direction the nation will take after next year's election. We appear to have an informed electorate who is aware that the massive problems accumulated over the years cannot be erased in a short period of time. We live in a great nation and I am sure that with determination and resolve, many of our major problems will be resolved with the help of God.

I wrote this book to tell my story and the path I took to lead me to where I am today. My objectives in life were to be a good man, husband and father to my children, only God can answer for me.

I am particularly indebted to many people without whom this book could not have been written. The list starts with my parents and continues to the present time. The names of all the people who have touched my life are too numerous to count. My family was a major influence on my life in addition to teachers and many people who crossed my path during my journey on this earth.

Without a doubt, God has blessed me with an abundant life. I have had the opportunity to meet many wonderful people not only in the United States but also in many foreign nations around the world during my military service.

I am frequently asked whether I am bitter about the treatment I received from some individuals during part of my military and civilian careers. My answer always is a resounding no. Bitterness hurts mainly the person who is bitter. Human emotions affect individuals both psychologically and physically.

In the scriptures, (Deut. 32-35) and (Rom. 12-19), the Lord said vengeance is mine; I will repay. I will not allow anger or bitterness to distort my faith in the word of God. I am at peace with myself.

Mervin McKinley Mosley Sr.
and Queen Vashti Taylor Mosley 1925

Alma, James and
Mervin Jr.   1931

Great Grandchildren →

Nya   Dariana

James M. Mosley Sr. HM1 (SS) USN Yokusuka, Japan 1957

Mr. & Mrs. James Milford Mosley Sr.

L-R Patricia Ann, Thomas Robert & Lillie Mae

Ellen Theresa   James Milford   Mervin McKinley

James

James Milford Mosley Sr.

12 August

James

Ellen Theresa Mosby-Ed
"Ellie"

Daughter,
Miasha
Nadine
Edwards

James

James

Mr. & Mrs. James Milford Mosley, Sr.

Linda Wiley

Joseph & John Wiley

James & Gloria

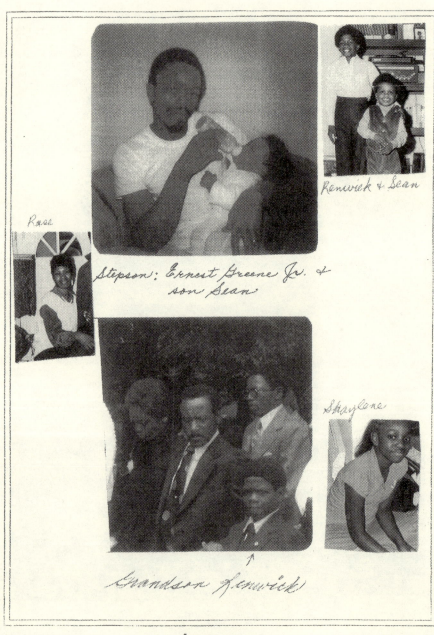

Rose

Renwick & Sean

Stepson: Ernest Greene Jr. & son Sean

Shaylene

Grandson Renwick

James

James

L - R Austin, Mero & Alana

Mero

Mr. + Mrs. Mervin McKinley Morley "Joyce + Mero"

L-R Austin, Joyce + Elana

James

Felicia Anne Mosley (Granddaughter)
University of Connecticut
School of Social Work
May 5, 2007

Alma Lee Mosley-Kitchings

2 May

Mervin McKinley Mosley, Jr.

9 September

William Roger Mosley

4 July

Harold Lloyd Mosley

24 January

Donald Murray Mosley

19 October

Norma Jean Mosley-Lampley

28 June

Yvonne Mosley-Johnson

11 January

Phyllis Ann Mosley-Colquitt

16 August

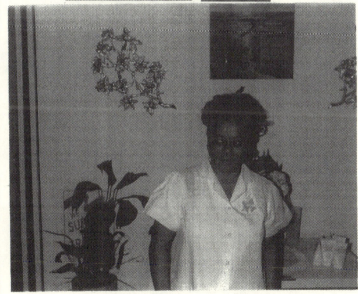

Madge Marie Mosley-Maydwell

2 February

Vashti Lorraine Mosley-Hayes

26 December

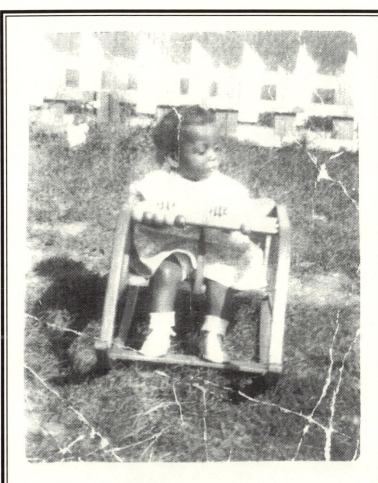

Marvina Mosley

29 October

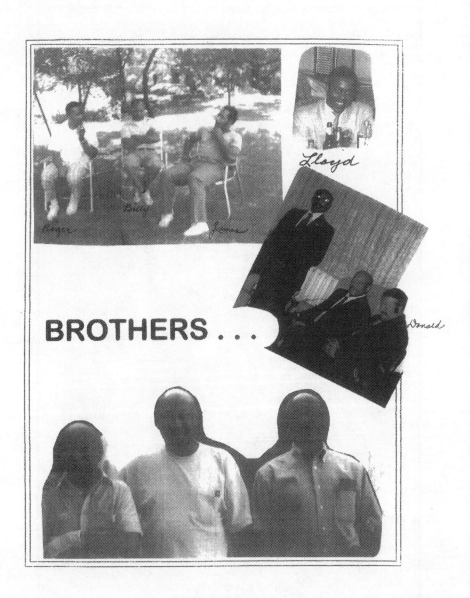

BROTHERS . . .

and SISTERS...

L-R Madge, Alma, Phyllis, Jean, Lorraine * Yvonne, Franciene

U.S. Army

LLoyd

REPORT OF ENLISTED PERFORMANCE EVALUATION
NAVPERS 792 (Rev. 8-65)
0105-402-3001

PERIOD FROM 17 FEB 67 **TO** 14 JAN 68

NAME (Last, First, Middle): MOSLEY, James Milford
SERVICE NO: 364 86 68
RATE AND ABB: HMCS (SS)
PRESENT SHIP OR STATION: USS SAMUEL GOMPERS (AD-37)

INSTRUCTIONS
1. For each trait, evaluate the man on his actual observed performance. If performance was not observed, check the "Not Observed" box.
2. Compare him with others of the same rate.
3. If the major portion of his work has been outside his rate or pay grade during this reporting period, evaluate him on what he did. Describe what he did in the "Comments" section.
   a. Pick the phrase which best fits the man in each trait and check left or right box under it. Left box is more favorable.

1. PROFESSIONAL PERFORMANCE: His skill and efficiency in performing assigned duties (except SUPERVISORY).
NOT OBSERVED	Extremely effective and reliable. Works well on his own.	Highly effective and reliable. Needs only limited supervision.	Effective and reliable. Needs occasional supervision.	Adequate, but needs routine supervision.	Inadequate. Needs constant supervision.
X	*				* *

2. MILITARY BEHAVIOR: How well he accepts authority and conforms to standards of military behavior.
NOT OBSERVED	Always acts in the highest traditions of the Navy.	Willingly follows commands and regulations.	Conforms to Navy standards.	Usually obeys commands and regulations. Occasionally lax.	Dislikes and flouts authority. Unsoldierlike.
	* X				* *

3. LEADERSHIP AND SUPERVISORY ABILITY: His ability to plan and assign work to others and effectively direct their activities.
NOT OBSERVED	Gets the most out of his men.	Handles men very effectively.	Gets good results from his men.	Usually gets adequate results.	Poor supervisor.
	* X				* *

4. MILITARY APPEARANCE: His military appearance and neatness in person and dress.
NOT OBSERVED	Impressive. Wears Naval uniform with great pride.	Neat and correct in appearance.	Conforms to Navy standards of appearance.	Passable. Sometimes careless in appearance.	No credit to the Naval Service.
	* X				* *

5. ADAPTABILITY: How well he gets along and works with others.
NOT OBSERVED	Gets along exceptionally well. Promotes good morale.	Gets along very well with others. Contributes to good morale.	A good shipmate. Helps morale.	Gets along adequately with others.	A misfit.
	* X				* *

6. DESCRIPTION OF ASSIGNED TASKS
"H" Division Officer. Supervises administrative functions of the Medical Department.

7. EVALUATION OF PERFORMANCE (E-5 and above include comment on ability in self expression and command, orally and in writing, of the English language)

HMCS (SS) MOSLEY has been instrumental in the development of the Medical Department aboard SAMUEL GOMPERS. His alert and energetic manner makes him technically proficient and very desirable as a peer. HMCS (SS) MOSLEY's command of the English language, orally and in writing is considered excellent.

* 8. THESE ITEMS MUST BE JUSTIFIED BY COMMENTS IN SECTION 7 ABOVE. HMCS (SS) MOSLEY has demonstrated unfaultering ability to administer the Medical Department of SAMUEL GOMPERS from it's very beginning during the construction of the ship until the present. His military behavior is always of the highest order in his associations with his superiors and with the men who work for him. HMCS (SS) MOSLEY's leadership is of a quite and highly efficient manner. His (Cont)

9. REASON FOR REPORTING: [ ] SEMI-ANNUAL [X] TRANSFER [ ] OTHER
10. DATE: 14 JAN 68
11. SIGNATURE OF REPORTING SUPERIOR: CDR C. E. CHINN, USN

NAVPERS 792 (Rev. 6-65) BACK

12. SERVICE SCHOOL(S) ATTENDED DURING PERIOD OF THIS REPORT

INCLUSIVE DATES	SCHOOL	GRADUATED (YES-NO)	CLASS STANDING
	NONE		

13. SPECIAL QUALIFICATIONS NOT INDICATED BY RATING OR PRIMARY NEC ATTAINED DURING PERIOD OF THIS REPORT

(Continued from Item 8)
ability to extract the best possible performance from the men in his charge is outstanding. HMCS (SS) MOSLEY has never been seen in other than an immaculate uniform, which he indeed wears with great pride. HMCS (SS) MOSLEY exhibits exceptional latitude in his personality in order to achieve the most amiable and effective relationship between himself and all others.

NONE

14. OFF-DUTY EDUCATIONAL ACHIEVEMENTS (USAFI, college courses, correspondence courses, etc.) COMPLETED DURING PERIOD OF THIS REPORT.

NONE

```
            U.S.S. SAMUEL GOMPERS (AD-37)
              FPO SAN FRANCISCO 96601        15 January 1968
```

From: Commanding Officer, U.S.S. SAMUEL GOMPERS (AD-37)
To: HMCS James Milford MOSLEY, USN, 364 86 68

Subj: Letter of appreciation

Ref: (a) BUPERS ltr Pers-E33-VSK-sm of 20 January 1967

1. By reference (a), the Chief of Naval Personnel has authorized and directed that you be transfered to the Fleet Reserve Class F-6 and concurrently released to inactive duty not earlier than 16 February 1968.

2. On this date, your enlisted service record indicates that you will have completed 19 years, 09 months, and 15 days active naval service on the effective date of your transfer to the Fleet Reserve Class F-6 and concurrent release to inactive duty. During that period of time, you have received the following awards and commendations:

    Good Conduct Medal (Fifth Award)
    National Defense Service Medal (Second Award)
    Navy Unit Commendation (First Award)

3. Your records further indicate that you have served in an impressive number of ships and stations, some of which are:

    U.S.S. VOLADOR (SS 490)
    Nuclear Power Training School, New London, Connecticut
    U.S.S. SKIPJACK (SSN 585)
    U.S.S. THOMAS A. EDISON (SSBN 610)
    U.S. Naval Submarine Base, New London, Connecticut
    U.S. Naval Submarine Medical Center, New London, Connecticut and the
    U.S.S. SAMUEL GOMPERS (AD-37)

4. In behalf of your shipmates, it is indeed a pleasure to take this opportunity to express the Navy's sincere appreciation for the long and faithful years of service which you have so willingly given. In bidding you farewell, the most appropriate words at this time are "WELL DONE." May fair winds blow and whatever Seas you Sail be smooth.

                                        HARRY RISCH, JR.

United States Naval Submarine Base New London
Groton, Connecticut 06342

NB/5800 (01)
Serial:
14 September 1966

From: Commanding Officer, U. S. Naval Submarine Base New London
To: HMCS James H. MOSLEY, USN, 364 86 68

Subj: Brig Counselor; performance of duties as

Ref: (a) SECNAV Instruction 1640.7 of 8 Jan 63
(b) Department of the Navy Corrections Manual (NavPers 15826 Rev) of 26 June 63

1. You are hereby assigned as a Brig Counselor on a collateral duty basis.

2. You will be guided in the performance of your duties by the instructions contained in references (a) and (b). Specifically, you will interview each offender assigned to you, observe him and keep an informal record of his progress, and make recommendations to the Commanding Officer, via the Brig Officer, with regard to the offender's eventual disposition. You will, when appropriate, refer the offender to other members of the command for specialized assistance as needed.

3. The Brig Officer and Brig Warden will coordinate your duties as counselor and the assignment of offenders to you for counseling.

W. A. McGUINNESS

Copy to:
Brig Officer
Brig Warden

U. S. NAVY UNDERWATER SOUND LABORATORY
FORT TRUMBULL, NEW LONDON, CONNECTICUT

USL NOTE 3050
6 October 1965

USL NOTICE 3050

From: Commanding Officer and Director
To: Distribution List A

Subj: Civil Defense Disaster Control Training Sessions

Encl: (1) ADP Attendance Cards

1. <u>Purpose</u>. To announce a schedule for the subject sessions.

2. <u>Background</u>. Much thought and planning has been predicated upon enemy action involving atomic, biological and chemical warfare. While these forms of attack are major considerations in a Disaster Control Program, it is intended that Disaster Control shall include measures taken to reduce the probability and minimize the effect of damage in peace or war due to natural or man-made causes.

3. <u>Information</u>.

   a. Civil Defense Disaster Control Training sessions will be held at the Laboratory on 11, 12, 14 and 15 October 1965. The sessions will be conducted by J. H. Mosely, HMCS, Head of the Submarine Base Disaster Control Branch.

   b. Each session will be held in Christopher Columbus Auditorium, Bldg. 34, from 0830 to 1200, and will consist of lectures supplemented by films, slides, and demonstrations of various radiac equipment.

4. <u>Action</u>.

   a. All Laboratory personnel, including the military and their dependents, are strongly urged to attend one of the sessions.

   b. Supervisors are requested to schedule approximately one quarter of their employees for attendance at each session.

   c. Automatic Data Processing Cards are enclosed for the purpose of recording attendance. Each attendee should turn his/her card in at the door of the Auditorium.

   d. The time involved for attendance at each session is chargeable to Job Order 6-2-090-01-00.

5. <u>Cancellation</u>. This Notice is canceled on 18 October 1965.

R. L. CORKRAN, JR.

Certificate of Chapter Charter

The National Association for Uniformed Services

Hereby charters the

GROTON CHAPTER - CT1

as a chapter of the association and as such is entitled to all benefits
and privileges of the association

Chapter Officers

President	MCPO Paul F. Dillon, USN (Ret.)
Vice President for Public Affairs	LT Ernest V. Plantz, USN (Ret.)
Vice President for Communications	MAJ John D. Monahan, USA (Ret.)
Vice President for Legislation	SCPO James M. Mosley, USN (Ret.)
Legislative Team Member	LCPL John P. Walker, USMC (Ret.)
Legislative Team Member	CAPT Pierce F. Connair, USN (Ret.)

Dated: 14 October, 1997

J. C. PENNINGTON
MG, USA (Ret) President

2006 INDUCTEES

SN(SS) Leo A. Amero USS CHIVO SS 341 1956
EM3(SS) Joseph E Banack USS BARRACUDA SSK 1 1956
ETC(SS) Fred Block USS CORSAIR SS 435 1956
ET1(SS) Howard Haines Brown USS IREX SS 482 1956
LCDR Donald Cameron USS CORSAIR SS 435 1956
MMCM(SS) Dee C Cheshire USS CORSAIR SS 435 1956
CPO(SS) Paul D. Cook USS TIGRONE SS 419 1955
TM3 (SS) Elmer Flanagan USS SPIKEFISH SS 404 1956
TMCM(SS) George I Foster USS GREENFISH SS 351 1956
SoS1(SS) Joe Frederick USS HARDER SS 568 1956
SN(SS) Joseph W. Gilbert USS CORSAIR SS435 1951
QMC(SS) Charles R. Hall USS ATULE SS 403 1956
CWO4 Peter B. Howell USS PICUDA SS 382 1956
EN1(SS) Stanley R. Hungerford USS ATULE SS 403 1956
MMCSS Don Kamuf USS BANG SS 385 1956
ICCS(SS) Charles R Kostoskey USS BECUNA SS 319 1956
MMCM(SS) Robert W Lindsay USS TANG SS 563 1956
CAPTAIN William L. Martin USS HARDER SS 568 1956
RMC(SS) Richard Mccannes USS SEA LEOPARD SS 483 1956
HMCS(SS) James M. Mosley USS VOLADOR SS 490 1956
EMCS(SS) George E. Moyer USS BERGALL SS 320 1952
YNCM(SS) John E. Mumford USS TUSK SS 426 1956
RMCS(SS) Morris Newkirk USS SABLEFISH SS 303 1955
YNC(SS) Elton T Nolan USS GROUPER SSK 214 1956
EN1(SS) Daniel R. Orcutt USS BECUNA SS 319 1956
LT Bill Parker USS VOLADOR SS 490 1956
HMCS(SS) Robert D. Perry USS HARDER SS 568 1956
EM2(SS) Robert J. Price USS TRIGGER SS 564 1956
MMCS(SS) Advah H. Reynolds, Jr, USS SPIKEFISH SS 404 1956
COW2 Thomas M Roan USS ODAX SS 484 1956
EMC(SS) Earl "Robbie" Roberts USS GRENADIER SS 525 1956
TMCM(SS) Stanley H. Robinson USS RUNNER SS476 1956
SO3(SS) David S. Socha USS CROAKER SS 246 1956
CWO3 Rollie D. Stephens USS ANGLER SSK 240 1956
EM2(SS) Paul Streickert USS SABLEFISH SS 303 1956
ET1(SS) Theodore A. Swanson USS BATFISH SS 310 1956
CWO3 Robert Tompkins USS BECUNA SS 319 1956
LCDR Ronald G. Trahan USS TENCH SS 417 1956
FTBC(SS) Teddy G. Vaughan USS TANG SS 563 1956
FTBC(SS) Emil J Vestuti USS RAY SSR 271 1956
EMC(SS) Kenneth C Vining USS AMBERJACK SS 522 1956
EN2(SS) Raymond F Williams USS BUGARA SS 331 1956
RMCM(SS) Walter L. Wooten USS ATULE SS 403 1956
STSCS(SS) Walter Wyllie Jr. USS CUBERA SS 347 1956

**USSVI GROTON BASE
200 HOLLAND CLUB
INDUCTION CEREMONY**

June 10, 2006

Dealey Center

Naval Submarine Base New London

Groton, CT

Mitchell College

NEW LONDON, CONNECTICUT
06320

ROBERT C. WELLER
PRESIDENT

<u>NATHAN HALE AWARD</u>

Almost 200 years ago, a young New London schoolmaster gave his life for his country. By both word and deed, he created a superior model for American men and women to follow in combining the academic tradition with good citizenship and service in the Armed Forces of the United States. The Nathan Hale Award is given to the student who, in the opinion of the President of the College, has most closely followed this example of service to country, community, and college.

The Award this year is given to a man who entered the United States Navy after high school graduation at Homestead, Pennsylvania. His service of twenty years in various parts of the world included duty aboard various battleships, submarines, and shore stations; and he retired as a Chief Hospital Corpsman.

While in the Navy, he graduated first in his class as a submarine medicine technician at the Submarine School in Groton, Connecticut. He enrolled first at Mitchell College as a part-time student in 1966. He was transferred to the West Coast in 1967, finished his enlistment, and returned to this area to live and work; and he re-enrolled at Mitchell in 1974. He compiled an outstanding record in the Navy, particularly in service schools; and his academic record at Mitchell is such that he was recently inducted into the Mitchell Society of Scholars.

He is presently the Minority and Small Business Administrator at the Electric Boat Division of General Dynamics, a position of responsibility for encouraging and aiding the minority small businessman to compete for sub-contracts from the industrial giant of this area.

Married, the father of six children, a homeowner, he has still found time over the years to be a coach in the Waterford Little League and to attend services at the Submarine Base Chapel.

The winner of the Nathan Hale Award for 1976, our Bicentennial Year, is

JAMES MILFORD MOSLEY of WATERFORD, CONNECTICUT

New London, Connecticut
May 22, 1976

Robert C. Weller
President

Mitchell College

NEW LONDON, CONNECTICUT 06320

(203) 443-2811

April 28, 1976

Mr. James M. Mosley
25 Dayton Road
Waterford, Connecticut 06385

Dear Mr. Mosley:

It is a pleasure to inform you that you have been elected to the Mitchell Society of Scholars which was founded in 1966. This is an honorary society authorized by the Faculty and Administration to recognize exceptional scholarship and to encourage a valid intellectual life at the college. You have been chosen by the Faculty Department Heads after a careful review of your academic achievement and character.

The Faculty and Administration of the College are giving a dinner on Friday, May 7, in the Clarke Center Cafeteria at 7:00 PM to honor you, and others who have been selected for the Society. Your wife is also invited.

It is necessary to know of your intent by Wednesday, May 5. Will you kindly inform us whether or not you plan to attend. This can be done by notifying Linda Susi in the Dean's Office (telephone 443-2811, Ext. 243).

In conclusion, may I offer my congratulations.

Sincerely,

David W. Harvey
Dean of the College

ls

Award presentation by Admiral E. W. Grenfel after being a member of the US Navy Atlantic Fleet Fast Pitch Softball Tournament Champions. (1964)

tional Naval Medical Center Fast pitch Softball Team (1951)

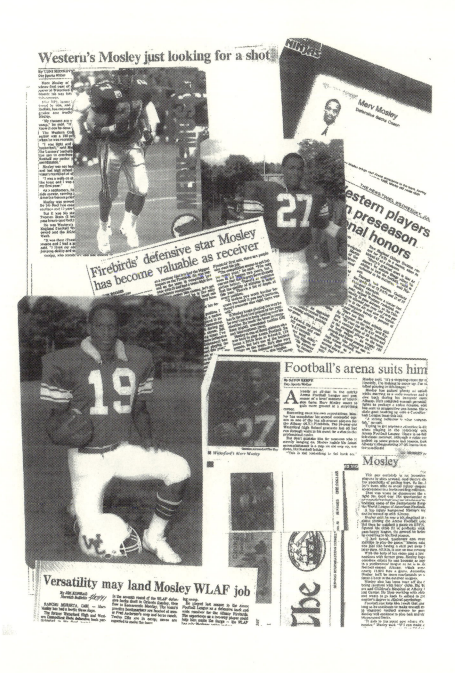

**Submarine Force, US Atlantic Fleet Sea Raiders
Fast Pitch Softball Team
Connecticut State Champions, 1964**

Submarine Force Sea Raider Fast pitch Softball Team prior to the All-Navy tournament in Seattle, Washington. We finished runner-up to The Submarine Force, US Pacific Fleet. (1964)

HOLLAND CLUB HISTORY

The Holland Club was established in May 1964 and was adopted as part of the Constitution and bylaws that year.

The Holland Club was originally established to recognize those members who had been qualified in Submarines 50 or more years. Truly we are talking about the pioneers of our Submarine Navy.

One of the first HOLLAND CLUB MEMBERS was a Submariner by the name of Ring Bennett, from Florida. Ring was recognized at the 1966 USSVI convention as the oldest living Submariner. He originally Qualified in Submarines in 1906. At the time Ring was in his high 70s, and USSVI was just 2 years old.

Of the original listing of 67 names there were 5 Admirals and at least one Medal of Honor winner, USSV Base Commanders, Chapter Presidents USSV WWII, National Commanders, National officers and commissioning crews of both organizations. The men of Holland Club

Later the USSVI Bylaws were changed that to be eligible for the HOLLAND CLUB you had to be a member of USSVI as a Life Member for 5 years. This remained in effect until 1998 when a change was voted to allow Sub Vets of W.W.II members who had been Life Members in good standing for at least one year the opportunity to become HOLLAND CLUB members. Today the requirements have been changed back to the original requirements where any Life Member who joins USSVI having been Qualified in Submarines 50 or more years is immediately eligible for the HOLLAND CLUB.

In 1996 the Perch Base submitted a Holland Club Patch as indicated on the front cover designed by Frank Rumbaugh, current District 8 Commander, denoting the 50 years of service.

These are the men who lead the way, the men we learned from and who trained and taught us to be the best Submariners in the greatest Submarine Navy the world has ever seen. In Wartime or in Peacetime. They are the men who showed us the way. Instilled us with Pride. Helped us to earn our Dolphins and set the high standards for all US Navy Submariners to achieve. They are the submariners who created our Submarine heritage. The men who served on R-boats, S-boats, O-boats, Fleet boats. From Diesel Power to Nuclear Power.

It is certainly an honor to be a member of the Holland Club. They are legends of the Submarine Force, and this is our salute to our senior shipmates. Pride Runs Deep

THE SUBMARINE VETERANS OF WWII CREED

"To perpetuate the memory of those shipmates who gave their lives in submarine warfare; to further promote and keep alive the spirit and unity that existed among United States Navy Submarine crewmen during World War II; to promote sociability, general welfare, and good fellowship among it's members; and pledge loyalty and patriotism to the United States government."

June, 10th 2006
USSVI GROTON BASE
HOLLAND CLUB INDUCTION CEREMONY

Attention To Colors

National Anthem

Pledge Of Allegiance

Invocation

Opening Remarks

National Commander

Class of 2006 Induction

SV WWII Creed

USSVI Creed

Benediction

Retire Colors

Group Picture

THE USSVI CREED

"To perpetuate the memory of our shipmates who gave their lives in the pursuit of their duties while serving their country. That their dedication, deeds and supreme sacrifice be a constant source of motivation toward greater accomplishments. Pledge loyalty and patriotism to the United States Government."

Meeting wht the Purchasing Manager to develop ways to purchase allocated Stock for the Maintenance Department of the shipyard (Not for construction Contracts). 1968

Member of the State of Maine Economical Development Council and Small Business suppliers meeting with members of the Purchasing Department at Electric Boat Division.

1973

Representatives for the Company at a Small Business Seminar. This seminar was for potential suppliers in the Northeast. 1974

Small Business supplier of the year award was presented to Mr. Slosberg by James M. Mosley (Small Business Administrator of Electric Boat Division) and Mr. Ray Rossi (Northeast Regional Manager of the US Small Business Administration). 1975

Luncheon Meeting with members of the Purchasing Department
General Dynamics Corporation/Electric Boat Division

Quality Assurance Meeting (Purchasing, Engineering, Quality Assurance, Manufacturing and Nuclear Engineering) with officials of the Earle M. Jorgensen Steel Company of Seattle, Washington. This company was to manufacture the hull steel plates of HY-100 and HY-130 for the Seawolf Submarine Program.

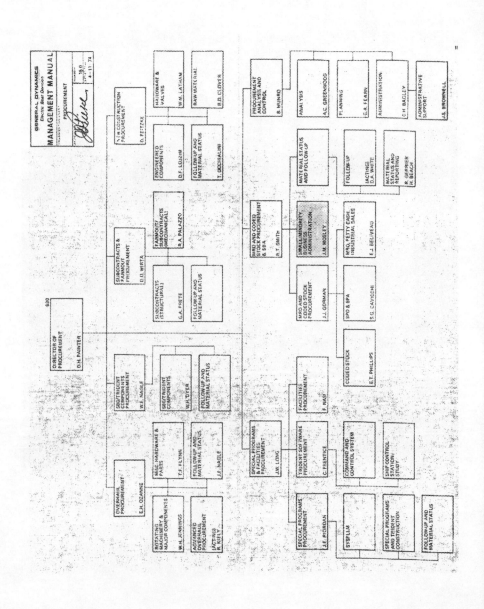

THE NATIONAL MANAGEMENT ASSOCIATION

CERTIFICATE OF MEMBERSHIP

JAMES M. MOSLEY

as a duly qualified management member of The National Management Association is entitled to all rights and privileges as provided by the Constitution and By-laws.

This member under the Association's Code of Ethics is dedicated to management development, the advancement of the management profession, and the promotion of the free enterprise system through the NMA affiliate:

Done this 24th day of September 1971

NMA President

NMA Executive Vice President

1991

awards this

Life Retirement Membership

to

James M. Mosley

in special tribute and recognition for advancing the management objectives of The Electric Boat Management Association through participation in its activities; for supporting its professional goals, and for adhering to its Code of Purposes.

This manager is hereby awarded Life Retirement Membership in E.B.M.A. and is therefore entitled to the privileges provided to such honored members.

_____   _____
EBMA President   EBMA Representative

GENERAL DYNAMICS CORPORATION
ELECTRIC BOAT DIVISION
GROTON, CONNECTICUT

THE PROCUREMENT DEPARTMENT

AWARDS THIS

CERTIFICATE

TO

J. M. MOSLEY
FEBRUARY 22, 1971

in evidence of successful completion of the
Electric Boat Division's prescribed course in

TRUTH - IN - NEGOTIATIONS

SEMINAR

ADMINISTRATOR
PROCUREMENT EDUCATION & TRAINING

MANAGER OF PROCUREMENT

GENERAL DYNAMICS CORPORATION
ELECTRIC BOAT DIVISION
GROTON, CONNECTICUT

THE PROCUREMENT DEPARTMENT

AWARDS THIS

CERTIFICATE

TO

J. M. MOSLEY

November 19, 1971

in evidence of successful completion of the
Electric Boat Division's prescribed course in

COST/PRICE ANALYSIS

(20 HOUR WORKSHOP)

George L. Hoyt
ADMINISTRATOR
PROCUREMENT EDUCATION & TRAINING

MANAGER OF PROCUREMENT

GENERAL DYNAMICS
Electric Boat Division

CERTIFICATE of APPRECIATION

Awarded to

James M. Mosley

In recognition of invaluable service, personal interest and participation in the plant-wide inventory.

January 22-29, 1978

W.G. Potts
Director of Material

P.T. Veliotis
General Manager

The American Graduate University

CERTIFICATE OF TRAINING

This is to certify that

JAMES M. MOSLEY

has successfully completed the course in

Negotiation of Contracts

GIVEN AT
General Dynamics, Electric Boat Division

October 3, 1980
Date

Paul R. McDonald
Paul R. McDonald, Director

The American Graduate University

CERTIFICATE OF TRAINING

This is to certify that

JAMES M. MOSLEY

has successfully completed the course in

Contract Pricing Techniques

GIVEN AT
Groton, Connecticut

October 23, 1931
Date

Paul R. McDonald
Paul R. McDonald, Director

TO: J. M. Mosley, -630   May 13, 1975
FROM: D. L. Suydam
SUBJECT: OC 15.0, Procurement

Attached, for your information, is a copy of Organization Chart
No. 15.0. You will be provided with a copy of each future organization chart on which your name appears. A file of these can serve
as a personal record of the management positions you have held at
Electric Boat.

                                D. L. Suydam

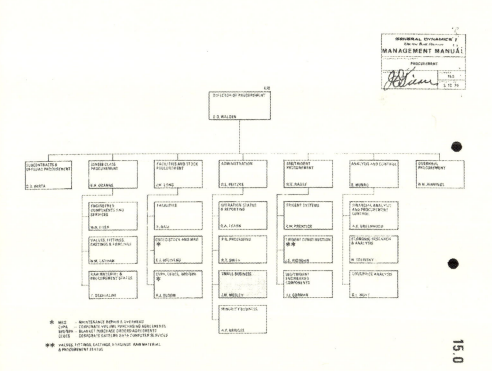

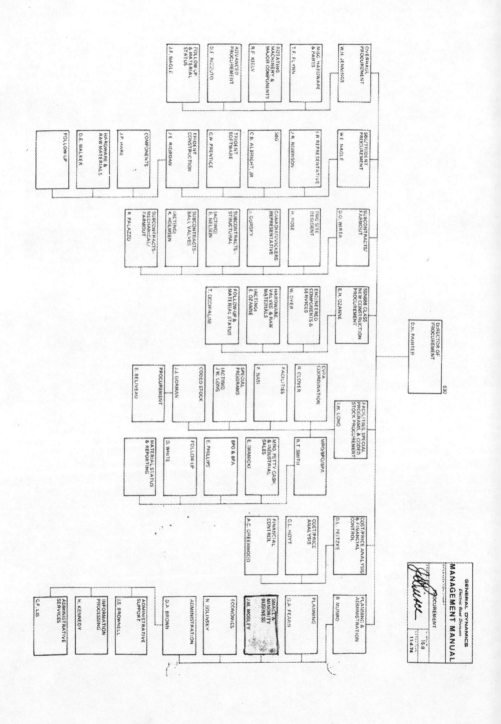

GENERAL DYNAMICS
Electric Boat Division
Eastern Point Road, Groton, Connecticut 06340

JAMES M. MOSLEY
Small Business Administrator
203 446-6721

GENERAL DYNAMICS
Electric Boat Division
Eastern Point Road, Groton, Connecticut 06340

JAMES M. MOSLEY
Minority and Small Business Administrator
203 446-6721

GENERAL DYNAMICS
Electric Boat Division
Eastern Point Road, Groton, Connecticut 06340
203 446-7306

James M. Mosley
Buyer Specialist

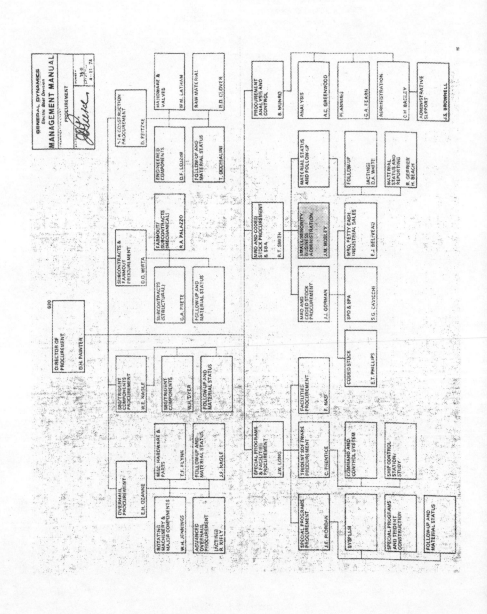

■ *Rear Adm. Cecil Haney, commander of Submarine Group 2, was a guest of honor Friday at the Submarine Force Museum's kickoff of its celebration of Black History Month in Groton.*

Struggles, triumphs of black sailors noted at submarine museum lecture

From B1

Waterford resident James Mosley, who served in the Navy from 1948 to 1968, said he saw a lot of fluctuation during his career.

"Quite a bit of tensions changed, opportunities changed," said Mosley, who said he found out two weeks ago that he holds the distinction of being the first African-American to attend the Submarine Medical Technician School in Groton in 1956.

Mosley, who went on to a civilian career at Electric Boat, said he was also the first African-American to attend the Navy's Nuclear Power School.

Standing beside him, Rear Adm. Cecil Haney, commander of Submarine Group Two, said the stories were "refreshing."

"Although there was segregation in the job, the camaraderie of the sailors is still the same," he said, noting that the small crews operating submarines have to work as a team. Haney said that his father, who was in the Army in World War II, felt the confines of segregation heavily in Portsmouth, Va.

"The opportunities he had compared to mine were incredibly different — like night and day," Haney said.

SATURDAY, FEBRUARY 10, 2007   The Day   www.theday.com

DANA JENSEN / The Day

■ Tina Rice of Norwich watches as John O'Meally of Teaneck, N.J., far right, signs a picture of himself that appears in the book "Black Submariners in the United States Navy, 1940-1975." The book's author, Glenn A. Knoblock, left, is signing books after giving a lecture Friday at the Submarine Force Museum in Groton.

'LIKE NIGHT AND DAY'

Lecture kicks off African-American history month at sub museum

By SHARMA HOWARD
Special to The Day

Groton

AS PART OF GLENN A. KNOBLOCK'S lecture on his book, "Black Submariners in the United States Navy, 1940-1975," a photo of a young African-American flashes on the screen. He is serving a pot of piping hot coffee to an officer seated at a desk and talking on the phone.

Knoblock appeared Friday at the Submarine Force Museum to talk about the role of African-American men in the history of the submarine force.

"One of the main focuses today is that these men were sailors first. They were indeed fighting men, but it's important to realize," said Knoblock as the crowd that included some of those very trailblazers.

The lecture and book signing opened up the museum's African American History Month, which includes an exhibit throughout February, African American Submariners: Profiles in Service and Sacrifice.

One pivotal figure was retired Master Chief Melvin Williams Sr., who submitted a plan to change the Navy's steward branch to its current rating of culinary specialist. The plan went to Adm. Elmo Zumwalt, Chief of Naval Operations, and was accepted by the secretary of the Navy in 1975.

Williams, who traveled from Maryland for Friday's event, recounted some of his disappointments, such as remaining at the same pay scale for eight years after he advanced to a higher rank.

"The Navy fell behind, but they're still ahead of the civilian world," he said, adding with pride that his son, Melvin Williams Jr., is a vice admiral.

See STRUGGLES page B3